A

Grievous Angel

Grievous Angel

an intimate biography of

Gram Parsons

JESSICA HUNDLEY
WITH POLLY PARSONS

THUNDER'S MOUTH PRESS
NEW YORK

GRIEVOUS ANGEL
An Intimate Biography of Gram Parsons

Published by
Thunder's Mouth Press
An Imprint of Avalon Publishing Group
245 West 17th Street, 11th Floor
New York, NY 10011

AVALON
publishing group incorporated

First printing November 2005

A portion of the proceeds from sales of *Grievous Angel* will be donated
to MusiCares, an organization dedicated to helping musicians overcome personal,
medical, and financial hardships. For more information, visit their Web site at
www.grammy.com/musicares.

Library of Congress Cataloging-in-Publication Data is available.

ISBN: 1-56025-673-7
ISBN 13: 978-1-56025-673-1

9 8 7 6 5 4 3 2 1

Book design by Jamie McNeely
Printed in the United States
Distributed by Publishers Group West

FOR TRUE MUSIC LOVERS—PAST, PRESENT, AND FUTURE

Contents

When you read these, I, that was visible, am become invisible;
Now it is you, compact, visible, realizing my poems, seeking me,
Fancying how happy you were, if I could be with you,
and become your comrade;
Be it as if I were with you.
(Be not too certain but I am now with you.)

—WALT WHITMAN (the original "Cosmic American"),
from the poem "Full of Life, Now" in *Leaves of Grass*

Introduction

THERE IS SOMETHING about Gram Parsons that works its way slowly into skin, blood, and bone, something about his music, his aesthetic, legacy, legend, and myth that seduces, even now, three decades after his death. It's difficult to pinpoint when I first fell for him—somewhere in the desert, the summer air like warm milk; in a smoke-dark bar, his voice on the jukebox; or alone, "Hot Burrito #2" spinning a lonesome tale on the stereo.

Writing a book about someone else, someone you never knew, is a surprisingly cathartic, self-revelatory experience. The past few years of research and interviews have led me on an unexpected and enlightening path, a true adventure, and I've watched with awe as both my own life and Polly's have transformed and transcended.

And all along there has been an unshakeable feeling, deep in the gut, that Gram himself was somehow pointing the way, guiding us. There were too many instances of fate, coincidence, destiny, whatever your word for that moment where everything *clicks*. Gram wants us to know him, to hear him, and so he hovers on the edges of modern pop culture and continues to quietly draw us in.

Someone asked me recently what Gram's music means to me, and I realized that the magnetism that draws me to him is less about the music than the feeling he gives, or rather, the *freedom* to feel. He was not afraid of emotion, of passion, of giving yourself entirely to the moment. He was a son, a friend, and a father—a long-haired, brown-skinned, diamond-bright boy who could shoot fire out of his fingertips. He was who he wanted to be and if you listen hard to what he tells you, you'll catch hold of something truly rare—that dusty-road, wind-in-the-hair, hard-won mix of elation and fear that comes in the brief, luminous moment just before art is born.

Gram inspires because he tried his best to live in that moment continually—sometimes for better, sometimes for worse. He donned his glitter, his space-cowboy-cosmic-American-rhinestone-superhero guise, picked up his guitar, laid his fingers against ivory, and made himself into something greater than the sum of his parts, something beautiful and wholly new.

—JESSICA HUNDLEY
Los Angeles, California
June 2005

A Word from Polly Parsons

The following is culled from an interview I did with Polly as we were completing the long journey of this book. In these past three years she has changed immensely, has grown stronger and more beautiful and is now not only a new bride but a radiant mother-to-be. I like to think this book and all that has come with it has helped us both grow and evolve and become the women we've always wanted to be.

—Jessica

THE MEMORIES OF my father are feelings and smells and touches and moments. They're the in-between moments of life, they're not "and then we went . . ." I can tell you that my feeling—viscerally, the tactile way I experienced my father—was of a very loving, strong, tall, long man. And I can hear his voice—it was very booming.

He was protective of so much about my upbringing. I remember him being very opinionated about the food I ate and the sleep I got and I could tell that he was doing the best he could with the time allotted. But I remember feeling rushed. My time with him was always brief, so there was a lot of concentrated input in a short amount of time whenever he was in my world.

I think he did fatherhood like he did life. I think he had this pure sense of intention directed toward me but the love that he surrounded me with had to be enough and he had to be on his way again. He was a whirlwind. My father loved deeply but moved quickly and I think that is obvious throughout his short but intense life. Everywhere you look, people were touched—immensely touched—but the moments with him were very brief.

I think it's really important for us as fans to remember how much he got done in a six- or seven-year period, to change the face of music as we know it today. It's such a short amount of time, and to have been so potent about his message at such a young, young age . . . I think it's an amazing thing, and I think that is what draws us to Gram Parsons. He has an element about him that's very swashbuckling.

Yet there's an element about him that is very human, too. He was a little bit of an everyman and a little bit of the love of every woman and there's something very romantic and heroic about that type of persona. It's an insatiable feeling and we yearn for that in our everyday lives.

I was not exposed to my father's music as a child because it was too painful for my mom. And therefore it became painful for me . . . because all I understood was that my mother's pain was tied to my father, therefore tied to his music. But finally I could no longer deny who I was or deny the demons I was battling or pretend like they didn't have a direct connection to not coming to terms with my father's death or my legacy.

So I was up against a wall, and the writing on it was, "you are at a crossroads here and you can go down this road that is very thick in your blood and it's very simple to do because it is in your lineage and it is written deep."

I didn't know how to do that. I didn't know how to begin. But my world, peripherally, had already been doing it for years. In a way, I felt like I was supposed to be something that I wasn't. I was supposed to be an aficionado and I was supposed to be knowledgeable and I was supposed to have his catalogue memorized frontward and backwards and I was supposed to be a historian and I was supposed to know, just because I was borne unto him, that I was supposed to be the key for these people that they so needed. But I would not and could not go there.

So I had to rediscover my father on my own terms. That was difficult. That was a really, really heavy time in my life. I just entrenched myself in his music and his writings and my memories and my journals and my writings and my fear and the things I would write as a child. I listened to all the music and of course I knew all the words because that is something you don't realize you know, but you do. I listened to the things that he wrote and he said and I remembered things that were in those songs that were about my mom and about my childhood and I picked up on things that nobody ever told me.

Finally, once I felt like I had come full circle, I felt a resurgence of joy and understanding. I settled with who I was and where I came from and who he was and where he came from and what he'd done. I had forgiven and I had accepted. Then it was time to give back because I needed to take it full circle somehow, as if he were here. Like making an amends and then living out that amends. What could I do that gave back and honored him and brought joy? And that's what this is all about, the concerts I've been putting on, the DVD [*Return to Sin City*], and this book. Giving back.

He's still a really active spirit in so many people's lives. There are people across the country who write me or who I meet who say that during some of the darkest times in their lives they felt like my father was there for them, they know it, and his music got them through. . . .

—from an interview with POLLY PARSONS
Los Angeles, California
May 2005

Nancy and Polly
in 1968. PHOTO BY
EARL CRABB.

Prologue

WHEN GRAM PARSONS was twelve years old, his father shot himself neatly in the head with a .38-caliber pistol. It was just before Christmas, 1958, and Gram had seen his father last on a Monday. It had been hot for that time of year, the sky a deep, bruised blue. Gram had stood at the station in Waycross, Georgia, that afternoon with his mother and younger sister, watching a man load their bags onto the train. They were going again to Winter Haven, Florida, to visit his mother's family for the holidays. His father was staying behind.

Cecil Sr. had held Gram too tight at the station, had said, "I'll see you in a just a few days," without looking into his son's eyes. Gram had wondered about that. He was a smart kid for his age, with a sly, lopsided grin and a keen sensitivity he had already begun to cloak in swagger.

He was young, but he noticed things. He had felt the sinew of tension between his parents, had found the empty liquor bottles hidden in the bottom of the trashcan, had seen his father somehow shrink in recent years, as if something important was slowly leaking from him.

When the train pulled out, Gram leaned his head against the window and saw Cecil waiting on the platform, standing very still. He watched until the gray figure of his father became small, smaller, and then the tracks curved to the right, and there was only Georgia streaking by in a green, wet blur.

When they finally arrived in Winter Haven, the house seemed hollow. There was the same bright sheen across the lawn, the same heavy wetness in the air, the same white glint off the blue waves of the town's forty-one lakes. But this was the first Christmas without Grandpa John, the family patriarch who had built the Snively estate, the well-kept, sprawling clapboard home that clutched at the side of Lake Eloise.

Gram's grandfather, a self-made man, had squeezed a fortune from the orange groves. He had arrived from Altoona, Pennsylvania, in 1911 and had built an empire out of little more than blind stubbornness and gumption. Where there had been swaying palm and swampland, there was now a vast swath of citrus fields, acres of trees heavy with fruit, the land owned and operated by two generations of the Snively clan.

Papa John had been a big man with a hangdog face and enormous pale hands. Without him, without his presence pressing against the tastefully decorated walls, his looming figure heavy-footed in the halls, the house seemed to have lost its spine. There were too many women suddenly.

Gram's mother and little sister, both named Avis, and his aunt Evalyn all bustled about, leaving the heady scent of their perfumes. His grandmother Hanie seemed smaller than he remembered, but she still lorded over the cooks and the servants in the haughty, straight-spined manner of a Southern belle.

Within a day or two, however, Gram was beginning to enjoy himself. Christmas at the estate was rooted in tradition, and there was something soothing for him in family ceremony. There was the tree trimming, placing fragile antique ornaments on the towering spruce by the fireplace, and the baking of pale yellow sugar cookies that he and his sister cut into reindeer shapes.

Back in Waycross, Cecil Sr. was still working. He headed the boxing division of Papa John's Snively Groves, overseeing the construction of the slatted crates that held the family orange crop. Late Tuesday afternoon, he left the office, drove home, and closed the front door gently behind him. In the bedroom, he carefully loaded his pistol, sat down stiffly on the flowered bedspread and, staring across at the white wall, placed the steel barrel against his temple.

Gram would not be told his father was dead until well after the holidays. Instead, he would sing carols with a thin, cracked voice, play the piano as he always did for his grandmother, tear at gift wrap, and tease his sister. His mother, aunt, and grandmother would cross their arms and hold their smiles tight.

More than a week passed before Gram and his sister learned that their father had had an accident. It would be many years later before the family admitted it was suicide, but Gram—who had gone deer-hunting with his father, who had listened to his war stories—must have known better. That Cecil had taken his own life was obvious, but his reasons for doing so were a mystery to Gram. He and his father had been close; Cecil was scoutmaster of Gram's troop, the leader of camping trips, the tosser of baseballs. He was gentle and sweet tempered, with moist eyes and a wide, white grin.

The loss of his father would simultaneously close Gram up and tear him open. It would instill in him a certain carelessness, a vague distrust of other people, and an innate knowledge of the precariousness of things. It would make him crave love, too, and make him hungry to fill what was missing.

But even before his father's death, melancholy had hovered around Gram like a cloud of perplexed sadness that he tried to offset with prankish humor. The burden of family secrets and obligation weighed heavy on his young life, and Gram was too perceptive not to feel the press.

IN KIWANIS SHOW—"The V
ter Haven musical trio, will be on
County Kiwanis Talent Show Friday
Mayo Hall. (1963)

From top: Birthday party;
The Village Vanguards make the
paper; Gram the folkie. ALL PHOTOS
COURTESY OF THE SNIVELY FAMILY.

From top: Gram wows the crowd; Gram solo.

From top: Gram's mother, Avis; Christmas in Winter Haven; Prom night with Patty.

Sing Me Back Home

THE EARLY YEARS, 1946–1965

GRAM WAS BORN in Winter Haven on November 5, 1946, but by then his parents had already relocated to Waycross. Cecil (known to friends and family affectionately as "Coon Dog") had been sent to head the boxing division of Snively Groves. The job had been a gift from Papa John to his favorite girl's husband, but Waycross was far removed from the luxuries of the Snively nest, and Avis went home often to Winter Haven, bearing her first child close to the family and the superior medical facilities of Florida.

Gram spent his childhood moving back and forth between the two towns, and he managed to dig his roots deep in both places, the southern-fried feel of each town indelibly marking the man he would become. Waycross was in the thick of Confederate country, perched at the edge of the sprawling, spongy mass of the Oke-fenokee swamplands. It was a small, neat Deep South town, a crossroad stopover turned tidy and industrious. Everyone knew everyone else, and lives intertwined in wet heat and long-held convention.

Winter Haven was a world away. It had formed around citrus fields and had evolved quickly from a rough-and-tumble outpost to a small American town in the center of paradise with aspirations toward the cosmopolitan. Gram arrived just as postwar optimism was beginning to burst, the nation anxious to put the economic, cultural, and political woes behind, far in the past.

The Snivelys had toiled for two decades in the Florida dirt, but by 1947 they were resting pleasantly on their laurels, enjoying their role as the city's ad hoc royal family. These were good days, shiny and polished bright, the sky scrubbed clean. The Snively family would congregate on the shore of Lake Eloise for barbecues or boat races, sitting in the cool green grass to watch the water skiers perform at the Cypress Gardens amusement park next door.

Built on land that had once been owned by the Sniveleys, the Gardens were a sprawling estate filled with intricate ornamental flowerbeds, wooden bridges, rose arbors, and towering magnolia trees. In 1936, a local entrepreneur had transformed the area into a Disneyesque tourist lure with a *Gone with the Wind* feel. Orchids bloomed, girls in antebellum gowns wandered through eucalyptus groves, and professional water-skiers performed feats of daring for New Yorkers, who wiped sweat away while they soaked up the Florida sun.

Snively Groves OJ ad. COURTESY OF THE SNIVELY FAMILY.

Papa John more or less owned Winter Haven, whose streets and schools bore the names of various family members. He ran the family business with an iron fist, lording over not only everyday matters at the office but also more personal matters at home. In keeping with the social structures of the day, the Snivelys were expected to display strict decorum at all times, keeping a firm grasp on their role as pillars of the community. They did this in large part by refusing to admit to their

John Snively, Sr.

John Snively, Sr., President and Director. Citrus producer since 1911—Director of the Florida Citrus Exchange from 1917 to 1934—Director of the Tavares and Gulf Railroad—Director of Florida Citrus Producers Trade Ass'n., Past President of the Cooperative Fruit and Vegetable Association, Washington, D. C. Past Director of the Exchange National Bank of Winter Haven, Florida.

John A. Snively, III

Pate Snively

"The younger generation of the Snively Family whom we expect to carry on in the Citrus Industry; looking ever forward to progress, harmony and better economic conditions in the Industry."

Rob Hoskins

Gram Connor

Snively Groves brochure.
COURTESY OF THE SNIVELY FAMILY.

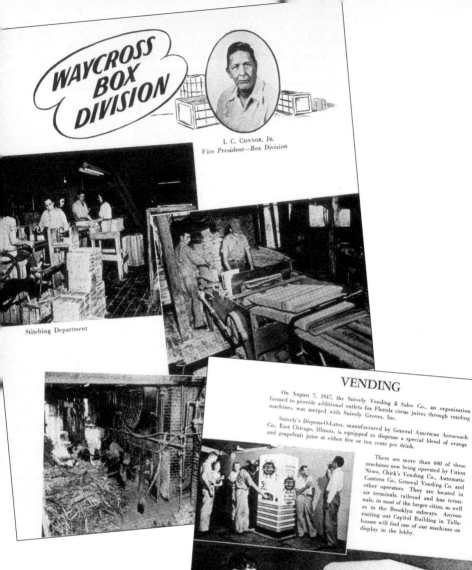

WAYCROSS BOX DIVISION

I. C. CONNOR, JR.
Vice President—Box Division

Stitching Department

VENDING

On August 7, 1947, the Snively Vending & Sales Co., an organization formed to provide additional outlets for Florida citrus juices through vending machines, was merged with Snively Groves, Inc.

Snively's Dispens-O-Lator, manufactured by General American Aerocoach Co., East Chicago, Illinois, is equipped to dispense a special blend of orange and grapefruit juice at either five or ten cents per drink.

There are more than 600 of these machines now being operated by Union News, Chick's Vending Co., Automatic Canteen Co., General Vending Co. and other operators. They are located in air terminals, railroad and bus terminals, in most of the larger cities, as well as in the Brooklyn subways. Anyone visiting our Capitol Building in Tallahassee will find one of our machines on display in the lobby.

Snively Groves brochure.
COURTESY OF THE SNIVELY
FAMILY.

own vulnerabilities. Even at a young age, Gram was aware of the artifice, the face his family put on for the world versus the one he witnessed at home.

Both in Waycross and in Winter Haven, the Connors did their damnedest to meet expectations. On the surface, they adhered to the neatly drawn conventions of the times. Gram may have been indulged materially, but rarely emotionally, as high drama and suffocating mother love were looked upon with distinct distaste. Avis lived first for herself. Her children were to be scrubbed clean and their clothes neatly pressed. They were expected to have impeccable manners and to conduct themselves, as well as they could, like adults.

This was the South before the civil rights movement tore open scabbed-over wounds, a South where segregation was the norm. The Snivelys were not overtly racist in any way, but the tired framework of tradition remained intact. Upper-class families like Gram's had black servants working as cooks, maids, and drivers.

Gram grew up surrounded by a slew of black faces. Despite the circumstances, he developed an intimacy with some, which sometimes blossomed into friendship. One of the servant's sons taught Gram how to ride his bike and brought him to Sunday mass at the local Baptist church so he could hear the singing.

Despite the stiff decorum, there remained a dreamy sort of intimacy within the Connor family. At night Gram and his sister Avis would play outside while the adults gathered in the sunroom at the back of the house and drank with their friends. As summer nights pressed in, Gram would lay down in the front yard, staring up at the pinprick stars and listen to women's laughter and the chilled rattle of ice against glass.

There was music always, everywhere—swarthy crooners of the day, those voices that made Avis swoon, old bluegrass tunes on the record player, and local country hits on the car radio. Coon Dog was particularly obsessed, finding some solace in music, something that soothed the emotional wounds he had suffered in World War II.

Coon Dog had been in the Air Force and was at Pearl Harbor when the bombs dropped. He had flown more than fifty combat

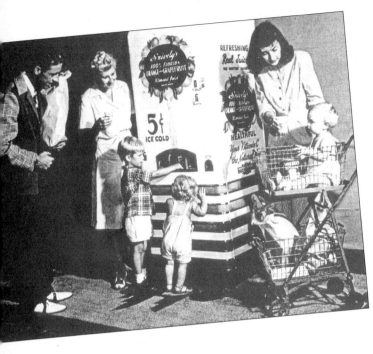

From top: Snively OJ; The Snively family factory. COURTESY OF THE SNIVELY FAMILY.

The Snivelys in *Cosmo*. COURTESY OF THE SNIVELY FAMILY.

COSMOPOLITAN

April, 1957 • 35¢

Arthur Godfrey and his daughter, Pat, on Biscayne Bay

FABULOUS FLORIDA
America's Lush Playground

Eight-page Fashion Forecast of Wonderful Summer Clothes

Where It's Fun to Be Old

Florida's Most Amazing Business Woman

Are Florida Coeds Prettiest?

What Effect Does Climate Really Have on Your Health?

Fiction

THE HEAT
Complete S
by John
Plus Fou

missions and had been made a major and a squadron commander. He had seen death, had dropped it from above, and the memory of it haunted him, surfacing in a melancholy that had increased each passing year. He'd been taking music lessons in Hawaii before the Japanese attack, and the sound of those old songs was a poignant reminder of the young man he had been before the war.

He had become an avid collector of vinyl over the years, and he and Gram spent long afternoons sifting through his old 45s and long-plays. On lazy Saturday mornings, they would drive downtown and spend the day together at the record shops, searching out new finds.

Together, the whole family would gather around the radio each week and listen to a local show called *The Hoot Owl Jamboree*, which featured folks like Carl Perkins, Hank Williams, Guitar Slim, and Lloyd Price singing "Kawliga" and "The Things That I Used to Do." Coon Dog would grill burgers while Avis curled Little Avis's hair. Gram would sit cross-legged with his ear up to the speaker, eyes closed, mouthing the words to his favorite numbers.

Coon Dog and Avis saw their young son's interest in music early on. They saw the way he responded to the radio, even as the baby fat still lurked in his cheeks. They gave him piano lessons with a neighbor, Mrs. Maynard, and filled the house with instruments—a children's drum set, a trumpet, and a toy piano that the family kept in the light-filled enclosed porch at the back of the house.

Rock was in its raw and nascent form then, birthed in the blues of the South and just about to find its own feet. After school Gram would bike to the boxing factory to wait for his dad on the concrete stoop. He'd watch as the workers gathered for after-hours jamborees, pulling out guitars and banjos and embarking on noisy renditions of the favorites tunes of the day, songs by Patsy Cline, Lefty Frizzell, and Hank Williams.

Music threaded through Gram's daily life, too. It floated out of car windows and blasted out over Waycross's main drag during Saturday night sock hops. There was music at home and with friends. Everywhere music was filling up Gram's young head. Certain sounds especially drew him—moth to flame—the earthy, sexual swagger that Jerry Lee Lewis coaxed from the piano keys, that enticing boogie-woogie strut that spoke of grown-up daring and something else, something masculine and slightly predatory.

During his piano lessons, Gram carefully pecked out the tunes he loved. He was diligent and focused, and he found his way across the keyboard with a preternatural ease. He learned the standards his mother loved, Cole Porter tunes and swinging Nat King Cole numbers, and then found his way through his own quickly developing tastes, trying his best to play with the same yearning and high emotion he saw in his heroes.

Summer evenings were spent with fingers pressed to the keys, the blurred chirp of insects outside, the low-tide smell of the swamps mixed with the sharp, sweet scent of Mrs. Maynard's sugar cookies. When Gram was eight years old, he wrote his first song, his fingers skittering across the ivories, tapping out a makeshift ramble he brazenly dubbed "Gram Boogie."

Meanwhile, the world rolled on. Chuck Berry was singing "Maybellene." The Teenagers were asking, "Why Do Fools Fall in Love?" Rosa Parks refused to give up her seat on the bus, James Dean had just died, wrapped in the bent metal frame of his Porsche Spyder, and Elvis Presley was about to conquer a nation with a thrust of his pelvis.

Gram was only nine when he went to see Elvis for the first time. He had heard Elvis on the radio, had seen pictures of the chiseled cheekbones, the dark-eyed sneer, and he had begged his parents for tickets. Gram almost always got what he wanted, and on February 22, 1956, he was there to see his hero, live and in the flesh.

He had come with two giddy young bobbysoxers in tow, already the ladies' man. He tried to act cool and smooth in front of his pretty companions, but he was excited beyond words, butterfly-stomached and fidgety with anticipation. He played the gentleman, nonetheless, waiting patiently with the girls in the long line of ticket holders, leading them through the crowd, a hand on the small of their backs. He sat between them in the echoing auditorium, looking up into the high domed ceiling, listening to the restless noise of the audience, the quick intake of a thousand breaths as the lights finally went low.

Elvis had recorded his first demo at Sam Phillips's Sun Studio in July of 1953, and by the time he arrived in Waycross, he was riding a crest of regional popularity. In a few months, he'd appear on the Ed Sullivan show for the first time and seduce the world in the process. But in Waycross that night, he was still young and hungry, not yet the superstar, not yet the "King" in the polyester rhinestone jumpsuit.

Just a few days before the Georgia shows, Elvis had stopped in at RCA in Nashville to record some tracks for his upcoming self-titled album. He had laid down "Lawdy Ms. Clawdy" and "Heartbreak Hotel" just forty-eight hours before arriving in Waycross. He had been on tour for months by then, playing that night with Little Jimmy Dickens as the opening act, two shows a day, one at seven and another at nine.

Gram on the couch in Waycross. COURTESY OF THE SNIVELY FAMILY.

When Elvis finally took the stage in Georgia, he looked young, impossibly young, full-cheeked and grinning, brown eyes catching the lights in the rafters, hair greased, black and immovable, liquid bright. He started the show by blowing through what were to become classic hits, "Hound Dog," "Don't Be Cruel," and "Love Me Tender." The tiny amplifiers did their best to beat against the screams of the crowds.

Cocky, beautiful, and completely fearless, Elvis threw himself into the performance with a desperate energy. He was just realizing the effect he had on his audiences, and he was wielding that power joyfully, aware of the ripple that shook the room at every thrust of his pelvis, aware of the picture he made in his sharkskin suit.

Gram watched everything with saucer eyes—the hip shake, the raw ache in that beautiful voice. And he watched the crowd, too. He watched the way the girls' faces had gone pink, mouths slightly open, a slight glint of moisture on the lips. He watched the way they closed their eyes and swayed, the way they clutched the backs of the seats in front of them, knuckles white as they held themselves up, the way the music took hold of them and shook something down deep.

When the show was over, something went empty in the room. A hot longing rose up from the crowd. Later Gram would make his way backstage, pushing along the auditorium hall and sidling past instrument cases and groups of young women fanning themselves with damp programs, their curls in disarray. He would march straight into Elvis's dressing room, where he would demand an autograph and offer congratulations with the mix of audacity and good breeding he had learned from his mother.

For Gram, the allure of music was obvious. He had always gotten the most attention when he was performing, all those impromptu piano recitals at his grandparents' house, the time spent strumming guitar on the front steps of his house in Waycross, and his belting out "Jailhouse Rock" for the neighborhood kids. After the Elvis show, he was hungry to learn and began to take Ms. Maynard's piano lessons even more seriously. He was a natural. His fingers were thin and graceful, beautifully shaped, and impossibly long. He was also an innate performer, content in the spotlight and always craving adoration, even from a crowd of strangers.

He spent long afternoons perched on the front steps, lip-synching to the worn grooves floating up from his singles collection, the local girls gathering to watch the show. Elvis would come through the tiny speakers of the portable record player, echoing across the lawn through the needle scratches and heat-warped vinyl, and Gram would sing along. He would mimic the snarl, the smooth ballad ringing, the deep-throated pleading, all the while trying to find his own way through the songs.

Gram loved the way the music rose up in him, unbidden, the way his mouth formed well-loved words, his hips jerking as he took sly sideways glances at the girls. Even at ten years old, he was eyeing the smooth foreheads, the lean tan legs beneath pleated skirts, that long arc of calf muscle leading to the innocence of white and black saddle shoes half-buried in the tall grass.

Before his father's suicide, Gram's life was, in many ways, charmed. He was king of his own hill, the good-looking, talented, bright young son of a moneyed southern family. There was the air of the elite about him, and the clean safety of wealth.

Even in Waycross, Cecil and Avis managed to stay at the center of a hectic social whirlwind, with church groups, bridge club, and late night parties. Gram and his sister Avis were showered with gifts and instilled with a sense of privilege and a touch of unapologetic decadence. Whether it was food on the dinner plate or presents under the tree, abundance was the order of the day. For the Connors, showing Waycross that they had come from something more was a social obligation.

Gram spent summers and holidays in Winter Haven under the moral and social guidance of Hanie and Papa John. He was encouraged in his musical ambitions, but he was pressured to keep up his grades. The expectation was that he would one day inherit a piece of the family business. In keeping with this line of thought, Avis decided private school would be most appropriate place to educate her only son.

Bolles School in Jacksonville, Florida, was an all-boys military academy doing its best to mimic the high-end prep schools of the Northeast. There were arched walkways, colonnades, neatly manicured campus lawns, cathedral ceilings in the dining hall, a tightly structured course load, and a prim, professional staff. At Bolles, it was trumpets at dawn, English, math, rifle practice, science, and football drills.

Gram hated it. He was only eleven and sick with loneliness. The lack of women was a hole driven deep. Gram missed the Waycross bobbysoxers, their cotton dresses wet and wilted from the heat. He missed his sister, who was always in his shadow, and he missed his mother's perfume. He would wander into the music rooms and pick out melancholy tunes on the piano or sit in his dorm room and write angst-filled poetry in his spiral-bound notebook.

He paid only vague attention to his classes but read voraciously on the side. The Beats had only recently made their way to the South, and Allen Ginsberg's *Howl* had just turned up on the shelves of the Jacksonville bookshops. Gram was instantly enamored of the Beat writers and the freedom that pulsed beneath their verse. He fell in love with Kerouac and Ferlinghetti, sometimes submitting their work as his own in his English classes.

It was at Bolles that he began to understand the true power of a well-placed word or a flow of phrase he could bury his loneliness in. Music was first, but books were a close second. They were a doorway to another reality, that strange, raw experiment the Beats were carrying out in faraway San Francisco and New York. His respect and curiosity for his favorite writers inevitably lead to his own explorations. Matching guitar chords with inquisitive lyrical expression, Gram found an affinity for the confessional at a time when most kids were burying emotions under towering adolescent egos.

Not that Gram lacked confidence. He willingly stepped into the spotlight at school dances, wooing the girls with a slick, steady gaze that made him seem older and more experienced that he really was.

Luke Lewis interview
Interview by Shirley Halperin

As Grammy Award–winning Mercury Nashville chairman and founder of the Lost Highway label, Luke Lewis is one of the savviest men in the modern music business. With Lost Highway, Lewis has helped to nurture the careers of everyone from Lucinda Williams to Ryan Adams, providing a home to musicians who sit decidedly outside the Nashville country mainstream. Lewis's vast contribution to the industry is in part due to his own close ties to his high school buddy Gram Parsons, a boyhood friend who helped nurture Lewis's own true love of music and music making.

Q: The first thing I wanted to know is just your first impressions of Gram. Do you remember the first time you saw him, the first time you got introduced to him? Take me back.

A: It was a long time ago. You know, it's funny, I'll tell you what I remember most, and this is freaky, I guess, but we both had sort of longish hair, I wouldn't say *long*, but long enough that we took shit for it. We'd get people saying "are you trying to be a Beatle?" I'm talking it was barely over the ears, you know what I mean. I was trying to grow a ponytail because there was a film called *Tom Jones*. Albert Finney had a ponytail and I thought that was cool so I was trying to grow a ponytail and Gram was just being Gram. As far as first recollections, probably those are from football. Believe it or not, the guy was on a football team. We were on it together. We were in the same class. I remember he always had a little twinkle in his eye. He had presence, even then, you know what I mean? He had some presence about him, and it wasn't like, you know, we were sixteen, you don't look at one of your peers and say he's a star, you know what I mean? No way. But he was mischievous and pretty sly. I don't remember him ever getting caught. There was a whole bunch of us that got thrown out of that school. I didn't get invited back after my junior year. They sent my dad a letter and said we don't want you son here anymore.

Q: What did you do?

A: Lots of things. We had this service club kind of a thing, it was really like a fraternity, it was called Centurions. It was like a gang really because we were paying off the night watchmen so we could slip out at night and go downtown and run around with the girls and stuff. We'd also pay the guys who were in charge of punishing us. The place was a military school a year prior to when we went there and it still had vestiges. Like if you got in trouble you had to run twenty laps around the football field or some goofy shit like that. We would get caught for something and pay the guys that were counting so we wouldn't run any laps, that kind of thing. Anyways, so it was seemingly kind of petty but the school frowned on it. They had so many rules you couldn't breathe without breaking some of them.

Q: What year was this?

A: I think that was '62 and '63 because all of us that were old enough can remember where we were when Kennedy was killed. I remember that night—I'm pretty sure it was a full moon—and the school we went to was on the St. John's River, a really beautiful location. It had this really long dock that stuck out into the river and it had a boathouse on it. There was a sitting area out by the boathouse and a bunch of us, the night that Kennedy was assassinated, went out there and Gram played and sang for hours. I still remember the song was called "You Heard My Voice and You Know My Name." I think that's the title of it. He sang that song that night and I never forgot it. I used to make him sing it afterwards every chance I got. But I have this really distinct memory of that night being pretty special, because of that song, I think. By then we had become good enough friends that we went home to each other's homes for the holidays. I went down to Winter Haven with him one Easter and he came down to West Palm with me a couple of times. I taught him how to surf there, and he got to be a pretty good surfer. He was really a pretty good athlete. He was also full of mischief. Once in a while, when everyone was sitting around playing songs, he would play an old Scottish folk ballad or something and tell everybody he wrote it, those kinds of things. It was fun to bust him if you happened to know the truth.

Q: Was he playing old country songs?

A: No, he wasn't at all, not yet. We were Ray Charles fans, all of us. Dylan was having an impact, and all the folkies were around and Gram was playing at hootenannies and stuff. It wasn't anything to do with country, it was all folk and R&B music. The country thing, I don't know where he first heard the Louvin Brothers, but when he got to Boston I know that you can start to hear it in his music. I only saw him a half dozen times because I was going to school in upstate New York and he was in Boston. But I'd go over there because that's where we went to party and see him.

Q: Back in those school days did he ever say "This is what I wanna do when I grow up"?

A: Absolutely. There's no question about that. Honestly, we were sixteen, seventeen at the time and he was already going off, making some money on weekends doing it. And he practiced all the time. He had some serious musical roots or just chops. But he practiced endlessly. Vocally too, vocal exercises. He would sing songs that were particularly hard in order to work on his voice. There wasn't much doubt that he was pretty committed to it.

Q: Tell me about your own involvement in the music industry.

A: It was after Gram. I had heard every record he ever made. The *Sweetheart of the Rodeo* record was just life-changing for loads of people. That one was like, "Holy shit, he's on his way!" He managed to fall in with the people who were my kind of musical heroes, if there was such a thing, and who made the music that I loved, that whole shelter group with Leon Russell and then the Byrds. He went everywhere I would have gone. Where I went with my musical tastes, he was already there. I'd like to say in some cases he led me because I don't know if I would be sitting in the desk I'm at right now if it hadn't been for him. I didn't know about country music. I mean I had heard Ray Charles sing some of it but not really, you know? It was Gram who turned me on, otherwise I don't think I would have paid much attention. If it wasn't for Gram, I don't think I would have known who the Louvin Brothers were. I would have just been a pure rock and roller. I mean, his records weren't big records, so if I hadn't been paying attention to what he was doing I wouldn't have found my way I don't think.

Q: Did you ever get to work together in any capacity?

A: No. It was one of those things that looked like it was going happen, but then he went off and died. I guess the year he died I went to work for CBS Records and there's no doubt that our paths would have crossed a bunch of times if he had made it. So that's always been sad to me. But you know, I've got nothing but fond memories. He was just a good buddy to run with and we had a lot of laughs and warm times and my parents really liked him. He was a real southern gentleman. He was a gentleman who carried himself well and you could take him home to mom and dad and he knew how to act. He got raised right. He was a really charming guy. Pretty witty, good sense of humor. But he had some darkness because he had experienced some tragedy, before most of us do, in his life.

Q: What do you think the country music industry thinks of him today?

A: I think there's reverence and that's a cool thing. It isn't like the guy was a superstar and had zillions of hits and sold hundreds of millions of records or anything. But I could walk up and down Music Row and take a poll of how many people know of him or know his music and there'd be a whole bunch of them and that's a pretty strong statement. You'd get the same response from kids who are music aficionados or anybody who's a hard-core music junkie.

Q: What about your favorite Gram song? Do you have one?

A: It's probably "Hickory Wind." In that song you can tell he had found himself. He had reverence and respect for where he came from. Like somebody talking about their home in a prideful way, soulfully and sincerely. All of those things came across vocally, in everything he did. I can go to some Burrito stuff that makes you shake your ass and is great, but "Hickory Wind," that would be the one.

Gram was still young and incredibly vulnerable, and those miles that separated him from his family seemed impossibly far.

During the spring at Bolles that would follow his father's suicide, Gram fell more or less apart, skipping most of his classes and talking back to his teachers. His already low tolerance for authority was wearing dangerously thin. The death of his father was a black space in him, but there was no one to explain his troubles to, no one to listen.

Instead, an immense anger settled in his guts, and he turned against the suffocating discipline of Bolles. To be told what to do was something Gram was not accustomed to. He had so rarely been denied his whims at home that he had an innate sense of his own maturity and intelligence over his peers. He grew aloof and blew off classes to hole up somewhere with his guitar. Sometimes he would wander into Jacksonville to flirt with the public-school girls who haunted the local soda fountains.

Coon Dog's death certificate.

A few months into the semester, his mother sent him a letter that shook him deeply. He fingered through it repeatedly, alone in his room or on the campus grass, searching for clues to what might be in his mother's impenetrable heart.

After the tragedy, Avis had opted to remain in Winter Haven. She had asked the servants to pack up the Waycross house and send her belongings down to the Snively mansion, where she and her daughter soon settled in to the luxurious, orderly surroundings. She felt safe in the house where she had grown up.

After a few months at Winter Haven, Avis had a met another man. Bob Parsons, a successful local businessman, was pursuing her with stubborn persistence, lavishing her with the kind of amorous attention that had been missing from her marriage to Coon Dog. Avis was still young, a vulnerable thirty-four-year-old widow who was anxious for male attention, and Bob Parsons was Cecil Connor's opposite.

Where Coon Dog had been melancholy, with his sleepy eyes and sad, fleshy face, Bob was neatly put together and defiantly optimistic. He had a strong chin and glass-cut cheekbones. He was a dapper gentleman of the world, and his appearance and demeanor contrasted in every way with Cecil's homespun, humble charm.

The Snively clan was less than enthusiastic about unseemly arrival of Parsons, his courtship of Avis cutting uncomfortably close to the accepted period of mourning. His sudden adoration of the favorite Snively daughter fueled suspicions that he was trying to dig into the family fortune. Avis, however, had always done as she pleased, and Papa John was no longer around to dictate his family's decisions or to steer its intimacies. Avis was flattered by Bob's attention and smitten with his well-cut suits and suave demeanor.

From Bolles, Gram tried to dissect Parsons's motivations in an attempt to understand the desperation and subtle desires that fueled his mother's attraction to this man. At a stiff introductory dinner during a weekend break from school, Gram met Parsons for the first time. Gram had cut his hair for the occasion, had scrubbed himself pink, and had made it a point to shake his mother's lover's hand with a straight back and as much of an air of superiority as he could muster.

By dessert he was surprised by how hard and how often he had laughed at Parsons's jokes and was taken aback by the vague but unmistakable feeling of admiration that rose up in him at the sight of Parsons's silk handkerchief and spit-polished shoes. When the after-dinner drinks arrived, Gram noticed the flutter of his mother's eyelashes, the way Bob Parsons touched the underside of her wrist distractedly as he spoke. When Avis and Bob looked at each other, Gram's heart went numb. He saw something pass between the two adults that he only slightly understood but knew he could not compete with.

After his return to Bolles that Sunday, Gram sank further into a paralyzing despondency that nothing, not even music, could penetrate. He skipped classes and wandered, dazed, through the approaching heat of a southern summer, watching the magnolias grow heavy with blossoms and the afternoon sky crack with thunder. By June the school's discipline board declared Gram, "unfit for continued academic study" at Bolles, a decision that simultaneously humiliated his mother and set Gram free.

Although Avis was shattered by her son's failure, she was kind and wise enough not to punish him for it. She knew he was hurting and that his missed his father and his old life. In the hopes of helping her children heal, she packed the family into a first-class train car and set off on a cross-country escape.

Train travel in 1959 could be as luxurious an experience as any four-star hotel, and Avis spared no expense. Days were spent in the glass-roofed observation car as the swampland of the South slipped away in a red dirt, green-leafed blur. The tracks dragged them slowly north, diagonally across the country. The train ground to a stop at the jagged edge of the Grand Canyon, where Gram climbed over the burnt orange rock, looked down into that deep tear in the earth, and felt his heart go clean and empty.

Back on the train, rushing through desert and shrub, something began to spread inside Gram like a flapping of wings in his chest.

The dry ground spread under an infinite sky. Everything was as perfect and sterile as bone, washed in clear heat and white-yellow sunlight. Watching the desert from the train window, Gram fell in love with the rawness of the landscape, the way nothing could hide there and everything was true to itself.

By the next morning, they were in San Francisco, falling out of the train car and into the city, with its clusters of Victorian clapboard houses washed in the light off the Bay. San Francisco was the place where Gram's Beat heroes had been birthed, inspired, where Ferlinghetti groped for words in wharf cafés, finding poetry in the smell of black coffee and sea salt. Gram woke up early in one of the grand hotels and wandered the streets while the fog still clung to the red brick and worn wood buildings.

Later, crossing the Bay Bridge, he looked down at the blue gray Pacific and the cypress-strewn hills that lined the mouth of the harbor. The family took a northern route toward home, boarding a train that cut through the buffalo plains of Montana, through South Dakota, the wildflower flatlands of Kansas, the thick maple forests of Pennsylvania, and finally pulled into the ornate cavern of Grand Central Station.

Gram's first step into the steel canyons of Manhattan was as revelatory for him as it was for any curious young kid before him. Avis noted the slow closing of a wound in her son's heart and was determined to finally rid her family of the sorrow of the past year with a dazzling whirl of activity and decadence. To start, there was the best hotel, starched white sheets, linen and silver, afternoon tea, and finger sandwiches.

They rode the carousal in Central Park, and in the evenings, Avis snuck Gram into the fashionable Upper West Side supper clubs. In a pressed suit and tie, he looked older than his twelve years and carried himself as if he had already seen too much of the world. Grief had aged Gram, thinned the plumpness from his cheeks, made his eyes aloof, and turned him from a chubby, soft-faced child into a strikingly handsome young man. In the heart of high-class Manhattan, Gram sat by his mother's side in white leather banquettes, sipping martinis with a twist and watching some of the era's great crooners, such as Nat King Cole and Tony Bennett, sing live.

By the time the family returned to Winter Haven, Gram was nearly whole again, ready to move away from the pain and the hollow ache of the past. He was enrolled at St. Joseph's, the city's Catholic school (despite the fact he wasn't Catholic), and he settled into academia with an unexpected ease. He joined the debate team and embraced his studies, particularly his English classes. Poetry and novels were still an evolving obsession. Music, however, was at the center of Gram's life; it was the glue that held his fragile ego in place.

The radio that year was playing change, rock's early roots pushing out of the southern soil and crossing the ocean in both directions. Chuck Berry, Fats Domino, Jerry Lee Lewis, all of them brewing spitfire, turning the drawing room piano into an instrument of imminent destruction, into sex and bad-boy blues.

The Billboard charts revealed the evolution. "Love Potion No. 9" by the Clovers was making way for the coming psychedelic sound, the Isley Brothers' "Shout" was stirring up mischief, and the Flamingos were singing their dreamily obsessive "I Only Have Eyes For You." The Winter Haven station played rock 'n' roll dosed liberally with country, with artists such as Johnny Cash and the Tennessee Two belting out "Folsom Prison Blues" and Carl Perkins strutting through his own version of "Blue Suede Shoes."

A few months later, Bob Parsons officially announced his engagement to Avis. Gram wasn't exactly happy, but he kept himself closed tight, protecting his sister with soothing words and reluctantly offering his approval for his mother's new lover. At thirteen, Gram was already well aware of his lack of control over the situation and opted instead to make the best of it.

Avis and Bob were wed in a small private ceremony that took place less than a year after Coon Dog Connor's death. Gram, hair oiled and smile thin, watched his new parents dance together, and he slowly headed over to the piano. He picked out the songs his mother loved, careful not to play anything reminiscent of his real father, his heart pounding against his ribs as he watched his sister's eyes.

In his pale tuxedo, Gram was no longer a boy. His cheekbones had gotten higher, and a pale dusting of sandy hair crossed his upper lip and clung to a slightly receding chin. Little Avis was prim, preening, in white frills. Both she and Gram were charmed, despite themselves, by Bob Parsons's brilliant, mischievous grin and a constant shower of gifts.

The new family moved into a midsized ranch house on Piedmont Drive in Winter Haven, located in a neighborhood of tasteful brick houses with wide green yards, sunrooms, spacious two-car garages, and basketball nets. The driveway was poured just after they moved in, and Gram leaned over the wet cement and carved in his sister's name and his own, marking Piedmont as his territory and transforming the house into a home. He wanted desperately to start again, to have his mother happy and sister safe, and although he barely knew Bob, he liked something about him, enough to try to make it work.

Bob Parsons, for his part, was not fool enough to ostracize his new bride's oldest son. He might have been studiously dismissed by the rest of the Snively family, but Bob was intent on making an impression on the kids, and he immediately began to spoil them shamelessly. Attempting to buy Gram's allegiance with a slew of new instruments, he built a music room off the garage, a true rehearsal space stocked with guitars, drums, and a piano.

Gram's bedroom had its own separate entrance, and Gram began immediately to carve out his independence, coming, going, and doing as he pleased, correctly assuming that Parsons would be reluctant to punish any indiscretions. He grew his hair out from boar's bristle to a soft fringe that hung close to his eyes and curled slightly at the tips, and he spent most of his time in the music room listening to scratch-needle 45s.

After a few months at school, Gram met Jim Carlton, a young musician and another non-Catholic enrolled at St. Joseph's to avoid the perils of public school. The two formed a bond based on

A party at Piedmont Drive. COURTESY OF THE SNIVELY FAMILY.

their mutual love of music, learning loose numbers for guitar and piano from their combined collection of singles by artists such as Ray Charles, Chuck Berry, and the Everly Brothers.

Jim and Gram sought out every new record released, making weekly trips to the local record store, hungry for anything that felt fresh, anything that resonated with some sort of soul. Gram was still hooked hard on Presley and had little patience for soft-edged crooners like Bobby Darin. He tried his best to emulate his hero when he played guitar, standing cocky, legs spread, collar up, and with a slight sneer at the edges of his lips. Friends flooded the house for afternoon listening sessions, picking up the scattered instruments and working their way through rough-and-tumble jams.

Gram was happy again. By the end of the spring semester at St. Joseph's, he had brought his grades back up and regained his emotional equilibrium. Avis, anxious to get her son back into boarding school, took the opportunity to enroll him for fall at Graham Eckes School, in Palm Beach.

Gram was not pleased. He had liked St. Joseph's, liked living at

Dearest Connie,
    Did you get the braclet?
I'm off at bording school now. It's all [...]
I'm not crazy about it. All the girls here [...]
up. But you're the only girl I need anywa[...]
Send me a few pictures of you. The bo[...]
picture with me is Tony Andamo from [...]
he's a great guy. I play elec. guitar for a [...]
called the "red coats now." I'll send yo[...]
as soon as they come out. ▬ Please [...]
it would mean alot. All my Love,
                                    Hram

Connie O'Connell
Suwannee Dr.
Waycross, GA.

...ME

I can only
offer a
SHABBY
EXCUSE
for Not Writing...

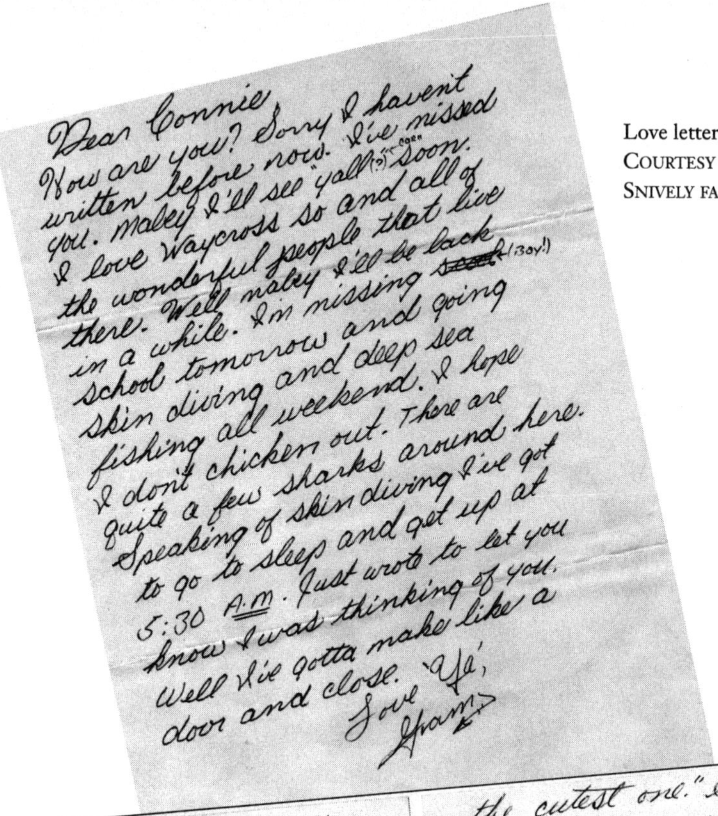

Dear Connie
How are you? Sorry I havent
written before now. I've missed
you. Maby I'll see "yall(?)" soon.
I love Waycross so and all of
the wonderful people that live
there. Well maby I'll be back
in a while. I'm missing ~~[illegible]~~ (Boy!)
school tomorrow and going
skin diving and deep sea
fishing all weekend. I hope
I dont chicken out. There are
quite a few sharks around here.
Speaking of skin diving I've got
to go to sleep and get up at
5:30 A.M. Just wrote to let you
know I was thinking of you.
Well I've gotta make like a
door and close. 'Ya',
Love
Gram

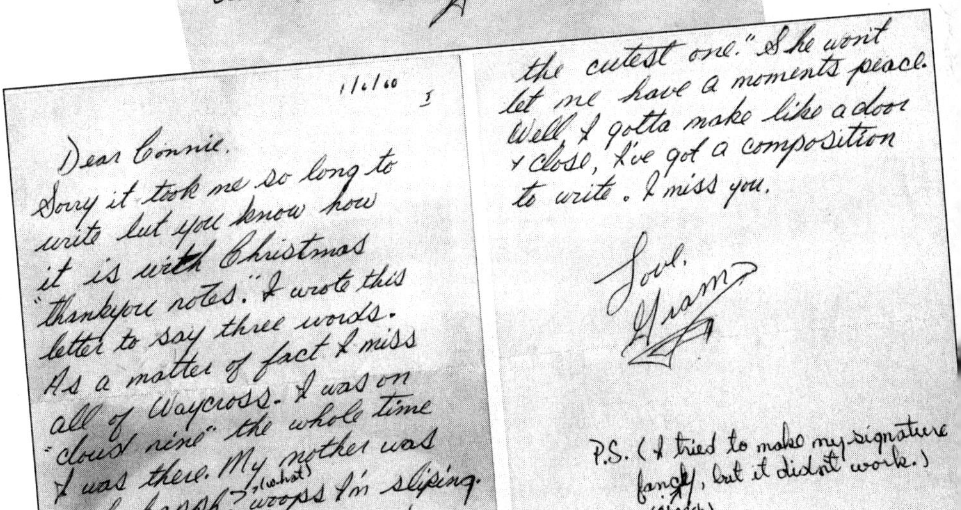

1.1.60 1

Dear Connie,
Sorry it took me so long to
write but you know how
it is with Christmas
"thankyou notes." I wrote this
letter to say three words.
As a matter of fact I miss
all of Waycross. I was on
"cloud nine" the whole time
I was there. My mother was
real happh?(what) woops I'm sliping.
What I meant to say was
happy (yes I've got it now), when she
heard I liked you. She said,
"I always told you she'd be—
the cutest one." She wont
let me have a moments peace.
Well I gotta make like a door
& close, I've got a composition
to write. I miss you.

Love,
Gram

P.S. (I tried to make my signature
fancy, but it didnt work.)
(Sheesh)

Love letters to Connie. COURTESY OF THE SNIVELY FAMILY.

home, and didn't want to leave Jim and his new friends in Winter Haven to board somewhere hours away. Going to Palm Beach felt like deliberate abandonment.

Lonely, Gram wrote weekly letters to one of his girlfriends in Waycross, Connie O'Connell, that were full of an increasing longing. He wasn't used to being told what to do. He missed his dog, missed being able to smoke, which his family had allowed, and he missed Connie with an adolescent's heated ardor.

"I'm off at boarding school now," he wrote. "It's all right, but I'm not crazy about it. All the girl's here are stuck up. But you're the only girl I need anyway. *Please* send me a few pictures of you . . . please write, it would mean a lot. All my love, Gram."

He tried to make the best of Eckes, however, keeping cheerful and making friends with Tony, a South American exchange student with whom he raised some preteen hell. He also formed his first band at Eckes (Red Coats Now) and carried his guitar with him everywhere.

But by Christmas, he'd had it. Calling on Bob Parsons to help his cause, he managed to convince Avis to let him come back home, moving back into his room on Piedmont and settling back into the groove with his Winter Haven pals.

He and Jim Carlton continued their easy friendship. They went to shows together, seeing Jerry Lee Lewis and Roy Orbison when they came through town, standing together in the midst of a packed house and soaking up Lewis's wild-eyed stage antics, that splash of hair over the eyes, the sweat, the white shoes, and the tight suits. Orbison's voice floored them; it was high and sweet and capable of making the hairs on their arms rise.

In the spring of 1960, Gram decided to put together a ragtag band, the Pacers, a group that could pull off Top Forty numbers at teen clubs and Saturday night dances. Gram made himself lead man, doing his imitation Elvis pelvic thrust at their first gig in an echoing train depot in Dundee, Florida. There were only fifty or so kids in the audience, but they were shouting with real enthusiasm between songs and seemed hungry for more.

Avis

Dec 24, 1976
. Now I'll recall Christmas past:
As a child living in Waycross Ga.
I became aware of Christmas every
year when Waycross had its Christmas parade.
    But christmas was not spent in
Waycross. No we always went to Winter
Haven for Christmas. Sometimes we'd
drive there, sometimes we'd catch
the train in Pahunta. Someone
would meet us when we got off at
Avon Park. There was no train station
there. We'd just step down onto the
grass of the park in the middle
of town. It would usually be
warm and sunny. We'd seek the
shade of a palm tree if our ride
hadn't come. Usually Travis would
be there waiting with his big
strong arms He'd lift me down
from the train, his blakk face
radiant with glee.
    Gram and I would sometimes
be able to speak to Poppa John on
the car radio & let him know
we were on our way. And
we'd always have a contest

Sister Avis recalls Christmas in Winter Haven.
COURTESY OF THE SNIVELY FAMILY.

Soon, a moist heat pervaded the room as the jittery twang of a
Ventures intro beckoned the crowd forward. Gram looked out at
the upturned faces; a hundred eyes watched his hands as he played
and watched his face as he held a note in his throat. Something
that had been shattered inside him suddenly slipped together
again. He felt his lungs swell and his cheeks go hot. He smiled,

Jim Carlton Interview
Interview by Jessica Hundley

Jim Carlton first met Gram in Winter Haven in 1959. He played in Gram's high school band, the Legends, establishing a friendship that would last throughout Gram's life.

Q: Tell me a little about what you were doing and where you were at when you and Gram first met?

A: It was toward the end of 1959. I was transferred to a new school, St. Joseph's. My parents were fairly well-to-do. Country club members, they both worked and they were interested in my getting a decent education. The public school system in central Florida was, basically, run by primates. So they sent me to a Catholic school, even though we weren't Catholic. Gram was not Catholic either. I transferred there around the latter part of '59 and saw this kid, who was, for lack of a better term, this rather magnetic kid. He was not pretentious in any way, he was just . . . God did a little dance around him, I think. When I finally met him, we just hit it off. I think he could tell I was pretty much on his same wavelength. I remember we just became fast friends. Immediately. My dad was a well-known musician in the area and Gram was attracted to that, I suppose. He had a piano in his room, but he wasn't in a band yet. Obviously he was one of the brighter kids in school. This was in the eighth grade. I remember the nuns would use Gram to monitor the lower classes. And if a teacher missed a class or missed a day, she'd ask Gram to go sit in that class and tell the kids stories. I mean that kind of confirms his intellect. He was a very bright kid, he had a tremendous sense of humor, and he would have been a great comedy writer. Gram always had great clothes, I don't know where the hell he got them. But he always had better clothes than most of us. He was just urbane and sophisticated, but, and I stress this, not in any pretentious way. He just fell out of bed with it. He would invite me home to his house after school and we'd walk in the house and he had this foghorn by the door. And he would get this foghorn and it's like "Gram's home!" Even though there was nobody there, possibly the maid. We all had maids back then, it was just a common thing.

Q: So Gram's family had servants then?

A: He was close with them. There was a cul-de-sac where people would pick the kids up after school and we saw this station wagon full of black people, and Gram says "I wonder who they're here to pick up?" because, believe me, this is long before integration and I laughed and said "I have no idea." And then Gram got in the car! And I said, "What in the world?" and he said, "C'mon, it's okay." It was Johnny, a guy who worked for the family, and his wife. Gram had no trace, not a shred of bias or prejudice in his attitude, and that was rare enough in the south. Gram was just totally free of that, which was very refreshing. So we got in the car and I'd go home with him and he'd hit the foghorn and then we'd ride around in his go-kart. I mean how many kids had go-karts? He was a privileged kid. We'd ride up and down the street and we'd take his BB guns out at night. I'd end up spending many afternoons and weekend nights over at his house and we'd get up and we'd have English muffins with peanut butter and Pepsis. And I thought now this is my ideal, living here. As an adolescent boy, this was fun. It was all fun because he had a room of his own and he had a double door on his room, back to back, to filter out noise because he had a piano. He had a television, which is common now, but back then kids having a television in their room was not. So I could see that this was a real playground, in fact we used to kid about that. I used to call his house the "playground of the stars." He would play a little piano for me or anybody, and he was writing these songs and they were always with some girl's name in them. So he had a way with the ladies even back then. He was always writing songs about his current girlfriend.

Q: He had a lot of girlfriends?

A: Gram was forever getting slugged by other guys to the point where he actually knew how to take a punch. Other guys were jealous. I can think of two instances right now where he got slugged.

Q: And when did you start playing music together?

A: Gram was in a band called the Pacers that I wasn't involved with, then in '62 Gram hooked up with Jim Stafford. Stafford was three years older than us and was an excellent guitar player, even back then, at sixteen years old. Together we had a band called the Legends, and Gram's family bought him a VW bus, so the band could travel to their gigs. I had a bass fiddle, so this was really early, nearly authentic rock and roll. Stafford played lead guitar, Gram played rhythm and sang. We had this little PA system called Premier System. It wasn't much bigger than a sewing machine. We had one microphone, I think. Gram would sing and play guitar. His folks bought him a Fender Stratocaster, which was a helluva good guitar. That guitar would be worth a few bucks today, a '62 Strat. We started going back and forth to this music store in Lakeland called Casswin Music, to buy records and there was a place called Fat Jack's Deli next door and on the other side there was a little folk music club called the Other Room that Gram would later play in.

Q: What kind of shows did the Legends play?

A: We played in the youth centers back then, the teen centers, the sock hops and stuff like that in the gym. I think our first gig together we all made eight bucks each. It was at the high school gym after the football game. We'd go out on weekends and play the teen centers in the various neighboring cities. Occasionally a long road trip over to Tampa. Gram was too young to drive and so Stafford would drive or one of the older guys in the band would drive. But Gram's parents bought him a car before he was old enough to drive, so that's the kind of money that was around, ostensibly around. Gram had a little Austin Healy Sprite in high school. My folks had a Nash Rambler with foldout seats and Gram would call me late at night and say, "Hey meet me halfway, I have a date with XYZ girl." We'd switch cars and he'd take mine with the foldout seats. He was off exploring his sexuality and the girls and what have you. So yeah that's the car we would always drive, the Austin. We would blast the music and we would just have a ball with that little convertible. You know we were just two youngsters with the world by its tail.

Q: And the lineup of the Legends was changing all the time, is that right?

A: The Legends was kind of a loose organization. Gram's parents had bought these red jackets that had this "L" across the front. There might be four people in the Legends or there might be eight people one night. We didn't much care about the money, we just cared about playing and having fun. Sometimes we had a horn section sometimes we didn't. It was great fun learning that stuff. It was just a meat-and-potatoes rock and roll band. We played "Johnny B. Goode" and a lot of Ventures stuff. When we would go on the road trips to Tampa we'd stay overnight and we though it was real hip to build a pyramid of beer cans in the motel room. So it was just sophomoric, kids having fun. We'd play and smoke cigarettes and drink beer, you know, we were away from home. So it was just adolescent high jinks. Not a bad rock and roll band, authentic for its time.

Q: And the band eventually dissolved after Gram went off to Bolles again.

A: That's right. Senior year Gram went to Bolles and by that time the folk music thing was going pretty strong and Gram and I would go over to that same music store, Casswin Music and would play a little club, the Other Room, that was right next door. It was a little folk music coffeehouse. Gram had gotten a couple really nice folk guitars, then. He got a really beautiful Martin that he kept his whole life. Around that time, in '64 I guess, he got hooked up with the Shilos.

Q: But you two remained close?

A: Oh yeah. He would come home from Bolles for the weekend and we would hang out and have fun and play music. He was also playing some five-string banjo at that time, and I would accompany Gram on guitar, because I was playing guitar by that time. We always liked to hang out with the adults because they were a real party crowd. Gram's parents were fun. We didn't really care to hang out with our high school friends that much because the adults had all the best stories and they had all the liquor. And they would always party and they treated us like adults, for whatever reason. Gram was kind of a mature kid. I guess we both were by that time, kind of past the beer-can stage. We would entertain at these parties and just hang out with the adults and so forth and then he would gig some with the Shilos whenever that opportunity arose. They were all down in Winter Haven and by that time Bob Parsons had bought a club for Gram called the Derry Down. Bob Parsons, I think, has gotten a lot of bad press, but he really loved Gram and he respected Gram. I saw no evidence of any animosity in any way. Bob was kind of a, for lack of a better term, a "Hugh Hefner" type. He was also very sophisticated and urbane and well dressed and they were always throwing parties and Bob was a great chef. It was always a lot of fun around that household. At least that's what I always saw. His mother was sweet, but usually she had a drink in her hand from what I remember. She was kind of, I want to say "poignant." She was a very, very sweet woman who loved her son very much. She was very social, always had friends over, but I am afraid she was in the clutches of alcohol by that time.

Q: And you would see him when he came home to visit after he left for college?

A: Yes. Shortly after that Gram went to Harvard. He was hanging out in the Village, and in Cambridge, and he would come home with all these great new folk songs. He was hanging out with Fred Neil, and he was playing a club called the Night Owl, and was making a little noise as a folk singer. I think that's where he met many of his influences, in particular Fred Neil. He would come home with these Fred Neil songs and I would tape them. I remember one time he came home and he brought back some hash. We smoked that and we'd go out and lay on top of the family's boathouse and look up at the stars. This was all so innocuous, but still we thought we were really living large, and I guess for a couple of eighteen-year-old kids, we were.

Q: Then he headed out to LA.

A: Yeah, and I remember he would come home for his stipend every six months or so, and he would stay at the Cypress Gardens Sheraton. I remember one of the last times I saw him he had several thousand dollars spread out on the bed—he had just gotten his money. I was on my own at that time and he was very, very generous. About every afternoon the family secretary would stop by with some more savings bonds and give them to Gram and we would have these terrific lunches, and I'd say "Thanks so much," and he would say, "It's on some old relative!" He gave me money to get my car fixed and stuff like that. He was very generous and gregarious. I really loved him.

Gram's note to Jim Carlton.
COURTESY OF JIM CARLTON.

gazing into the pale face of a girl in front for just a moment too long, felt her surrender, saw the boys and their envy, and for the first time in his life, felt whole.

Through family connections and Bob Parsons's enthusiasm, the Pacers got regular work at the local sock hops and private parties at the Snively mansion. Their usual repertoire consisted of Chuck Berry tunes, some Ventures numbers, and Pat Boone for the more grown-up affairs. By 1961, Gram had earned a reputation for emotive vocals, an uninhibited stage presence, and his stepfather's generosity.

Jim Stafford, a local guitar impresario a few years older than Gram, decided to woo him away from the Pacers, anxious to add Gram's charms to his own impressive efficiency on lead guitar. Gram invited Stafford over to the Piedmont house, needing the safety of his own turf as a buffer when they played together for the first time. By then Gram was a good enough guitar player, solid and quick to learn, but Stafford was nimble-fingered, a natural.

Gram's own fingers, lean and graceful, were much better suited to the piano, but it was the guitar he wanted to play. He liked the way holding it felt, its heavy wooden neck in his palm. He loved the mobility of it, the independence. He could write and play any song he chose on those six strings, picking out his own melodic chords to back Stafford's intricate solos.

The Legends evolved quickly out of that first jam session. Gram agreed to play with Stafford, bringing on local star drummer Jon Corneal and recruiting Carl and Gerald Chambers, then members of another Polk County act, the Dynamics. Jim Carlton became an occasional member as well, adding his impressive skills on the stand-up bass.

The young group put together a formidable act with the financial help of Bob Parsons, purchasing a PA speaker system and a VW bus for local touring. The Legends may have been teenagers, but they took themselves seriously. Soon, the band was working every weekend, playing gigs all over southern Florida at teen rec centers, weddings, and high school dances.

It was a whirlwind, a small but potent taste of fame. Within a year the band was hot enough to book some TV appearances, driving up to Tampa for a residency on *Hi-Time*, a local teen show on Channel 8. Photos of the band appeared in the Tampa papers, with Gram's big sad eyes gazing into the camera lens, revealing a mixture of hope and longing.

There were girls, too, giddy nervous girls with wet palms and lowered lashes, bawdy girls who smiled coyly and climbed into the back of the van. Gram was in love with them all, in love with the stage, with the music, with the glimpse of a life outside of the Snively expectations, beyond the petty indiscretions that were beginning to affect his mother's new marriage, beyond the norms of a suburban American life, the purgatory of flickering television sets and a slow death. Gram decided early on that he would not let go of what he'd found with the Legends, he would hold onto it like a drowning man until it pulled him up and out of the life he had known and into the future he was aching for.

Meanwhile, a new kind of sound was beginning to pervade the airwaves; groups like Peter, Paul & Mary and the Kingston Trio were wedging their way onto the charts. Gram bought a Journeymen album, placed the needle in the groove, and was hooked from the start.

Folk music—with its focus on guitar, fluid melding of vocals, and, most of all, its words—had a purity to it that appealed to him immediately. There was none of rock 'n' roll's da-doo-run-runs or sha-la-las, none of R&B's sly sexual innuendo. Instead, folk lyrics were about emotional, cultural, or political truths, about pulling open a secret spot inside yourself, about exploring tragedy and the American myth with poetic phrasing and a fearless sincerity. Gram began to explore this new sound on his own, searching for words to match what he was feeling, the swell inside him, the pain, the excitement, the raw desire.

HE HAD FALLEN in love for the first time by then, and fallen deep. Patti Johnson was lean and long with golden brown hair that coated her shoulders and brushed against the small of her back. She was a year older than Gram, a cheerleader with milky skin and wide eyes, and best of all, a pretty, high voice that melted into Gram's own. The two began to sing together, and it wasn't long before Gram had established a side project with Patti and another friend, Dick McNeer, that he named the Village Vanguards.

The Vanguards played shaky, slightly ragtag versions of the popular folk songs of the day, songs by the Cumberland Three and Peter, Paul & Mary. Gram and Patti got lost in each other. Together, the two good-looking, popular teens felt undefeatable. Their gigs took place mostly during the intermissions of Legends shows, their sweet lilting numbers giving the crowd some breathing room before the frantic rockabilly and swing began again.

Gram was elated. At fifteen he already had two bands and a beautiful girlfriend, and he was giddy with the promise of things to come. He spent as much time as he could with Patti, driving the back roads in the little MG convertible Bob had bought him, taking midnight adventures to skinny-dip, the two of them floating in the warm water, watching the moon hit the skin of Lake Eloise.

Back on Piedmont Drive, however, things were becoming increasingly complicated; the air was thick with deceit and a growing resentment. Avis was pregnant again, too soon after the wedding, and already Bob Parsons was beginning to show his true colors. His need for attention was fueling various flirtations, and there was a hint of real indiscretion. Avis, with a swollen belly and sore feet, sat in the sunroom, growing larger and more moody by the minute. The awful truth of the situation began to weigh on her, pressing her down, but she kept a smile on for Gram and Avis.

Gram was too absorbed in his own happiness to notice the lines forming at the sides of his mother's mouth, the blue hollow under her eyes, or the tension between her and Bob. Parsons did his best to keep a smooth appearance on things, indulging his stepchildren at every opportunity and creating the façade, at least, of good times. Money did a fine job of disguising the wounds, and Gram and his sister were kept blissfully ignorant of the trouble brewing in the adult world.

Slowly, however, Gram was becoming an adult himself, delving further into his sexuality and beginning to experiment in other ways as well. One afternoon he cut his finger while pressing too hard on a new set of steel guitar strings. He went searching for a bandage, and in the mirrored bathroom cabinet, discovered a small private pharmacy, a pill for every one of his mother's ills.

Without thinking, Gram grabbed a sampling for himself, filling his pockets with reds, blues, and yellows. Somewhere brewing inside was a dark resentment, a streak of orange spite. His mother, the skin growing tighter around her womb—his mother who ignored or coddled him, depending on her mood—his spoiled, arrogant, beautiful mother, she was revealed to him for the first time as her own person, unaffected by him or attached to him, and he hated her for a moment, hated her for her indulgences, her foolishness.

Stealing pills became an act of rebellion that turned quickly into habit. He found that if he mixed Valium with his grandfather's good bourbon, it felt as if his shoes were only lightly, delicately brushing the ground. With the right combination of Librium and cold gin, you went underwater, everything blue-tinged and swaying. Two of the yellow pills and you'd go hard and fearless. On stage Gram would stretch to the ceiling; look down at the crowd as from the top of the township water tower. Patti's hair slid through his hands as if oiled, and at night the streetlights colored her white.

The two of them would grope in the back of the van, yearning fogging the windows, leaving a dew on the seats. Junior year, just as spring was beginning to press with warm palms, Gram asked Patti to marry him. She breathed an affirmation, and the two held the impending elopement between them like a sweet on the back of the tongue.

Gram gathered his money, built an escape hatch out of lies, and finally, one night, the two of them packed up the car. They were just about to take the pavement north to Georgia when their parents showed up and cancelled, with furious finality, the young lovers' plan.

The end of Patti and Gram meant the end of the Village Vanguards and the end of Gram's patience with his family, whose thumb he was under. He felt too old for his skin and was angry at being treated like the child he actually was. In retaliation, Gram flunked out of school, took more pills, and turned up the amplifiers until the plaster chipped.

Avis was livid at this second embarrassing display of academic failure, and she was determined that Gram pay for his belligerence. Using the Snively's significant political and social sway, Avis got her son reenrolled at Bolles, a hefty contribution to the scholarship fund winning Gram a repeat of his junior year and a record wiped clean.

Gram just nodded his head at the news, his lips a small tight line, his eyes ice. At the Legends shows that summer, his stage repertoire grew wilder. He outfitted himself in velvet jackets and silk shirts, and tight pants made long with pinstripes. When he was alone in the music room, he played melancholy folk tunes, poking at his self-pity like a sore tooth.

His mother heard his voice through the thin walls and felt overcome with remorse. She was only trying to do the best for him and didn't know what to make of the tall, longhaired stranger who had suddenly appeared in the place of her little boy. To assuage her own guilt, she decided to try to win Gram over the best way she knew how—by hiring him a personal manager.

Gram had met Buddy Freeman at a dinner party a few years before. Freeman was twenty-two then, an equestrian star, and the slick product of a healthy trust fund and good breeding. Sometime between the third course and dessert, Buddy had asked Gram to show him his stuff on the restaurant's grand piano.

Gram had given a small smile, excused himself, sat down on the bench, and brought his fingers to the keys. Everyone went silent when he began to play; he was just thirteen years old but sang with a voice full of unexpected emotion. A few girls at a nearby table giggled nervously, watching Gram with hot eyes. Freeman knew a good thing when he saw it, and when Avis called him up in 1963 and asked him to help guide her son's music career, he accepted.

Within a few months, Buddy was negotiating hefty fees for the now fifteen-year-old Gram, booking him for parties and radio appearances. His first real coup as manager was snagging Gram a five-hundred-dollar stint at the Greenville Memorial Auditorium in South Carolina. The event was a local hootenanny competition, a collection of bands competing for grand-prize glory, and Gram was booked as both a member of the judging panel and as a solo intermission entertainer.

For the occasion, Gram wore a blue silk shirt, which was one of his favorites, and a gold medallion he'd borrowed from Bob. He planned to play a few songs on his

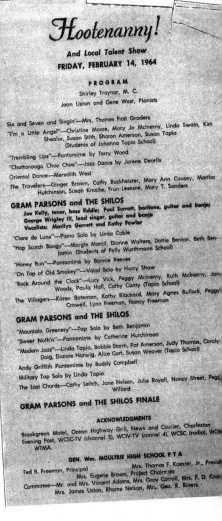

Hootenanny.
COURTESY OF PAUL SURRATT.

guitar and then spend the rest of the evening eyeing the girls. When he saw there was a band on the bill called the Shilos, he tracked them down to make sure they weren't planning on playing a song he'd decided on for his own brief appearance, "The Hills of Shiloh."

The Shilos ham it up. COURTESY OF PAUL SURRATT.

Paul Surratt and Joe Kelly's first impression of Gram was of a tall, nicely tanned kid who acted a hell of a lot older than he looked. The Shilos were young themselves, in their mid-teens, but they were talented and absolutely devoted musicians.

The two boys explained that they weren't playing the song, but by then the conversation had veered into folk music, and the three musicians were forming a fast connection based on their shared enthusiasm. One of the finest folk groups of the time was John Phillips's Journeymen, one of the bands that had introduced Gram to the genre, and whose 1963 album *New Directions in Folk Music* was one of the best of the recent bunch.

Gram, Paul, and Joe spontaneously began to sing a Journeymen song together, a cappella, in the drafty backstage hallway. Something happened then, their three voices bouncing off the concrete walls, going soft in the air and melting together into a thing golden and stunning, a sound that surprised them all. Their voices were good together, better than good, their combined vocals blending into beautiful harmony. Gram's medallion flashed in the fluorescent glare, Paul grinned wide, and Joe let loose with a deep, satisfied chuckle.

It was the start of something, and they all knew it.

The Shilohs had a third member, George Wrigley, who hadn't made it to the hootenanny because he had caught the wrong side of a fist in a teenage brawl. Paul and Joe asked Gram to fill the gap, and with Gram conveniently serving as one of the judges, they managed to take home the title of best band.

By the next morning, their new friend had become an official Shiloh.

Buddy Freeman was less than enthused about the new band. He had signed on to rep Gram as a solo artist, and now he suddenly had four precocious teenage boys to deal with. But Gram got his way, and Freeman was quickly making a good living from his cut of the Shilos' show profits.

For a local folk act consisting of four kids under the legal

```
dear bear—
the pictures are tremendous. whoever took them
really xxx knew how to capture the spirit of the
group.
i've been thinking. if we want to make it as a
x group we're going to have to do some serious
rearranging. the people want a really different
sound, and ours isn't different enough yet. of
course, we might not like all the changes but
i do think they're necessary. for one thing i
think we should sing all new music with a few
exceptions. i think we should work on my material.
i know it will sell. music, believe it or not,
is turning towards a more xxxxxxxx intellectual
vein. we should go into serious rehearsals, now i
know we've said that before but now it is a nec-
essity. i'm sure that my music is going to be as
big as dylans, and after my album we will have the
advantage of owning my music plus dicks. we are
going to have to cash in on this thing dylan's sta
rted, and like it or not we'll be associated with
him. i still want very much to make it with the
shilos. i always have.
    there is a bigger chance for us than i imagined,
even at spring. don't get too excited though. it
is going to take a tremendous effort on our parts.
write me as soon as you get this and tell me what
joe and george think.
```

Letter to Paul Surratt.
COURTESY OF PAUL SURRATT.

Gentlemen:

We would greatly appreciate your giving the enclosed tapes your most careful consideration. We believe we have the newest and freshest style to come along in the folk field for many years.

As performers, we have won tremendous acclaim in night clubs, coffee houses, college campuses, radio and television. Youth is on our side since no one in our group exceeds eighteen years of age.

Regretfully, our tapes are not of the highest quality. We had no time to achieve proper balance through reverb and possible overdub.

We feel that we could be of significant value to your company.

Sincerely yours,

THE SHILOS

RE F.
~~Enclosures~~

WFBC	Andy Scott	Greenville, S. C.
Club Jamarta	Mr. Posey	Greenville, S. C.
Ivey's Fashion Show	Ed Wickliff	Greenville, S. C.
WCSC	Carol Godwin	Charleston, S. C.
The Citadel		Charleston, S. C.
Derry Down	*Helen Page*	Winterhaven, Fla.
Cafe Rafio	Ed Gordan	

The Shilos state their case. COURTESY OF PAUL SURRATT.

drinking age, the group was remarkably successful. Cypress Gardens, by now a thriving amusement venture and one of Florida's premiere tourist draws, sent the band to Chicago to record a theme song for the park. The result was "Surfinanny," a slightly goofy, giddy folk number used to promote the inland surfing on Winter Haven's string of lakes.

What followed were three-hundred-dollar gigs, tours of the southern states, local TV appearances, and the Shilos becoming a booming business. In celebration, Gram had Avis and Bob buy him a few new guitars for the band, a Martin and a twelve-string Goya that had a warm, waxed glow and a shimmering sound.

In the humid summer of 1964, the Shilos scored a month-long residency at Myrtle Beach, where they strummed songs for sun-burned girls in string bikinis, and the Atlantic licked the sand just a few yards from the dance floor.

Gram was sixteen, cocky as ever, and happy as hell. He and his friends were on their own, making good music and necking with hot-skinned girls in sand that still held the heat of the day's sun. The band rented a house close to the beach, brought friends over for late night jams, smoked dope, gobbled Gram's stash of pills, and drank cold beer from the bottle.

When Buddy finally showed up to check in on the band, he stumbled into a den of teen debauchery, clothes strewn across the living room, young girls sleeping on the huge, cigarette-burnt couch, empty Jack Daniels bottles, and the Shilos looking like made men, faces shadowed in stubble, eyes shot with red.

Freeman put his foot down, attempting to clean house and shake a scolding finger at the teens with all the parental authority he could muster. The boys responded with bemused laughter, and then calmly showed him the door. The Shilos could take over from here on in, thank you very much, and Buddy could say goodbye to his percentage of the take. He had been hired by Gram, and now he was fired by Gram, plain and simple.

A few weeks later, fall finally arrived, uninvited, a sweet summer of freedom forgotten in the first frantic weeks at Bolles. The school had changed since the last time Gram had been a student. It had dropped its military stiffness and was concentrating instead on offering up a loose liberal-arts education. Gram carried his guitar to classes, slung across his back, and slipped it into his hands at any moment the desire struck.

Searching the school grounds, Gram found a secret refuge on the Bolles campus. If you walked the wood-planked paths behind the school, you'd find yourself on the soggy banks of the St. John's River. At night there was the furious din of insects, the water's lips against the shore. A guitar sounded good out there, the notes drifting across the river, held aloft in the heavy air.

There was a stone gazebo, too, where Gram liked to sit between classes, hear the pluck of steel strings echo off the damp ceiling. Invariably, kids gathered to watch him, intrigued by his willing seclusion and impressed by his easy talents.

He met another girl that year, a long-legged, chestnut-haired southern belle with doe eyes that fluttered under long lashes. Margaret Fisher was a doctor's daughter, whip smart as well as beautiful, usually opting for books over boys. But Gram was an exception. Gram drew her out of her shell, pulling secrets from her in exchange for some of his own. He told her about his father's death, his mother's new husband, and the problems that were brewing back in Winter Haven.

On weekends, when many of the students went home, Gram stayed behind, avoiding his family with a shiver of guilt, preferring the quiet campus to the slow but inevitable disintegration of Avis's second marriage.

Avis was just in her forties, but alcohol had already burned canyons at the sides of her mouth and above her brows. She was doing her best to care for her third child, she and Bob's new daughter, Diane, but she was distracted and fading. She had become quite good at ignoring the obvious, pretending not to notice the hungry looks her husband shot the eighteen-year-old babysitter. It didn't matter, anyway. By midafternoon she would be numb with drink, staggering slightly, but with a warmth in her gut as a welcome obliviousness descended, blurring her vision and masking the hurt in her heart.

Instead of going home for the extended break, in the summer of 1964, Gram made up his mind to make his way north, convinced that he needed a taste of the authentic folk scene. Friends hooked him up with a loft in Greenwich Village, and he eventually spent the summer sharing a bed with a cabaret singer named Zah.

He brought the rest of the Shilos up as well, and the band made the rounds of the coffeehouses, playing late-night parties and ingratiating themselves as best they could, becoming kid brothers to a host of older up-and-comers. In New York the group met up with their heroes, the Journeymen, spotting John Phillips on the street and spending a few wine-soaked Manhattan evenings with Phillips and his wife Michelle.

The trip was revelatory for everyone in the Shilos, but it was especially so for Gram, who had his first taste of true freedom in New York, where he was on his own and away from the turmoil on Piedmont Drive. New York was another world, proof that he could live another way, that he might eventually begin to carve out of his own reality, a place removed from three generations of Snively obligation. When Gram returned to Bolles his senior year, he had a faraway look in his eyes. He knew if he kept moving forward, he would eventually be able to move *away*, away from the grip of southern conservatism and family expectation.

Meanwhile, Bob Parsons in Winter Haven, trying to win Gram's affections, perhaps out of real emotional need, or perhaps because he knew Gram—now more a man than ever, and ultimately one of the heirs to the Snively fortune—could make things unpleasant for Parsons if he chose. In a savvy attempt to impress his son (by this time Bob had officially adopted both Gram and Little Avis), he converted a downtown Winter Haven warehouse into a teen dance hall, with Gram as a featured attraction.

The Derry Down was a cavernous space with dubious acoustics and an Olde English theme. Gram had named the place in a moment of pretense, deciding it should echo with antiquated British formality and Shakespearean haughtiness. The bar served nonalcoholic drinks with names like Hotspur, Falstaff, and Midsummer Night's Dream.

The Shilos played at velveteen troubadours wandering the heather telling bawdy tales of love and loss. It was silly, but it was grand fun, a game that kept the rest of the band waiting breathlessly for Gram's arrival each weekend from Jacksonville. There were radio shows and recording sessions as well. The Shilos slowly refined their sound, attempting to keep pace with pop music's evolution and their own quickly unfolding adolescence.

By 1965, however, popular music was moving forward at a

Margaret Fisher Interview #1
Interview by Polly Parsons

Margaret Fisher was a close girlfriend of Gram's in high school. She would ultimately reunite with him years later, in 1972. She was with Gram when he died in Joshua Tree.

Q: How did you know Gram?

A: He went to the Bolles School for Boys. He was boarding. Bolles had two types of kids. They had upper-middle-class, very successful people, like my parents, and then they had the boarders. And half of the boarders were kids from small towns whose parents wanted them to get an education. And half of the kids were kids who were just an inconvenience. Their parents had a problem with them, their parents had habits, they were the throwaway kids. And that's what Gram was. His mother had her problems. God knows Bob Parsons didn't want those children, did he? Bolles was all boys, it was a prep school, and Bartram, where I went, was all girls. So we socialized with each other because nobody else would have us.

Q: When did you first meet Gram?

A: I had a friend who went to another prep school with him in Palm Beach. She always described him as a fat little kid dragging around a big guitar. He went around everywhere taking that guitar with him. He slimmed down when he got to high school. But I bet he was a chubby little kid and I bet he always had that guitar with him because one thing about him, he knew exactly how talented he was. He knew he was going to be something.

Q: Even in the middle of high school?

A: Oh yeah. The ambition was relentless. I was so impressed. I remember one time, the Shilos boys were in town and he asked me out. I was over the moon, I don't think I'd ever had a date before. We went down to the River Club, which in Jacksonville is like the premier club where the businessmen meet. And there we were, a seventeen-year-old boy and three rednecks, you know? And they didn't want to let us in. Gram took them aside and he got us in. I was so impressed. And I just couldn't believe I was at this premier club with this guy who just talked our way in.

Q: How old were you, seventeen?

A: He was about seventeen, I would have been fifteen at that time. And he had a hotel room and everything. But he didn't get anywhere with me. I had no idea. We necked and that was it. But then in high school, his senior year, I had a boyfriend and after that he would not talk to me. By God, you did not get a second chance with him. He was the child of alcoholic parents and he had been let down early in his life. And he was not going to let the world do that again. It's just the way he was. I tell ya, he sure didn't like Bobby Parsons. He was bad news and Gram knew it in high school. He wrote a story once about a boy whose father beat him up. He let me read it. I said, "Is this you?" and he said, "Yes it is. My father hits me." And it was just the way he said it—I couldn't say anything else. He never did either. He'd been hurt, but he knew he was going to get out of there. He knew it even then. I remember one time we were at my house and we were walking and he had given me a book by Jack Kerouac and he wanted to know what I thought about it. *On the Road* or something. And I said well, I didn't think he was much of a writer. And he said, "Well, Margaret Fisher, that just goes to show how ignorant you are." And we walked a little further and I finally looked at him and I said, "Well, if I'm so ignorant what are you doing here?" And he said, "Well, I'm here because you and me are going to see wonderful things in our life. And most of the people around Jacksonville aren't gonna see shit." And he was right.

GEORGE WRIGLEY   PAUL SURRATT   GRAM PARSONS   JOE KELLY

No Sale or Consumption of Mead, Stout Sac or Other Spiritous Liquors

BY ORDER OF

At the Derry Down, a night club for Winter Haven teen-agers, the rule of the house is posted conspicuously. — (Staff Photos by Dan Fager)

By JACK McCLINTOCK
Tribune Staff Writer

Have you ever eaten a derryburger?

Or a downdog?

Or drunk a Wales Sunset or a Midsummer Night's Dream?

Winter Haven has a new club for young adults that offers these and other bits of exotica on its menu. It has folk singing too. It's called the Derry Down, after a portion of the chorus of an English folk song.

Its operators bill the Derry Down as a place "In the Spirit of Olde England."

A long building with a high beamed ceiling and partly paneled walls, the Derry Down is the newest example of a current fad: "night clubs" for the non-drinking set—mostly teenagers.

• • •

IT IS SUPPOSED to look like an Eighteenth Century English inn. What it does resemble is a refurbished warehouse—which it is.

But the kids flock there at a dollar a head to hear Gram Parsons and the Shilohs, a merry band of teen-age folk singers with surprising talent. The group plays at the Derry Down during school holidays.

Parsons got the idea for Derry Down after a visit to Greenwich Village last summer, where he and the Shilohs sang at the Bitter End.

His father owns the building, but Gram and his band have done the work. They hired four high-school boys as waiters—girls would be too much of a distraction, they figured—and got two high-school coaches to act as bouncers.

• • •

THEY DREAMED UP—and borrowed—ideas for esoteric non-alcoholic drinks. Many of them are named after characters and events in old English literature: Midsummer Night's Dream, Hotspur, Jack Falstaff.

"We were really going to go old English," says Gram, "but the trouble is nobody here understands it. Even Hotspur is pretty far out for Winter Haven.

"All they want to know is what's in it."

The Shakespearean references may go over as obscure in Winter Haven, but that doesn't damage the popularity of the drinks. Some ingredients are: cinnamon, cider, cranberry juice and lemon juice, ice cream, and rum extract (non-alcoholic, of course, and hence tasting nothing at all like rum).

THROUGH a complex sound system—termed "decaphonic" by local disk jockey Jacque Phillips—customers can harken to the sounds of the Shilohs.

The Shilohs are Paul Surratt, 17, Joe Kelly, 17, George Wrigley, 18, and Parsons, 18.

Parsons is the only one of the quartet who has finished high school. The group, however, sings with a professional poise rivaling better-known groups who are riding the folk-song fad.

DERRY DOWN has been open only a few weeks, but was packed every night but one—the one before New Year's Eve. Phillips, who helps out with reservations there, says he's surprised at the musical taste of modern youth. It's the music that brings them, he says—that and getting out of the house.

"It's amazing how many kids like Sinatra and that sort of thing," said the bearded deejay.

"We'll be open just three nights a week from now on," he said. "Probably Wednesday, Friday and Saturday. It gives the kids some place to come to. If they want to dance, we're providing the music. If they want to have a party in the back corner, that's fine with us.

"We'll serve them the drinks and some pretty good hamburgers—I mean derryburgers—and they can have a ball."

From top: The Shilos at the Derry Down; Derry Down in the news.
COURTESY OF THE SNIVELY FAMILY.

frantic pace. Folk, R&B, and rock were putting out tentative shoots that pushed up and out of the soil of tradition and into the clean air of experimentation. Dylan had put clear words to the transition with his song "Blowin' in the Wind." Change was coming, and it was coming fast.

In California, the Byrds heard Dylan's battle cry, as did John Phillips, who had moved west and was forming a new band with Michelle called the Mamas and the Papas. The Beatles had come and conquered, the Kinks and the Animals were a sign of things to come, the Rolling Stones weren't getting any satisfaction, and the Who made a generation their own.

In Winter Haven's dandified Derry Down, the Shilos were suddenly out of touch, soft-spined, singing flimsy folk covers, Gram introing with a fake British accent, playing Falstaff to a room full of country kids. Gram knew he had to up the ante, get out of Dodge. On a whim, he applied to Harvard.

Despite the fact he'd flunked a year of school and could barely spell, Gram figured he had a chance. The school seemed anxious to enroll more creative, artistic types, and with the Snively trust fund, Gram certainly had the means to foot the bill. The application was indicative of a healthy ego and a growing desperation. Harvard seemed like an escape hatch to Gram, a hole to crawl through that would lead him someplace bigger.

He didn't tell the Shilos he was thinking of heading north. Instead, Gram put on a good show for his friends, giving them little reason to expect he was anxious to abandon them. In March the Shilos spent thirty-five bucks on studio time and recorded a few songs for posterity. Gram sang the lead vocals, leaning forward into the mike and closing his eyes, lending the tracks a trace of the bittersweet.

There was nothing particularly unique in the recordings, but the Shilos were tight, and they loved to play. On Gram's original "Zah's Blues," everyone hit his stride, Gram rising above convention with a cracked intensity that exposed something raw beneath the music. The lyrics seemed to come from a place that was already far in the

The Shilos in the studio. COURTESY OF THE PAUL SURRATT.

future, as if Gram were singing from somewhere up ahead, looking back over his shoulder at the Shilos and himself.

> *When I was young, the world was rich*
> *my heart was filled with pride*
> *my head was filled with praise*
> *I wore my youth like a crown*
> *and watched the sun comin' down.*

By May, Gram had an acceptance letter from Harvard. He may not have been able to spell, but he could talk and write, and he had been able to wow the admissions board with a heartfelt essay that verged on the truly poetic. He lay awake the night after it arrived, alone in his Bolles School bunk, dreaming of the New England winter, of cheeks tight from cold and the steamed windows of Cambridge coffee houses, a nameless girl's body hidden under a cable-knit sweater. He was gone already, putting distance between himself and the deep blue bruise of his past.

Meanwhile, in the wood-paneled den on Piedmont Drive, Avis was drinking, pushing her days away with a stubborn persistence, safe in a hole dug by old-fashioneds and midmorning martinis. Bob smoothed over the edges of his guilt, softening the blow of his barely veiled infidelity and dishonesty by filling the ice bucket and flashing his white grin. When he touched Avis, her skin shrank from his hand. He had somehow set something in motion, and suddenly everything was sinking, stuck deep in some soft, sandy place of longing and regret.

Gram wrote to his sister from Bolles, sent out a hand to grasp her, tried to keep her afloat in the deepening, darkening water. When he had the strength, he went home to see his family, playing loose, lilting songs on the piano, trying to reach his mother, to soothe her. Gram didn't blame Bob; he couldn't, not when he saw the fear in his stepfather's eyes and realized, with a sudden shock, that Parsons was as weak and lost as Gram himself. Panic had taken hold of him, punched him in the guts, and sent him reeling. No one was going to save Avis. She had always done exactly as she wanted, with an unyielding and stubborn arrogance. To kill herself slowly seemed to be her last, persistent desire.

The day of Gram's graduation from Bolles was hot, gray, and bloated, and clouds turned the air yellow and electric. There was a tent set out on the dew-covered lawn, the canvas flapping in the breeze. In his room Gram picked out a pressed pair of khaki pants, a dark blue school blazer, and a narrow striped tie, the businessman's uniform he had no intention of wearing again—ever. He had had his hair cut short for the occasion, but not so short as to lose the soft sweep at the top. He parted it on the side that morning, pushing the brown waves back with a wet palm.

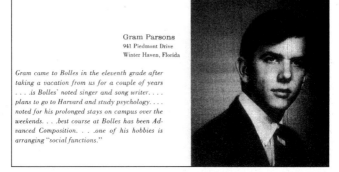

Gram Parsons
941 Piedmont Drive
Winter Haven, Florida

Gram came to Bolles in the eleventh grade after taking a vacation from us for a couple of years . . . .is Bolles' noted singer and song writer. . . . plans to go to Harvard and study psychology. . . . noted for his prolonged stays on campus over the weekends. . . .best course at Bolles has been Advanced Composition. . . .one of his hobbies is arranging "social functions."

Gram's high school yearbook. COURTESY OF THE SNIVELY FAMILY.

Row 1: Driscoll, S.; Cooper, H.; Broder, P.; Hupp, D.; Parsons, G.; Hastings, J.; Clark, R. W. Row 2: Prisant, D.; Wallace, T.; Murphy, F.; Wurn, Gifford, D.; Dick, J.; Glickstein, P.

in the Tower Auditorium. Mrs. Blocker will also be featured in a program of incidental piano and melodeon music in the Foster Museum.

PARSONS, A senior at the Bolles School, is recognized as one of the outstanding folk artists in the South and has sung in clubs and on other programs in New York, Charleston, and throughout the Jacksonville area. He has made one recording and plans another in the near future.

The young singer, who composes much of his material, will be heard in "Far Side of the Hill," "3:10 to Yuma," "Spanish is a Lovin' Tongue," "Soft as the Summer Winds" and "You've Heard My Voice"

ESPRE

EMORIAL AUDITORIUM

AY COCA-COLA HI-FI HOOTENANNY
STARRING GRAM PARSONS

From top: Pages from Gram's high school journal. COURTESY OF THE SNIVELY FAMILY.

His sister was downstairs, dressed in white, looking older and prettier than he remembered. Coon Dog's father Ingram, for whom Gram had been named, had arrived the night before and was staying in the same hotel as Grandma Snively. He heard the two grandparents come in together in the front hall, heard their greetings and then his sister's high, sweet voice calling him down.

Gram looked in the mirror, tried to smile, then walked quickly out the door. His sister Avis stood at the bottom of the stairs, gazing up at him with envy and pride. Hanie Snively had her arm around her granddaughter, grand and elegant as always, in a pillbox hat and pearls. Gram nodded good morning, took their soft hands, and walked them toward the tent, the wind smelling of cut grass.

By ten-thirty the heat was stifling. Scattered families sipped ice tea and made small talk until the ceremony began. Gram watched as one of his professors began to make his way toward his family's table. He rose to greet him but then saw something in his teacher's face that was both terrifying and familiar. The tightness in Gram's chest drew his ribs in and made his long piano-player's hands shake. He knew what the man was going to say before he said it.

Gram's mother was dead, but the news didn't come as a surprise to any of them. She had been hospitalized a few weeks before, her body poisoned and decaying quickly. She had been sick for some time, but Avis had waited until the day of her son's graduation to finally let go. In the moment he was told he had been orphaned; suddenly everything that had been between Gram and his parents seemed to evaporate.

He felt cut loose, floating, freed from grief. The fist in his chest slowly unclenched. He refused to leave, staying to accept his diploma as the sun poured out a thick, sensuous heat. Later, he threw the party he had planned and put on a good face for all his friends. When the next morning arrived, he hadn't slept. Instead, he had walked, walked all over Jacksonville, along the river and back again. As the sun went from pink to orange, he realized he was finally free, and he knew with sudden certainty how alone that would make him, how alone he was always going to be.

Havenite Brings Go-Go To Staid Harvard Yard

A Winter Haven student is rocking 'n' rolling to Variety's front page.

He is Gram Parsons, 19, of 941 Piedmont Drive, son of Robert E. Parsons, owner of the "Derrydown," teenage center on Cypress Gardens Road.

His success story is told by William Fripp in last week's Boston Sunday Globe:

"It's not that Gram Parsons can't adjust to the freshman grind at Harvard.

"It's all these other things, like calls from Ed Sullivan, frugging with the Beatles at Arthur, wrapping up that contract with RCA Victor.

"Rarified things like that, they keep a boy busy, on edge.

"Grams's go-go, part of The Scene. His rocking 'n' rolling has carried him to front-page Variety, coupled with the elegantes in whispery gossip columns, propelled him under the kleigs.

"But he's only 19, and Harvard with its hour exams and

GRAM PARSONS . . . As Photographed for Boston Globe's Report.

The Like in the press.

I Started Out Younger

GRAM ENTERED HARVARD in the fall of 1965 with a group of classmates that included the actor Tommy Lee Jones and the future vice president, Al Gore. Cambridge was bright and crisp with coming winter, the light sharpening the edges of things instead of softening them as it had in the South. The buildings of the old campus, built to mimic London townhouses, had settled into themselves, their brick walls colored to rust. It was another world for Gram. The trees were yellowing, expectation scattering leaves over Harvard Yard.

One of the first people Gram connected with in this new life was a young assistant dean, the Reverend James Thomas, known affectionately to friends as Jet. The age difference between the two spanned nearly a decade, enough to make Jet seem something like an older brother, but not enough to add the tension of parental superiority. In many ways, Jet was Gram's antithesis, a pragmatic man who had turned most of his aspirations into reality, devoting his life to both teaching and God.

Gram had chosen theology as his major, a decision that seemed logical despite the fact that Gram had never been overtly religious in the traditional sense. Instead, Gram found himself attempting to construct some spiritual bedrock, a foundation that would help to explain his parents' early deaths and help to determine the direction of Gram's own life.

He already adored gospel music and understood how worship

could be turned into sound. In his own way, Gram had been calling out to God for a long time now, and studying theology seemed a way to make the transmission clearer.

While Jet's faith was more traditional than Gram's, Jet was still young and curious and had a sharp mind that was open to exploration and philosophical pondering. Gram had been around smart people all his life-well—educated family members, Bolles professors, and a few other intuitive and well—spoken teens-but Harvard offered a bounty of intelligence.

Jet was not only an intellectual match for Gram but an instigator as well. He was older and more experienced, the kind of person who had spent many hours in self-examination. Gram found himself slipping into deep conversations with the young minister, going on ambling, utterly enlightening verbal adventures that drew Gram out of himself and took him to some higher place, a place where his emotional complications slowly became clearer.

Jet's God was a merciful one, helping to guide Gram back to himself. In many ways these long discussions were pretty much Gram's only encounter with academic study during his time at Harvard. He avoided classes in favor of gaining experience, and he devoured books by such authors as Walt Whitman, Allen Ginsberg, and William Burroughs.

There were girls, as always, most of them hungry and wide-eyed with newly acquired independence. And there was music. Cambridge still resonated with the raw poetry of its years as an important folk breeding-ground. Coffee shops that had nurtured the likes of John Baez, Bob Dylan, and Richard Fariña still kept up a brisk business in artistic, cultural, and political dissent.

Boston was a city big enough to pulsate with new ideas and artistic innovation but small enough not to intimidate, and Harvard Square itself, though a tiny village, had urban swagger. Gigs were easy to find, and fellow musicians were plentiful. It wasn't long before Gram had integrated himself into the scene, his defiant cockiness and gentle charm helping to push him fast into the fold.

He strummed his guitar on the quad lawn, gazing up from under long bangs to watch the girls watching him play. He took Jet to shows at the local clubs and made sure to befriend any musician he liked the looks of, regardless of genre of music being played. He kept exploring musically, listening to jazz, folk, R&B, anything he could find in the bins of Cambridge's dusty secondhand record stores.

After only a few months in town, he'd already formed a band, a group he called the Like, which featured Gram at the helm backed up by pros from the Berklee College of Music. They had only played a few local clubs when news of the venture reached the ears of the kids back home by way of a Winter Haven paper hailing its own with a story entitled "Havenite Brings Go-Go to Staid Harvard Yard."

Gram, however, found he had little in common with the technically adept but creatively stifled Berkelee crowd, a group of young musicians taught to play to perfection and to shun experimentation. Gram was looking for more than hired hands. He was looking for some whimsy and impulsiveness in his collaborators; he wanted musicians who could challenge him, take his ideas and run with their own.

One night, just as winter was beginning to truly take hold, he met a dapper British dandy at a girlfriend's house, a fellow musician with whom Gram immediately connected. Ian Dunlop was well-traveled and relentlessly hip. He sang and played saxophone and guitar for the Refugees, a band that was immensely popular on the New England rock club circuit.

Dunlop watched Gram play that night and was suitably impressed. The two had a mutual obsession with music and an inherent flash in their personal style, a unique aesthetic that melded rather than clashed. Like Gram, Ian was buoyant, mischievous, and blessed with a healthy ego. They both felt bred for better things.

Soon after the two met, Dunlop introduced Gram to his friend John Nuese, who at the time was rocking guitar with a group called the Trolls. The three of them clicked, bonded as they were by optimism and total faith in their own abilities. It was not long before Gram had wooed both men away from their respective groups and made them members of the Like.

Gram had learned the knack of integrating friends into his projects, instilling enthusiasm in others without losing his place as centerpiece. He wasn't egotistical, merely intent on making his own moment happen. Harvard and his theology studies faded into the background as his true goal became clear. Gram was going to be a musician and, if he could pull it off, a star.

There was nothing empty in his desire for recognition. Gram wanted his music to have all the heart and depth and soul of the music he admired. Ian and John were not only fine players, they were fellow searchers as well, intent on purity and truthfulness in their music and immediately dismissive of anything inauthentic.

Nuese loved the country music classics, the stuff that had been subtly woven into the soundtrack of Gram's youth. Nuese's enthusiasm for these early songs reignited a flame in his friend's quick mind. He and Gram would huddle close to the rattling radiators in icy Cambridge apartments, playing George Jones and the Louvin Brothers, staying warm with ample doses of hot mulled wine.

Gram was elated with his new friends, his new freedom. By this time his high school forays into his mother's medicine cabinet had given way to a serious interest in hallucinogens and high-quality marijuana. It was 1965, and Timothy Leary had just left Harvard a few years earlier and was now on the run from the law, hunkered down somewhere south of the border.

But Leary's LSD legacy was coming vibrantly to life, and Cambridge was the womb from which it had been birthed. Gram took Leary's philosophies of psychedelic psychiatry and ran, using LSD as a way to push deeper into the intellectual journeys he embarked upon with Jet, attempting to push open Aldous Huxley's doors of perception as wide as he possibly could.

Bundling himself in heavy wool sweaters and scarves, he would throw himself into the steely New England night, wandering cobblestone alleys, tripping hard on pharmacy grade LSD he'd scored from the med students and science geeks at nearby MIT.

The Charles River snaked black and cold under the liquid arches of old bridges, its banks outlined with walking paths and the green parallel of the Esplanade. If you walked far enough you'd hit the harbor, the hot lights of Faneuil Hall, the tiny restaurants of the North End, where everything was clouded with the smell of garlic and ground espresso.

Gram watched the sky move closer, stroked the neck of his ever-present guitar, and lay down in the frosted grass, his mind burning with ideas and inspirations. Memories flashed by: his mother's face, his father hunched over the morning paper, the scent of bacon and aftershave. Gram felt haunted, tragic, and electric all at once; he was nineteen years old and free to make his own mistakes.

By October, Gram, Ian, and John had a tentative deal with RCA, recording a track under the name Gram Parsons and the Tinkers. Gram may have been an avid drug user, a social whirl-wind, and a consummate lady-killer, but he was also a savvy businessman, his grandfather's blood running clean through his veins.

During his Greenwich Village stint the year before, he had made every friend he could, ingratiating himself with John and Michelle Philips and playing eager kid brother to the likes of music manager Marty Ehrlichman and Brandon De Wilde, a Hollywood child star just come of age. Erlichman was managing Barbra Streisand when he met Gram. De Wilde, a young man now with his own burgeoning music career, was just graduating from playing little Joey Starrett in *Shane* and Paul Newman's kid brother in *Hud*.

De Wilde had been born into a New York theater family. He had hit the stage young, starring in the Broadway production of *The Member of the Wedding* and then going on to an Oscar nomination at age eleven for his performance in *Shane*.

Gram had been thrilled by De Wilde's history, with its glamour and tales threaded through with hints of desperation and decadence. The two had become immediate friends, both possessing the knack of drawing people with a subtle and irristable charisma. After Gram had returned to Bolles, the two had kept in touch. When Gram had been matriculated at Harvard, it was not long before De Wilde arrived in Cambridge, checking in on Gram, the girls, and the music scene.

De Wilde was looking to make an album, and he had the talent to back up his ambition. He saw something in Gram that he knew would complement his own creativity, and when he returned to New York, he brought Gram and his new band along to help out with recording.

The group, with the help of Ehrlichman, laid down several tracks at RCA's expense. By this time, Gram and his friends had recruited a drummer, Mickey Gauvin, a white boy with funk who could bang out James Brown beats with the best of them. Mickey was tiny and had a jet-black shag and an ever-present pair of sunglasses. He was the real deal, and with his backing, the Like, or the Tinkers, or whatever they happened to be calling themselves that day, suddenly became a real band.

By February of 1966, Gram had officially withdrawn from Harvard and moved himself and the band to New York City. The group found cheap digs at University and 195th in the Bronx. They had eleven rooms of sprawling brownstone, decorated with torn upholstery and Depression-era frugality.

The musty, slope-ceilinged attic became a rehearsal hall, and the old house suddenly was a great ship lumbering toward new adventures. Gram was out on his own, away from Florida, and out from under the weight of Harvard. He had finally cut himself loose from family legacy and was more than ready to raise the roof and test his boundaries.

The house in the Bronx became the epicenter for exploration, musical and otherwise. Day-long acid trips threw the brick canyons of the neighborhood into hard relief against a sky that glowed white with city light. The boys changed the band's name again, giving themselves with the surreal and rather grand moniker, the International Submarine Band. Dunlop, who had a way with words, brainstormed the title, a keen sense for the whimsical psychedelia that was just coming into vogue.

The hi-fi was the boys' only addition to the collection of battered furniture already inhabiting the living room. Records lined the floors, were stacked high on scattered shelves, and strewn across couches, beds, and the kitchen table. There was an air of giddy chaos and a layer of dust covering most everything. Everyone sensed glory lurking just around the corner.

International Submarine Band publicity shot.
Courtesy of Jeff Gold / www.recordmecca.com.

Brandon De Wilde regaled the boys with stories of Hollywood glitz, the Bronx seeming just one step removed from the revolution brewing in California. Girls came and went, leaving lingerie between the couch cushions and the lingering scent of Breck shampoo and patchouli. The Manhattan winter breathed ice through the cracks beneath the door and drew jagged patterns across the windowpanes.

Gram got word from home that Bonnie, the eighteen-year-old babysitter, had officially moved in, sleeping in Bob's bed and doing her best at playing wife and mother. By then Bob Parsons had relocated, taking Bonnie, Little Avis, and he and Avis's daughter, Diane, to New Orleans, installing them in an ostentatious home off Audubon Park and doing his best to save face.

Gram took the news in stride. He cut through the last threads that tied him to his past and did his best to be a brother to Avis from afar, sending letters, tapes, photos, and jotting down colorful descriptions of life on 195th Street. He barricaded himself in the fantasy world he and the band had created for themselves. Fame, he was certain, was waiting just a few steps ahead.

Marty Ehrlichman was keeping a curious eye on the band, but he'd delegated day-to-day management duties to Monty Kaye, who had been working with the Modern Jazz Quartet. Kaye was savvy at scoring the band semi-regular gigs, but lucrative record deals were not forthcoming.

That spring, however, Kaye finagled a deal for a promo single, a track written for Norman Jewison's film *The Russians Are Coming*. Gram and his friends did a loose instrumental number and also recorded a raunchy version of Buck Owens's "Truckdrivin' Man" for the B-side.

The single was released on Ascot soon after, but it garnered ISB not a lick of major-label attention. After much coercing, however, Kaye was able to generate some interest from Columbia, and the band settled in to record a second single, which featured the tracks "Sum Up Broke," with lyrics by Gram and music by Nuese, and "One Day Week," which Gram had written on his own.

ISB "Russians Are Coming" single and sleeve.
COURTESY OF JEFF GOLD / www.recordmecca.com.

Unfortunately, the single went flat, forgotten by Columbia almost as quickly as it surfaced, but the boys refused to be flustered. There were enough bites, enough late-night club dates, and enough drinking and drugging sessions at the Bronx digs to keep their heads and their hopes above water.

In the late summer, Kaye pulled off a real coup, winning the Sub Band a gig opening for the Young Rascals in a Central Park show with a crowd of fifteen thousand. It was Gram's first experience with true, unadulterated fame, with the inexplicable, heady thrill of thousands of upturned faces and open ears.

ISB's set was short, but Gram tried to remember every moment, to etch the scene indelibly upon himself. He never wanted to forget the way the wood stage sloped beneath his feet, or the ragged, blurred sounds of voices screaming and hands clapping, and the echo of his guitar shooting across the Great Lawn and creeping up the brick homes that fronted the park. He was addicted to the nervous rush of energy, to the tingling fear that crouched in the silence between each song. There was nothing like this feeling, and Gram swore to himself he would have it again.

In the Bronx attic and Greenwich dives, ISB slowly began to hone their sound, pointing themselves south and west, integrating a loose country sway into their otherwise rock-based melodies. More records appeared on the shelves at home, discs culled from Village corner stores and borrowed from friends' collections. The notes of Buck Owens, the Louvin Brothers, and Jerry Lee Lewis floated, caught in the ever-present clouds of dope smoke. New York breathed with bright energy. Spring and then summer rolled across the island, leaving a strange and anxious heat, the odor of burnt sugar and exhaust coming through the brownstone windows.

In the living room, empty whiskey bottles held dried flowers, and the neighborhood girls came to sit on the ragged carpet and watch Gram. He was beginning to rely upon, almost crave, the hunger in their eyes. One night someone brought home the Ray Charles album *Country and Western Meets Rhythm and Blues*. It was late, and there was a pleasant party haze about everything. A few sweet-faced girls were dancing with bare feet, and someone, John maybe, was making eggs in the kitchen. Gram was on the floor, his back pressed against the old boards and his eyes closed when he heard Ray Charles start to sing Bill Monroe's "Blue Moon of Kentucky."

When the song was over, he felt numb. John silently walked in and set the needle back where it had started. They played the album again and again, day after day, until the grooves were worn deep. The boys were in love with those tracks, with the way Charles continued country tradition but added the sex and swing of rhythm and blues. They listened to that record's sound count-less times, played it until it began to seep into their own skins and surface in their own exploratory tracks.

As fall crept in, Gram took the opportunity to prolong some of the hope and heat of summer by flying to Los Angeles, where Brandon De Wilde was filming a new movie. He landed in the midst of one of the city's most colorful eras. There were riots on the Strip, and excitement infected everything; you could somehow taste the change.

Gram fell in love first with the feel of LA, the way its concrete sprawl led so quickly into wilderness, into the scrub brush canyons of Topanga, the cliffs of Malibu, and the winding, moneyed hush of suburban Bel Air. As in New York, there was neon, pavement, and a bustling, thrilling energy, but there was also pine and red-wood, coyotes and mountain lions. It was a cowboy-outpost-turned-fantasyland, a place where wilderness still clung to the ragged hills, coyotes lapped from swimming pools, and the wind blew in the sharp smell of the desert.

And there was the music. The city still resonated with the sweet clear notes of the West Coast pioneers, the Okie folk music of Dust Bowl émigrés and the songs of the matinee-idol cowboys. The echoes of Roy Rogers and Gene Autry could still be heard, and the promise of Manifest Destiny remained, hanging in the air like campfire smoke.

Young Hollywood kids and burgeoning rock legends had spread into the canyons, their houses clinging to cliff sides, hidden among groves of tall eucalyptus. With De Wilde as his guide, Gram moved straight into the center spotlight of a new scene, fitting in snugly with the help of Brandon's friendship, his family's money, and a southern charm he quickly discerned would set him apart and serve him well.

He drank homemade wine on tilted redwood decks, the orange glow of the city framing the arc of the Santa Monica hills. He met Dennis Hopper and Peter Fonda, Hollywood brats turned hippie royalty, whose money, fame, and taste for rebellion had spun a circle of talented friends around them. His old friends John and Michelle Philips had gone California dreaming, and Joni Mitchell, Neil Young, and Buffalo Springfield breathed in the jasmine-scented night and wove a story all their own.

LA had magic and a fresh and tingling excitement; something in the feel of the city teetered between elation and collapse. Gram took it all in and felt alive in it, invincible. Fortune and (more importantly) fame were woven into the fabric of his day-to-day LA experience. De Wilde integrated his friend seamlessly into his world, taking Gram to parties, concerts, and the set of the movie he was shooting.

One hazy afternoon, toward the end of Gram's stay, De Wilde picked him up and drove him through a maze of roads to Beverly Glenn, where they stopped in front of a beautiful mini-mansion nestled on a wooded acre just above Sunset Boulevard. The house belonged to David Crosby, who had grown up in Hollywood. The son of Academy Award–winning cinematographer Floyd Crosby, David had gone from wild child to cheerful pop star, churning out hits with the Byrds and getting his fair share of female attention thanks to his baby face and healthy bank account.

At the moment, Crosby happened to be engaged to an impossibly young, impossibly beautiful girl named Nancy Ross, another Hollywood hell-raiser. Her father was a retired captain in the Royal Air Force who had relocated to California. Ross had been raised in Los Angeles and had been tearing a path of cheerful destruction and seduction across town from early adolescence on.

When she was seventeen, she had dated the grandson of Eleanor Roosevelt, a union that lasted just a few tempestuous years. More recently she had been immersed in a torrid affair with Steve McQueen.

Nancy was chestnut-haired and pouty-lipped. She had enough experience under her belt to know how to handle a man and enough smarts to pretend she didn't. Rose-skinned and coy, she projected an image of sly naïveté. She had known David Crosby since they had both veered into adolescence, and she had recently accepted his offer of marriage with a mix of bemusement and curiosity.

The afternoon that Gram and Brandon arrived, the sun was slipping under the hills, and dusk was making everything soft. Gram stepped out of the car and fell straight into full-blown obsession, a glance at Nancy igniting something inside him that had been dormant for far too long. She was in the garden, moving toward the house, and Gram watched her, watched the way she walked, the way her hands fluttered over the wineglass she was carrying, the way her cotton skirt clung to her thighs.

Later, as the sky went from bruised blue to purple and finally to black, David started a fire while Nancy lit vanilla-scented candles and brought wine and cheese from the cupboards, which she had decorated with Day-Glo psychedelic frills. As Gram listened silently to David and Brandon reminiscing, he stole glances at the light flirting with Nancy's hair. David was leaving that night for a tour of the South, and he was nervously pacing around the room, anxious to get on his way. Gram and Brandon stayed a few hours, then finished their glasses and left, waving goodbye as they backed out the drive.

Gram was silent as they drove, eyes on the flash of palm trees and yellow-lit houses that lined the road. He and Brandon stopped for burritos at a roadside stand on Sunset and drank beers that felt like ice in their palms. The action on the Strip was just reaching a crescendo with cars backed up bumper-to-bumper and girls shouting from open windows. The two friends watched the scene with slight smiles, the beer and the girls sending out an electric shiver of LA evening, warming Gram from the inside out, flooding him with optimism.

After a long moment, he looked straight at Brandon and told him what had been on his mind since they had coasted into David Crosby's driveway, and he had seen that brown-haired girl standing in the long grass, wind pushing soft against her hair.

"I want you to take me back there," he said simply, and Brandon nodded as if that was what he had been expecting to hear all along.

By the time De Wilde dropped Gram off back at the house, David Crosby had left, and Nancy was alone. The house still glowed, the candles were still lit, and vanilla and wood smoke hung in the air. She didn't blink when she found Gram at the door, didn't protest when he picked her up and carried her barefoot and blindingly beautiful into the bedroom. She didn't say a word when he gently laid her down on the bed she had shared with David, who, by the next day, would be her ex-fiancé.

Gram touched down in New York City still vibrating from his trip west, convinced his destiny was waiting in California. It didn't take long to convince the Sub Band to make the trek. It was January in New York; the city was in the clutches of ice storms, and the streets were lined with exhaust-blackened snow.

The house on 195th was drafty and creaking, and with Gram's enthusiastic description of Los Angeles, the Sub Band boys began to envision southern California as a kind of new utopia—a place where the sun shone and the girls looked like angels. There was the allure of the new music scene as well, the Doors creeping along the Strip, Arthur Lee and Love blowing amps out at the Whiskey. And not far out in the desert, Bakersfield was coming into its hay-blown own, with artists like Merle Haggard and Buck Owens transforming Okie dustbowl protest into new forms of cowboy country.

There was also the seductive allure of the blank slate, of starting fresh in the golden glow of California. By February of 1967, the entire band had packed their bags and said goodbye to New York.

From top: Baby Polly;
Nancy and Polly at
the Sweetzer Home;
Gram and Nancy.
COURTESY OF POLLY
PARSONS.

Left: Gram with Dove; On the set of
Saturation 70. Right: Gram at the swap meet;
Burritos at Tom Wilkes's ranch.
ALL PHOTOS COURTESY OF TOM WILKES EXCEPT
"GRAM AT THE SWAP MEET," WHICH IS COURTESY
OF ANDEE COHEN NATHANSON.

From top: Burrito's *Gilded* shoot.
PHOTO BY TOM WILKES.
Gram at the Troubadour; Gram hanging out.
PHOTOS BY ANDEE COHEN NATHANSON.

Sin City
LA Casts Its Spell, 1967–1970

GRAM FOUND THEM A new clubhouse, a little home on Willow Glen that sat at the base of Laurel Canyon, wedged between the hippie havens and the vibrant energy caught at the eastern tip of Sunset Boulevard. Gram had laid his groundwork, and he was quick to contact his new LA friends, alerting members of that tightly knit network of his move to the West and bringing the rest of the band into the fold.

There were parties at Willow Glenn with Fonda, Phillips, and De Wilde, nights filled with late-night guitar playing and raucous jams on the oriental rugs in the low-ceilinged living room. Fonda, who was one of the most frequent visitors, was charmed by Gram's gregariousness and seduced by the proximity of up-and-coming rock 'n' roll talent.

Fonda came from a family of Hollywood notables. His father Henry and his sister Jane were already established firmly in the upper echelons of city society. Peter, however, was not interested in the film-studio rigidity that had made his father famous, nor was he interested in the brilliantined and spit-shined movie-star pose. He and his pal Hopper were defiant outsiders, outlaws with enough money to hold on to at least a bit of creative independence.

Peter felt comfortable with Gram in part because the young southern import seemed completely unimpressed by celebrity, interested only in good music and good times. Fonda, like De Wilde, was an aspiring singer-songwriter himself, with a decent voice and a nice touch on the guitar. The give-and-take of his friendship with Gram would eventually lead to Fonda's recording a cover of Gram's newest song, "November Nights," a single matched by a B-side cover of Donovan's "Catch the Wind." Trading Hollywood access for rock authenticity thrilled them both, and Gram was flattered and endlessly pleased with Fonda's appreciation.

Meanwhile, as the Sub Band dug in their heels, Gram fell deeper into his relationship with Nancy. The two were inseparable. Gram, who had so rarely committed himself, found himself needing her, nursing a hollow space in his chest when she left the room. Intellectually, the two of them had begun to pick up where he had left off with Jet, the young lovers exploring spirituality and metaphysics, the connection between the two of them building in its intensity.

Just a few months after Gram's arrival, he and Nancy set up house in a Tudor-style apartment at 821 Sweetzer, a pretty street in the Melrose flatlands. Nancy prided herself on her ability to carve out a nest for her lovers, and the apartment on Sweetzer was no exception. There were thick carpets, polished oak cabinets, antique brass candlesticks, and raw-silk curtains that closed out the afternoon smog and shut the two of them in where they could be alone together in an atmosphere reminiscent of an English manor house.

Gram moved his records from Willow Glenn, brought the Sub Band over for late-night guitar play and Nancy's home-cooked meals. Extensive jam sessions were relegated to the Laurel Canyon house, the band slowly developing their sound. The songs Gram was writing reflected the new world around him, incorporating Nancy, LA, and the excitement of starting fresh.

ISB got their first brush with West Coast success when Fonda asked them to appear in a party scene of a film he was working on. *The Trip* was another exploitation flick from Roger Corman, a savvy producer who had made a healthy living in B horror and biker movies. By 1967, psychedelic experimentation was widespread enough to warrant a cinematic depiction. Corman brought

Random lyrics in
Gram's journal.
COURTESY OF JEFF GOLD /
www.recordmecca.com.

There's a family Bible on the table
Each page is torn + hard to read
There's a family Bible on the side table
Was more than anything could ever be
the close of day when work was over
when the evening meal was done
They would read to us from the family Bible
And we would count our many blessings one by
And see us sittin round the table
When from the family Bible
...

SPEAKING ABOUT WEALTH A HEALTH
AND CARRYING OUT THE TOMB
JUST DRINK YOUR TEA AND CARRY YOUR KEY
THE SONG WILL SING ITSELF

DONT BE AFRAID TO SPEAK YOUR PIECE
CAUSE THAT'S YOUR HUMAN RIGHT
JUST GO YOUR WAY AND HAVE YOU SAY
AND SOON YOU'LL SEE THE LIGHT.

IF I SPOKE MY PIECE + HAD MY SAY I WOULDN'T BE HERE
BUT THEN I'D END UP LIVIN IN THAT SAME OL LAZY WAY

ITS IN YOUR HANDS IF YOU'RE KICK

YOU'LL HAVE TO WORK IT OUT

THERE'S A CHINK IN MY ARMOUR
SILENCE IS GOLDEN. Remember what peace there's in it
BUT PEOPLE LOOK AT ME WITH AFFECTION
AND HONOR.
GOOD Things Come of Changes We go Through.
And sympathy aside i depend on you + you depend on me
CEPT THE ONE'S WHO SEE ME AS A
MAN WITHOUT A COLOR.
I NOT color blind.
THANK-YOU DEAR FRIEND.

on Fonda to star and had enlisted a young actor, Jack Nicholson, to pen the framework of a script and direct. The Sub recorded a song for the film, Gram's "Lazy Days," but Corman dumped it, claiming it wasn't trippy enough for his acid movie.

The boys still got a taste of glamour, however, appearing in the film in a whacked-out nightclub scene, lip-synching to another band's song. It may have been a barely-there cameo, but it was enough to make Gram and his friends feel part of what was happening in Los Angeles, part of the movement in music, film, and art that they were all certain would change the world.

Gram, however, was less interested in a cultural revolution than a personal one. He focused his efforts in one direction, the integration of country and rock music, and he did his best to gain entrée into the thriving Cali country scene. Gram knew he had something with the mix, something original enough to feel dangerous and fresh. The sound he was making with the Sub Band was touched with rebellion, and Gram was convinced that if he put the right spin on things, both the hippies and the hicks would find his match appealing.

To test his theory, Gram headed north over the Hollywood Hills into the flat-bottomed bowl of the Valley. North Hollywood's Palomino Club was a squat, nondescript concrete box whose marquee had featured the names of some of country and western's finest. The club was true blue to its roots, its clientele streaming in the wind from the Central Valley farmland and outlaw desert, an audience of modern-day cowboys looking for an authentic country sound.

The mood inside was decidedly downbeat. A forum for traditional honky-tonk jam sessions and Johnny Cash cover tunes, the Palomino was steeped in down-home feel, cowboy grit brought in with the arrival of the Okies. It was not the place for a flashy young hippie, but Gram was not the type to back down from a challenge. The Palomino's open-mic night offered the chance for Gram to cut his teeth, and he was determined to fit in, no matter how out of the ordinary he might appear to the regulars.

Soon after arriving in California, Gram had sought out the famous tailor Nudie Cowen. Nudie had created a uniquely Hollywood haute couture, a style that matched cowboy cuts with Vegas glitz. He had clothed the likes of Elvis, Roy Rogers, and Dale Evans, and he had developed the "rhinestone cowboy" style, all honky-tonk flash and glitter.

Nudie's Rodeo Tailors was not far from the Palomino in a nondescript building that housed a treasure trove of custom-made costumes. Not long after settling into LA, Gram had tracked Nudie down and befriended him. So far his "Rodeo" wardrobe from the master tailor included some truly elegant Western shirts and a few pairs of perfectly fitted, custom-styled jeans.

With Nudie's clothes to lend him courage, Gram decided it was time to try his hand at the Palomino. Decked out in colored rhinestones, long-haired and long-limbed, Gram made his way to the stage and immediately sensed that he was unwelcome. There were cold stares coming from the bar and hoots and hollers from the back from the room. A man in wheelchair was finishing a decent cover of a Johnny Cash song. When it came time for Gram to step up for his turn, he threw down a shot of whiskey to keep up his courage and then gave it everything he had, singing with church-hall heart and clinging to his guitar like a drowning man clutches a broken plank.

When he finished, the crowd was quiet for a moment, the silence swallowing the room. Then, someone by the door began to clap, and it took hold; the rest of the club-goers added their cheers of approval. From that night on, Gram was inducted into the Palomino scene, taken under its audience's wing, and treated as the black sheep but beloved little brother, the freaky-deaky hippie kid who could belt out a honky-tonk number with the best of them.

John Nuese sometimes joined Gram on his Palomino visits and also accompanied him as he sought out other gritty Valley haunts—Chequers on Lankershim, Walt's Place, and Miller's Cave. The duo were always forced to engage in some sort of uncomfortable initiation rite, receiving threats and icy stares that eventually thawed into bemused acceptance once Gram opened his mouth to sing.

It was at the end of one of these wild Valley nights that Gram arrived home in a blue dawn to find Nancy waiting for him, her bare feet curled underneath her and her thick brown hair hanging loose. There was the smell of fresh coffee and incense, and the house was clean and ordered as always, the furniture glowing with wax and the arched front window opaque with the last hour of streetlights. Nancy had been crying; her cheeks were raw and salt stained. Gram was a little drunk and very tired, and when she told him she was pregnant, something went sour and caught in his throat. Cold clutched at his legs, made them impossible to move, leaden and swollen.

Gram was just twenty-one and doing his best to launch the career he had dreamt up for himself in Winter Haven. This dream had kept him afloat through his mother's slow death and helped him to face his father's persistent ghost. He wasn't ready to be a father, but the fact of it was there, as immovable and undeniable as stone. So he swallowed and smiled, took Nancy in his arms and held her, kept her there so she wouldn't see the tears in his own eyes. Outside a car passed, honking, and a bird sang the first notes of the morning. Gram was going to be a father now, and that was that, so he swore to himself he would be a good one.

Meanwhile, there were other changes happening in Gram's circle. Ian Dunlop and Mickey Gauvin were holding sessions of their own at the ISB house, playing soul and R&B with a host of Hollywood musicians. The glue that had kept the band together was slowly losing its strength. Without Gram's focus, attention was straying, and the cohesive unit that had made the move westward together slowly began to crumble. That first spring in Los Angeles, the Sub Band members had settled into the city in their own ways, Nuese and Gram heading for the northern hills to the country and western dives, and Dunlop and Gauvin embracing the rock 'n' roll of Laurel Canyon.

One night as spring slipped quietly into a California summer, Gram found himself standing outside at a party, sharing a smoke with music impresario Lee Hazlewood. Gram knew about Lee and the hits he had churned out with Duane Eddy and Nancy Sinatra (including Sinatra's huge song, "These Boots Are Made for Walkin' "). By 1967 Hazelwood had his own label, LH1, complete with high-tech studio facilities and a distribution deal. Gram decided to ask Lee for his help flat out, to lay his cards on the table and await the outcome of the game.

Hazelwood, surprised and charmed by the kid in the purple silk cowboy shirt, said yes with the stipulation that Gram use a Hazelwood-approved producer, in this case Lee's girlfriend Suzi Jane Hokum. Unfortunately, it was too late for Dunlop and Gauvin, who had already gone their own way on to new projects, and Gram, keeping the ISB name, found himself on a search for appropriate substitutes. Nuese stayed by Gram's side, the two bonded by their mutual love of traditional country and buoyed by the validation their deal with Hazelwood had given them. It would be a few months, however, before Gram could dig up a backing band, the right configuration of musicians to bring the music he envisioned to life.

He took a break from LA to head back to Florida in June, part of what was becoming a yearly ritual to collect his trust-fund money and check up on old friends. Winter Haven seemed the same as always with its lazy days and heavy heat. Gram settled in to a suite at the local hotel and hosted a slew of visitors.

On a whim, Gram decided to track down the Legends crew, hoping that some of his former cohorts might be willing to make the move west, adding some authentic southern flavor to the ISB lineup. Jesse Chambers was entrenched in Winter Haven, settled down and unwilling to take Gram's bait. Instead, he gave Gram the phone number for Jon Corneal in Nashville, where the Legends drummer had gone to try his hand as a studio musician.

Corneal heard Gram out and within a few weeks was toasting him in the yellow glare of California sun. It was late summer and liquid gold. Gram and Nancy were still entrenched in their Sweetzer hideaway, still floating. Corneal was installed at an apartment nearby, and Gram set out to complete the lineup, anxious to finally get his songs down on vinyl.

Eventually, Nashville session vet Earl Ball was enlisted on piano, and local pedal steel wonder JD Maness was brought in to strut his stuff alongside bassist Joe Osborne. The first session was booked for July, the time of year when the city was pressed flat by the heat of white afternoons, and the palms were dusted in exhaust.

The group settled in with Suzi Jane at the boards and a young Glen Campbell occasionally joined in on backup vocal harmonies. By the end of the month, they had two of Gram's songs down, "Blue Eyes" and "Luxury Liner." Nancy would visit sometimes, sit down and listen quietly in the corner, swaying, Gram's baby growing bigger inside her belly.

A second ISB session was booked for November, this time with a new bassist, Chris Etheridge, a veteran of the LA music scene who had most recently played with Judy Collins. The Sub Band finished the rest of the album quickly, due in part to Suzi Jane being at the helm, guiding Gram with a sure hand.

Working days started in the swollen late morning and lasted into the deepest part of the night. The work included straight country covers, a plea for authenticity that would include solid renditions of Merle Haggard's "I Must Have Been Someone Else You've Known" and Johnny Cash's "I Still Miss Someone" and "Folsom Prison Blues." Gram also included a version of Arthur Conley's "That's Alright Mama." Gram's own songs were full of revelation and unabashed emotion. A glance at his lyrics sheets, and it was obvious he was pushing himself to show a bit of his soul.

On "Do You Know How It Feels To Be Lonesome," he drew upon the loneliness he had felt after his father's suicide and after his mother's death, perfectly emoting isolation and a world-weary grief.

> *Do you know how it feels to be lonesome*
> *When there's just no one left that really cares*

Did you ever try to smile at some people
And all they ever seem to do is stare
And you remember how it feels to be cold again
When the happiness of love has gone away
And you never want to go out on the street again
And you only seem to live from day to day

Gram was thrilled with the results, the album shaping up to be the manifestation of what had merely been a cloudy vision, country music infused with a streak of youthful energy and the loose psychedelic groove of the times. The Doors were lighting fires that fall, and the Jefferson Airplane were looking for somebody to love, but Gram was defying expectation and making music completely his own, his most assured and poignant to date.

By the time *Safe at Home* was nearing completion, Gram had reconciled himself to fatherhood, had even begun to watch the swell of Nancy's stomach with a sense of excited anticipation. He was full of hope for the future, and he did his best to include the idea of family into the equation. There had been too much that had gone bad with his own mother's two marriages not to teach him some lessons in patience and mutual respect.

When his daughter finally arrived on December 1, 1967, Gram was elated. He sat by Nancy's bedside, taking the tiny baby they had made together into his thin arms. Everything about her, her wrinkled skin, the light fuzz of hair on her little head, her perfect, graceful feet, everything made him dizzy with pride. "Pretty Polly," he cooed, forgetting for a moment that he was young and scared and was filled merely with some new ache, a kind of love he had never tasted before.

When Gram finally got word the album was near release, he decided to head down to Florida again to clear his head and fill his bank account. In Winter Haven he tracked down one of his old friends, Bob Buchanan, and told him the good news. Once he had settled his accounts and made the rounds of friends and family, he suggested the two of them take the train to Nashville to celebrate with Nuese and Corneal, who had gone to Tennessee just after recording was complete, hoping to earn a few extra dollars on the studio circuit.

For the first time in a long while, Gram felt that perhaps things would finally fall into place, that the album they had just made would crack everything open, and he and his friends would ride off into a golden glow sunset. Nashville's easygoing glamour made for a warm homecoming. Nuese and Corneal were enthusiastic and happy to see Gram. The four of them washed down beer and barbecue and staggered in and out of the honky-tonk bars.

After a few debauched days, Gram booked a cabin on a westward-bound train. He and Buchanan boarded, leaving to go back to LA in the early morning, with Nuese and Corneal promising to follow by car. That first day on the rails, Gram sat watching the familiar landscape slip by, his notebook, spiral-bound and tattered, sitting on his lap.

His mind was cluttered with anxieties, excitement, anticipation, and a deep longing for some vague thing in his past, for the air he had been breathing in Nashville, the same thick and humid wet that had clung to the pines outside of Coon Dog's parents' house in Tennessee. As a kid, Gram had lain awake summer nights at his grandparents, listening to his father's rattling laugh coming up through the floorboards, looking out at the huge oak that seemed to hold the house in its boughs.

As the train rolled through swampland on hot metal track, lurching forward toward the life Gram had made for himself in LA, he found himself filled with nostalgia for a youth that hadn't been entirely his own, a nostalgia for a childhood he wished he'd had. He opened his notebook and began writing scraps of thoughts, one line, then two.

After a while, Bob Buchanan came and sat down next to him, and the two began talking, talking as the windows went black, and there was only the occasional brief glimmer of small-town lights and the moon high and huge in the sky. By the next morning, they had written the lyrics to what Gram knew immediately was the best song he'd dreamed up thus far, a song that encompassed the delicate balance of longing, desire, regret, and the ache of memory.

Its lyrics were simultaneously naïve and world-worn, the words distilled down to a feeling Gram recognized as truth. The song captured, like an old still photo or a scent, the feel of his youth, the way he saw his home in his own head, a messy incomprehensible jumble of smells and sounds—the ammonia scent of pine needles, campfires, banjo strings high and tight, his father's hands, the winds that carved at the tree branches and blew whispers into his adolescent ear.

> *In South Carolina there are many tall pines*
> *I remember the oak tree that we used to climb*
> *But now when I'm lonesome, I always pretend*
> *That I'm getting the feel of hickory wind*
> *I started out younger at most everything*
> *All the riches and pleasures, what else could life bring?*
> *But it makes me feel better each time it begins*
> *Callin' me home, hickory wind*
> *It's hard to find out that trouble is real*
> *In a far away city, with a far away feel*
> *But it makes me feel better each time it begins*
> *Callin' me home, hickory wind*

"Hickory Wind" was a song he could grab on to, that he could hold up as proof positive that he was onto something, that he had dug a sound out of himself that was uniquely his own, a song that would keep him afloat in an ocean of uncertainty and doubt.

Back in LA it was cold, colder than Florida-bred Gram thought California could be. At night, bright, icy winds blew, and a chill rain fell in the late afternoons. Not long before *Safe at Home* was finally due to hit the stores, Gram found himself in line at the bank, waiting to draw some quick cash from his Snively funds. He was out of his element amid the dim fluorescence and plate glass, his jeans slung low on his hips, flared at the bottom,

Jim Lauderdale Interview
Interviewed by Jessica Hundley

Jim Lauderdale is a talented solo artist with several successful, soulful, country-inflected albums under his belt. As a song-writer, his work has been covered by George Strait, Vince Gill, and many other immensely popular Nashville acts.

Q: How old were you when you first heard Gram's music?

A: I was a senior in high school when I first heard Gram's music and it was one of those things that stopped me in my tracks. Like the first time I heard the Beatles, the first time I heard George Jones. He has a real life-changing effect on people and he kind of changed the course of my life. I started writing fairly soon after that. When I first started listening to Gram I just couldn't stop listening and I wanted to find out everything about him. I eventually moved out to California because I wanted to walk the same streets he did and go to the clubs he used to play at and I started going out to the desert, to Joshua Tree, and just picture him being out there and hanging out. I never got to meet him or see him play, I wish I could have. I feel like the people that listen to him do know him in a lot of ways. I think that when I meet people and I find out that they are fans of Gram's, it's like you have this kind of understanding between yourselves. I have never experienced that with anybody else, ya know, Hank Williams or anybody else. There was just some-thing really magical about him.

Q: So you started playing your own music soon after that?

A: I was doing bluegrass music mostly. I was playing the banjo. Then I started switching off more to guitar, branching out, doing more country stuff. I went to business school and I was in a country band for a while, and I would always do several of Gram's songs during my set. Years later when I finally got a record deal, I had to resist making the albums like Gram's solo records, because to me, they were just perfect with the way they were . . . everything about them. From the song selection, the singing, the playing, the song sequencing, the production. They're just perfect so I really had to fight the temptation to make a record similar because he left just such a deep impression on me. There are several songs of mine that you could really hear his influence.

Q: What are some of your favorite Gram songs?

A: Some of my favorites are, "Hickory Wind." I used to live in South Carolina, my folks still live there. It's got that line "In South Carolina, there's many tall pines," and there was a bunch of pine trees outside our house. Everything he wrote, I think, just stands on its own. There was so much feeling in his music and his singing and I think that's one thing that draws people in. There's nothing contrived about it and he has a really unique voice. You definitely know it's him. I think that it was so important the way he brought to real hard country music this rock sensibility. I think Gram really expressed a lot of love through his music, too, and I think maybe that was the way he really loved. I know while he was here he must have touched many people, his friends and his family, and I think maybe another reason people love him so much is that there is this presence there. There's so much from the heart, there's not this goal in mind commercially, it's just wide open. There's just this real romance I think about his presence that nobody can probably ever explain it. Gram is just one of those guys that you just get goosebumps when you hear them.

and dragging a bit on the industrial linoleum. He was wearing a patchwork velvet coat and a scarf and had a bit of hair swinging over one eye.

Standing among the meandering trail of customers leading to the teller was another young man, blinking in the sea of polyester pantsuits and flower-print housecoats. At first it seemed as if the man was a reflection of Gram himself, a mirror image save for his hair, which was blond and wiry and curled up high toward the ceiling tiles.

Gram tried out his crooked smile on him, teeth white, and the other young man hesitated, then smiled back, sharing in their secret, that acknowledgement of youthful defiance, two natives of the underground, angels among thieves. The two edged closer together and began to talk.

By January 1968 Chris Hillman had built a solid reputation for himself both as a revered mandolin and bass guitar player (bred on California bluegrass) and as a charismatic showman. He had founded the Byrds in 1965 along with Roger McGuinn, David Crosby, Gene Clark, and Michael Clarke. The band had produced a string of successful hits, beginning with their tidy rendition of Bob Dylan's "Tambourine Man."

Hillman grew up on a ranch outside of San Diego, obsessed early on with the likes of Earl Scruggs and folk heroes like Pete Seeger. With the Byrds, he was writing songs, playing bass, and singing high harmonies with Roger McGuinn, Gene Clark, and (ironically enough) Nancy's ex, David Crosby.

But in January of 1968, Hillman was feeling lost, his band cracked and scattered to pieces, Clarke quitting, Crosby stalking off in anger, Hillman and the rest of the band still reeling, a weight in the pit of their stomachs from the less-than-enthusiastic audience reaction to their latest album, *Notorious Byrd Brothers*. What Hillman and the rest of the Byrds had been trying to do on *Notorious* was a slightly more hallucinogenic, outer-space take on Gram's own country-rock hope, a sprawling folk-rock freak-out laced with trippy touches borrowed from the English bands across the water. The Byrds were attempting to position themselves as merry musical pranksters, and although *Notorious* had not necessarily been a hit with the fans, it had impressed the critics with its fearless weaving and intertwining of genres as well as its impressive guitar work, a gift from the album's twenty-two-year-old session player, Clarence White.

That afternoon, in the echoing lobby of a Hollywood bank, Hillman looked Gram up and down, and a light went off deep inside his head. LA was not as big a town as it might have seemed. He had met Gram here and there, gotten word from Crosby about the rich kid from Florida who had walked into David's house and left with his fiancée. He had heard about Gram's trial by fire at the Palomino, about the Sub Band's exploits with Hazlewood, and about the catch-voiced ache that made Gram sound like he was singing at a camp revival.

The gangly, thin-legged kid standing across from Hillman suddenly seemed to be there—exactly on that day, at that place, at that time—for a reason. The two of them had been walking parallel, and now their two paths had crossed, at a bank of all places, a buttoned-down business place full of suits and stiff backs.

A couple of weeks later, Gram found himself in a smoky LA rehearsal space, auditioning for the Byrds. He played a few songs on piano, stroked some rhythm guitar, and sang straight from his guts. When he was done, he watched as Hillman and McGuinn shared a look and a nod, and he knew that he was in.

Soon, *Safe at Home* slowly began to emerge from stillborn status. That spring the LA airwaves were occupied with British exports. The Rolling Stones were growing raunchier and rowdier by the minute, and Beatlemania showed no signs of slowing. Music was beginning to vibrate, shake, and gleam; it was a sonic reflection of the LSD experience, acid dreaming reflected in the psychedelic experiment of the Beatles' *Sgt. Pepper's Lonely Hearts Club Band* and the Stones' *Their Satanic Majesties Request*. The Beatles' "Revolution," a grinding, gritty threat to the establishment, was the song to beat. Stateside, the sound of San Francisco was bleeding

Steve Earle Interview
Interview by Jessica Hundley

Raised in Texas, Steve Earle got his start singing in local coffeehouses in the 1960s. He is now one of the most revered and revolutionary singer/songwriters coming out of the country rock scene.

Q: When did you first hear Gram's music?

A: I started listening to Gram when he was with the Byrds. We just happened to have a little radio station out in San Antonio and it was our first, what they call underground rock station. It actually started out as a midnight to six program and an easy listening station then that evolved into KEXL and they played the Byrds record that Gram was on and they continued right on and played the Burrito Brothers. So I happened to live in a place where the Burrito Brothers got played on the radio. There weren't that many places that played them, but out here there was and in Texas no less. It was odd, because San Antonio is so conservative. Nowadays you would think I would have happened to hear them in Austin but I don't think there was a station in Austin that played that kind of stuff. I'll be fifty next year, so, I was probably twelve or thirteen when I first heard him. And then when Gram died I was eighteen, I guess, and I was still in Texas. I'd been on my own a couple of years. I was working for a swimming pool company. The crew that I worked with, we were like the trim and follow-up crew, we did the landscaping and cleaned up the mess after the swimming pool had been built. It was a lot of wheelbarrow and shovel work and everybody happened to be musicians. I started off playing coffeehouses, so I was kind of a folkie. I sort of gravitated toward some of the guys who had actually started out in rock bands and, you know, it was a real decisive thing, being in country-rock. In Texas it's either one extreme or another, you either gravitate toward country-rock because the country part of it was part of your culture, or you avoided it completely because it was part of your culture and you wanted to piss your parents off.

Q: So listening to the Burritos was an act of defiance?

A: It made me feel like I wasn't so weird because I wore cowboy boots and I had long hair. That's one of the reasons his music was really important to me. I was lucky enough to see him play as well. I hitchhiked over and saw the Fallen Angels at Liberty Hall in Houston. It was a really great show. There's a bootleg that exists of that very show—it was a really good one. They had couple of rough dates because they didn't rehearse much I guess, but by the time they got to Texas they sounded pretty good.

Q: What are some of your favorite songs?

A: "Luxury Liner" because it's Gram's first single. It's on the International Submarine Band record, which I heard, not when it came out, but because I backtracked because I was a Burrito Brothers fan. It was the best Gram song on that first record. He wrote it by himself. I also like "My Uncle," which is a Burrito Brothers thing, him and Chris wrote it over in Burrito Manor out in the Valley and it was the only antiwar song to come out of the band.

Q: When did you start making music yourself?

A: I was eleven or twelve when I first started playing and it pretty much took over and was pretty much my identity from the time I was thirteen. You know, I mean no one ever saw me anywhere without a guitar and everybody knew me as the pain in the ass with the guitar. I'm still a pain in the ass!

quickly into the mainstream, Jefferson Airplane leading a patch-work hippie hit parade down both coasts.

When *Safe at Home* was finally released, it fit into no one's pigeonholes. It was an undeniable country album, full of southern swing and hayfield romance, but strange enough and experimental enough to carve its own way. Gram had been adamant about keeping his own vision, his rock and country hybrid, his mix of tradition and defiance. It was still difficult, however, for the album to be easily digested or neatly categorized.

LH1 did its best to explain the album, marketing *Safe at Home* as country and including avowals of approval in the form of liner notes by Duane Eddy and Don Everly. The results, however, were mixed. Critics were either nonchalant or mildly enthusiastic, and audiences were more or less bewildered. The album fell flat, quickly relegated to forgotten back stacks of the record stores, a bargain-bin gem awaiting discovery.

Gram, however, had won some respect from his peers with *Safe at Home*, and although the disc had not shot out on a straight, clear path to fame, it was still evident Gram was in the game. He was uncertain how to take this response, however, desiring as he did adoration from his audience. Money was not the issue. With his trust fund, Gram could afford to make music for decades without ever producing a hit. It was ego, that deep hole in him, the place hungry for attention and acceptance.

As the album stalled, ISB splintered, and Nuese and Corneal headed back to Nashville, trying their best to keep their heads above water. Gram watched his friends leave with a shiver of regret and a sick embarrassment at the album's financial failure. For Gram, the breakup of the Sub Band was like a dull blow; he saw his past dissipating like morning mist just as his future spread its arms wide.

The Byrds moved in to fill the gap that ISB had left behind. Their reputation, their experience, and their string of successes and foundation of fans warmed up the cold doubts in Gram's heart—his doubts about Nuese and Corneal, his doubts about

Nancy, and about himself. With his entrée into the Byrds, all of these uncertainties warmed, melted into nothing, and slipped conveniently away.

The Byrds had already explored a substantial amount of the territory Gram was keen to travel. Both McGuinn and Hillman were unabashed music adventurers, artists who stepped onto their own paths without waiting for approval from either their fans or the commercial climate. They had flirted successfully with country before on *Younger Than Yesterday*, and they both had enough background in bluegrass, folk and blues, and enough knowledge of jazz and R&B to be able to play almost any genre with relative ease, to be capable of a melting-pot experiment.

It was easy for Gram to go from background player to the driver's seat, which he did on occasion. "Hickory Wind," which he reshaped and remodeled, was his proof to himself that he could hold his own with the Byrds, hold his own and more. What had begun as a search for a touring musician, a decent piano player and guitar sideman, had turned into a major redirection for the band, with Gram, more often than not, pointing the way.

ALMOST IMMEDIATELY AFTER meeting Roger and Chris, Gram took them to meet Nudie, who decked them out in customized rhinestone and flash. The three spent long nights together smoking hash, hanging out, and listening to tracks by George Jones and Hank Snow. Country became a new adventure, a door open to fresh air, and Chris and Roger were ready to breathe deeply, ready to shake the dust off their four years together and test out something new. Gram thickened his drawl and went to it, enthusing to his new bandmates on the revelatory nature of their upcoming experiment that would roll the Beatles and Hank Williams all into one, seducing two disparate audiences simultaneously.

Columbia Records was slightly wary of the concept, the label executives raising their brows at what amounted to a concept album, a time-travel journey encompassing Appalachian hoot and holler, defiant Dylanesque folk, sprawling space jams, and urban-cowboy country. Nevertheless, the record company agreed on the basic creative plan and gave the go-ahead when the Byrds announced that they wanted to record in Nashville.

That spring Gram returned to the South, swell-chested and triumphant. He brought on Jon Corneal as drummer for the upcoming album, along with *Safe at Home* alumni JD Maness and Earl Ball. McGuinn and Hillman invited Clarence White, who had by then become an unofficial fourth member whose playing was thrilling and imaginative, an indispensable addition to the mix.

In early March the band went into the studio and sat down to record two songs, Bob Dylan's "You Ain't Goin' Nowhere" and Gram's "Hickory Wind." With the guidance of producer Gary Usher and the skills of steel guitarist Lloyd Green and bassist Ray Huskey, the Byrds did right by Dylan, beautifully revisualizing "Going Nowhere," and they revamped Gram's "Hickory Wind" until it was silken and swollen with emotion.

In the midst of recording the song, Gram looked around the room at Jon on drums, at McGuinn and Hillman carefully executing notes that he himself had written, and he went numb with pride and anticipation. It was finally happening, finally falling into place; everything he had spent so much time building was emerging into a recognizable edifice.

The next night the Byrds were invited to play on the sacrosanct stage of the Ryman Auditorium, the broadcast venue of the venerable Grand Ole Opry. Gram was ecstatic. The Ryman had originally been built as a place of worship, a tabernacle complete with wooden pews and sacred ground.

When the Byrds hit the stage for their half hour of preacherman glory, a palpable wave swept through the audience, a mixture of curiosity, bemusement, and a hint of hostility. The Byrds had opted for full regalia, Nudie suits catching the spotlights, colors vibrating, rhinestones glowing, their hair stroking their shoulders, their long-legged hippie-kid ease a spit in the face of Opry tradition and an utterly alien presence on the Ryman stage.

They started out easy, breezing through Merle Haggard's "Sing Me Back Home," the audience sighing with relief at the familiar chords and settling in to see what these California kids could do. The next song on the set list was another Haggard number, "Life in Prison," but just as the weak applause was dwindling, Gram leaned forward into the microphone and coughed. He wasn't sure exactly why, but something in the audience's smug assessment made him angry, and defiance rose in his throat, tasting of bile and rebellion.

"This next song," he said calmly, flashing a grit-teeth grin, "is for my grandmother, who used to listen to the Grand Ole Opry with me when I was little. It's a song I wrote called 'Hickory Wind.'"

Hillman and McGuinn exchanged looks, shrugged, and started in on Gram's number. The crowd was uncertain what to think, and the stage manager was furious. Gram gazed out into the vaulted, echoing hall and played like he was born to do it.

After wrapping up their Nashville session, the members of the newly revamped Byrds lineup did a short tour of colleges up and down the East Coast, refining their new songs and streamlining old Byrds numbers and favorite covers. When they got back to Los Angeles, they settled in to finish their new album, whose title *Sweetheart of the Rodeo* was a clear indication of the direction in which the band was headed.

In their California studio, they recorded a Merle Haggard number; a classic Louvin Brothers piece; a traditional British murder ballad, "Pretty Polly"; and two of Gram's songs, "One Hundred Years" and "Lazy Days," the latter resuscitated from Gram's rejected contribution to the score of *The Trip*. Not only had Gram become a fully-functioning member of the band, but Hillman and McGuinn were also willing to let him play occasional front man, blending his high thin voice with McGuinn's graceful harmonies. The tracks they recorded over the weeks of sessions affirmed the mutual chemistry they were all feeling.

Gram, however, in his haste to ingratiate himself with the Byrds, had swaggered out of his contract with LH1, feeling untouchable

Dinosaur Jr. / J Mascis Interview
Interview by Jessica Hundley

As cofounder, guitarist, and singer of Dinosaur Jr., J Mascis was an integral member of one of the most influential groups of the late 1980s. The band's distinctive sound went on to fuel the massive indie rock movement of the past two decades. Today, Mascis continues his wall-of-sound "guitar drone" tradition, with a thriving solo career.

Q: When did you first hear Gram's music?

A: I think I probably heard it as a kid, but I first really started listening to it in the early 1990s. At the time I was into anything Rolling Stones related, so I came across him that way. I remember seeing him briefly in the movie about Altamont, *Gimme Shelter*, and thinking that the stuff he was playing sounded really cool. So I went and got some albums and I liked all his stuff immediately.

Q: What was it about his music that first drew you in?

A: I like everything, but his singing was what I think made me really sit down and listen. He could do covers and make them sound better than the originals, where most people do a cover and make it sound worse than the original. There was a lot of emotion in his voice, I guess that's what really got me from the start.

Q: What are some of your favorite songs?

A: Well, I think I initially liked "Hot Burrito #1" and "#2" and "$1000 Wedding." I liked his version of "Wild Horses" too. I liked some country music at the time, Merle Haggard and those guys. But I think he made me appreciate that music more. One of the things I really liked about him was that he had a really high, pretty voice, really soulful singing, whereas all those other guys, George Jones and Merle Haggard and Johnny Cash, were singing country with these really deep voices. I liked that he did it his own way, did it with this kind of graceful, high voice. I think he also made me appreciate the Byrds more too. I had originally thought they were too wimpy. I mean, I like all their stuff now, but *Sweetheart of the Rodeo* is what really made me first appreciate them. "Hickory Wind" was a song I really liked.

Q: Do you think his music had an effect on the music you were making yourself?

A: I'm sure he had an effect. I was writing things that were a little more country-ish for a while. I even did a cover of "Hot Burrito #2" as a B-side of a single, so yeah, he definitely had an effect on what I was doing.

Q: Do you think his music has resonance now?

A: Definitely. People still discover it and listen to it and relate to it. His music, I think because it's so soulful, has had a lasting quality.

and a little too proud. Hazlewood was a hardened veteran of the industry with little patience for kids with swollen egos, and when he got wind of Gram's involvement with the Byrds, he made a call to CBS, coolly reminding them that he still owned the rights to any and all of Gram's vocal performances.

The bottom suddenly dropped out of everything; Gram deflated like a punctured balloon, bumped back into place by the threat of a lawsuit, and CBS execs were was quaking in their shoes. What might have been a strong and spectacular showcase for Gram's talents, *Sweetheart of the Rodeo* became an exercise in careful erasure.

Gram's voice was either stripped off songs entirely or left as pallid backup harmony, and there was nothing the band could do. Everyone was at the mercy of the label and its lawyers, all of whom unanimously agreed to back off after Hazlewood's sly reminder. The threat of pricey legal hassles proved to be far more persuasive than the desire to stand up and fight for the new kid in the group, a singer who had originally been enlisted as a hired hand.

McGuinn and Hillman were apologetic, but Gram was devastated, furious, the entanglement yet another obstacle in his pursuit of fame, another frustration meant to bleed him of his optimism. In spite of himself, he began to let paranoia affect him and black suspicions descend. Did McGuinn merely want the spotlight on himself? How hard had Hillman fought for Gram? How much did they really care about having him in the band at all?

Things at home were rocky as well. Gram's relationship with Nancy had suffered from his obvious fear of fatherhood, and from the growing resentment that had begun to sour his interactions at home. He had proposed to Nancy, feeling a burden of responsibility, and she had accepted. But when the troubles with Hazlewood descended, Gram began to spend less and less time at the apartment, using any excuse to get away from home, all the while aching with guilt and wishing to recapture the energy that still existed between him and Nancy.

Somewhere inside himself there was a sick feeling, a feeling that perhaps his actions over the last year—his slow dissolution with Nancy, his fear of fatherhood, and his quick exit from the Sub Band—were coming back to haunt him, karmic retribution in action. He had become loosely enamored of Eastern thought. He had learned about Buddhism and Hinduism through his long talks with Jet at Harvard and had explored the embrace of Eastern mysticism and metaphysics with Nancy. His keen inquiry into the cosmic was not only his own long-held habit but part and parcel of the cultural clime.

Accordingly, he held onto a vague belief in the concept of past misdeeds coming back to affect the present. He had been unkind to Nancy and grievously self-absorbed in his dealings with his friends in ISB; that was certain. But, while he smart enough to recognize his lack of honesty with himself, he did his best to avoid looking too closely, afraid to see things as they truly were. Had he been more gracious in his dealings with Hazlewood, less contemptuous, things might have turned out differently, and the truth of this, in particular, sat in Gram like a stone.

The news of an upcoming Byrds tour, however, acted as a balm. It would be Gram's first trip abroad and would include a stop in Italy and then in England. Gram hoped the trip would give him some much-needed perspective, a little space between himself and the complications of his LA life.

The first week of May 1968, the Byrds packed their gear and took off from LAX, heading to Rome. Gram looked down at Los Angeles, at the maze of concrete and palm, watched as it slipped beneath him, giving way to the mountains that lined the bowl of the valley like a jagged backbone. He ordered a drink, winked at the stewardess, and settled in, feeling the impossible stretch of space between the plane's belly and the ground.

Only a few hours after arriving in Rome, the Byrds found themselves playing to a packed crowd at the Piper House. The show was a hit despite the fact that most of the audience only had a vague idea of lyrical content and even less of a clue about the country roots the Byrds were referencing. Whatever the pretty, longhaired American boys were playing sounded all right to the Italians. The music was soothing and exotic, a bit of mythic California on display.

By the second week of May, the Byrds had arrived in England, welcomed by sold-out shows at Middle Earth, a Covent Garden hotspot and London's answer to the Whiskey. Old friends had gathered to meet the band at the airport, a group that included Keith Richards, Marianne Faithful, and Mick Jagger, the Stones playing host for the Byrds' Brit stay.

Gram was in heaven. The brick and stone of London reminded him of Boston, and he was ecstatic at the proximity of the Rolling Stones, although he was careful to bury his excitement under a veneer of nonchalance. He was a rare bird in London, a child of the Confederacy, an authentic southern gentleman, complete with a lazy drawl and a history worthy of a Tennessee Williams play. The Stones had recorded a cover of a track by Grand Ole Opry star Hank Snow back in 1964, and Richards was an avowed Roy Rogers fan. The members of the band, particularly Keith, were immediately intrigued by the Byrds' new member, plying him with questions about country music and southern living.

The Byrds concerts were an immediate success and were attended by enthusiastic audiences that included friends, peers, artists, and musicians—the cream of the swingin' London crop. For Gram it was one of those rare lightning-strike moments when you realize that you have stumbled into exactly the right place at exactly the right time.

After the last show at Middle Earth, in the hash smoke and sweat of backstage, Keith, his girlfriend Anita Pallenberg, Mick, and Marianne made their way to the Byrds' dressing room. Within moments the entire crew had relocated to the plush interiors of two shiny Rolls Royce automobiles, each one carrying a substantial supply of weed and liquor, fully stocked for a trip to the countryside for an impromptu visit to Stonehenge.

For Gram, this was confirmation that he was heading for something big. Here he was, twenty-one years old, high as a kite, Johnnie

Walker warming his skin, and he was sharing a Rolls with the better half of the Rolling Stones. It was something out of his adolescent dreams, a moment to write home about, to regale his little sister and Winter Haven pals with—Gram Parsons and Keith Richards bonding over Roy Rogers ballads with the English hills, green and wet, roaring past in soft spring darkness.

By the time they arrived at Stonehenge, it was a pink and orange dawn, and Gram and his friends were floating on deep-cushioned clouds of Mary Jane, tongues thick with booze and talk and sleeplessness. The vast stone structure loomed ahead, massive and mysterious, the grass around it soaked with beaded dew. The edges of Gram's blue jeans went black with it, his boots seeping.

As he staggered behind the crowd, he paused for a moment to take in the slice of yellow sunrise, the moon still lingering in the sky, the girls' hair swinging and blond, and Keith, Mick, Chris, and Roger looking like strange medieval balladeers or court jesters, all patchwork color and crushed velvet, their silk scarves catching the early morning breeze. Gram paused there in front of Stonehenge, tasted dope smoke and the sharp echo of scotch whiskey, and smiled so wide it hurt his cheeks.

The Byrds arrived back in LA when *Sweetheart* was finally about to be pressed, Gram's vocals appearing and reappearing on the album like a ghost, a distant echo buried in the background, his traditional phrasing loping just under McGuinn's more contemporary country take. Gram's songs still were intact, Hillman and McGuinn adding their own vision, a sound they had developed years before and refined. Although the new country twang was a slight deviation from the norm, there was still enough of the classic Byrds sound on *Sweetheart* to make the fans feel like they were on familiar ground.

Still, Gram felt despondent. He clung to the idea that the album had not been mixed as they had wanted, that the country rock message, the blend they were striving for, had been watered down so as not to alienate fans on either side. He felt the album didn't stray far enough, didn't push any boundaries, that in the end

Keith Richards Interview
Interview by Jessica Hundley

Guitar man, rock 'n' roll rebel, and backbone to the Rolling Stones, Keith Richards has led an incredible life. He's been at the center of the cultural storm for three decades and counting. As one of Gram's best friends, Richards continues as keeper of the flame, shouting Parsons's praises from every rooftop and making certain Gram's legacy remains strong.

He granted this interview backstage just before performing his old friend's songs at one of the 2004 "Return to Sin City" tribute concerts organized by Polly Parsons in her father's memory.

Q: Can you tell us about Gram's influence on you musically?

A: You know when you play with someone for a few years, things rub off that you're not really aware of immediately. Later on you say "Oh yeah," you know. It's not a matter of "Oh, I'm gonna nick that lick or take that thing," it's just . . . it's like osmosis. We osmosed a lot! [Laughs] The other thing Gram loved was the finer points of country music—the difference between Nashville and Bakersfield, for example. Before I met Gram I didn't know there was a difference, you know what I mean? He pointed out the different styles and also he introduced me to an amazing new area of musicians in the country. James Burton—the great J. B.—and Al Perkins, who worked with the Stones on *Exile on Main Street*. Gram knew his country music inside and out and he had a real love for it. I learnt so much by being with him.

Q: What do you feel was Gram's biggest contribution to country music?

A: In the short time, really, that he had, his influence on it was enormous. After Gram every other country singer saw another new way to deal with it, instead of the old way. I mean new thoughts, really. That's what he did. That's what his influence is. I mean, he didn't have enough time to do enough stuff, although he's left us some great songs. He and I had some incredible times together. And I still feel him here, tonight, you know? He would have liked this, the fact that all these people are still listening to his music and getting it. You know, he was someone who had spent enough very lonely nights in odd places, very odd places, indeed. We had a lot of laughs together, Gram and I. And I always miss him. I miss him all the time.

it was just another Byrds album, containing some pleasant country-inflected numbers, yes, but none of the revolutionary sound they had been after.

Three tracks had been cut entirely from the album, including Gram's "Lazy Days," on which he had sung lead vocals, and "Pretty Polly," which he had selected as a tribute to his newborn daughter. Even though CBS and Hazlewood had settled amicably, the record execs had decided that it was better to keep Gram's involvement in the album as far in the background as possible. It was a blow to his ego. Worse still, there remained the persistent doubt that perhaps he had been partially at fault for the state of things, his own pride and insensitivity equaling obstacles to his success.

And then there was Nancy. Gram had felt a weight lift with his trip abroad, with the space he'd put between himself and Nancy. Everything at Sweetzer growing more nervous and strained, but the baby was beautiful and growing, a silver chain that bound Gram and Nancy tight to one another.

Gram didn't have the strength to cut himself loose. But it was obvious to both him and Nancy that their love had become a small sad thing between them, fading into nothing as they watched, each of them helpless to stop its diminishing. One night in bed, Nancy turned, her arms outstretched to hold Gram, and he flinched when she touched him, his skin pulling away from the warmth of her hand. In that moment that last loose link between them snapped, and Nancy knew with cold clarity that it was over between them, that Gram didn't love her anymore.

A second tour, scheduled to coincide with the new album's release, seemed to spell the end to Nancy and Gram's relationship. The Byrds planned to stop in London again and then continue on to South Africa, where the band had consented to a series of concerts regardless of the political clime and controversial policy of apartheid. Chris and Roger were hoping to play for black and white audiences alike, hoping, therefore, to make a defiant protest against apartheid in the process. Gram was just anxious to get out of California and back onto the stage.

In July of 1968, Gram found himself at Royal Albert Hall, playing in front of four thousand screaming fans, the Stones in the audience again, cheering the Byrds on. His friendship with Keith Richards blossomed over the next few days in a blur of decadent hotel-room debauchery. The two made their way through the stack of country and western records Gram had stuffed into his suitcase, drinking whiskey and swapping stories. All the while Gram played the perfect sidekick to Keith's outlaw gunman guise.

It was on one of those nights, the two of them soaked through with bourbon and dope smoke, that Keith nonchalantly mentioned the Byrds' next tour stop in South Africa. He and the Rolling Stones, along with hundreds of other international acts, had boycotted the country in a loosely defined protest against the apartheid policy.

Gram was curious. Over the past few years, he had been largely lost in his music, only vaguely aware of the turmoil evolving in culture and politics. He had never been actively involved with the protest movement, had never marched or held a placard shouting his stance, and had never joined a university sit-in. Even though he was coming of age in one of the most tumultuous periods in human history, Gram had been predominately concerned with music, girls, clothes, and a vaguely spiritual self-exploration.

Bob Parsons's business connections and Gram's brief stay at Harvard had kept the Vietnam draft card out of his mailbox, and most of his friends were rich, educated kids, lucky enough to not to have to worry, at least not directly, about the war. Vietnam was merely a distant, tragic unreality evidenced only by body counts on television and riots in the street, but not by anything that had touched Gram yet point-blank.

Bleary-eyed and riveted, Gram listened to Keith's CliffsNotes summary of apartheid and his comparison of South Africa's social structure to the Deep South during slavery, hitting Gram on his home ground. Gram remembered the "colored" kids he had ridden bikes with in Waycross. He remembered the cook at his grandparents' house, the woman with the wide pretty face who had made his Christmas cookies and his Easter ham each year in Winter Haven.

By the time dawn arrived, bringing with it the sharp, bitter beginnings of a hangover, Gram had decided that he would not go with the Byrds to South Africa, fame and fortune and previous contract commitments be damned. He made a brief statement the next day to the British newspaper *Melody Maker* announcing that he was refusing to finish the tour.

Hillman and McGuinn were furious. They knew that Gram had never displayed any political leanings in the past, and they saw his decision as both a disappointing show of disloyalty and a blatant move to ingratiate himself with the Rolling Stones. Gram pretended not to care. He stuck to his guns and refused to go. After a bitter argument and bad blood, the Byrds left for South Africa without him.

Gram opted to remain in London, and a few days after Chris and Roger's departure, Keith asked his new friend to join him at Redlands, Keith's country estate in West Whittering. It was midsummer and incredibly verdant, lush, and green. Britain was displaying its finest colors. The air at Redlands tasted of grass, and the sky was washed a pale blue.

Gram, Keith, and Anita (now Richards's common-law wife) spent lazy afternoons playing guitar, smoking hash from an enormous brass and silver hookah, and wandering dazed through the acres of woodland that surrounded the estate. The bond between the two young musicians grew, their new friendship fortified by their mutual passion for music and books. They each bled knowledge from the other. Keith regaled Gram with his Rolling Stones escapades, and Gram told tales of the American South, filling them both with that unnamed nostalgia, that yearning for a time and place that, in truth, neither had ever experienced.

They played guitar together on the stone patio and threw rocks into the moat that surrounded the estate. At dusk Anita would join them, bringing out whiskey and ice, the sun dipping below the roll of the hills. It was a magic time, touched with some electric charge. Gram was immensely inspired, even though he no longer had a band.

In playing country music professor to Keith's eager student, Gram was beginning to get a clear idea of where he was headed next, of the type of music he should be making, that sound that he had first touched upon with "Hickory Wind." He wanted to make music that made your ribs crack and your mouth go dry, goosebump music, a sound that raised the hair on the back of your arms. He dubbed it "Cosmic American Music," and he talked about it until his voice had frayed. Keith and Anita listened, watching with cats' eyes and sharing the last orange ember of a joint as Gram enthused about the true potential, the magic he saw in the mating of musical ideas. He was on fire with it and giddy with the freedom he had been handed by the departure of the Byrds.

Amid the gloss of smooth scotch, hot meals, and the best drugs money could by, Gram hatched a new plan for a new phase, a band that could manifest his new style of music—that creation of funk, folk, purebred country, and nitty-gritty rock 'n' roll that would sound like nothing anyone had ever heard and everything they wanted to hear, all at once.

Ecstatic, Gram began making calls from Redlands, already starting to recruit musicians who could make his music a reality. He contacted old friends such as Chris Etheridge, who had played on *Safe at Home* and had impressed Gram with both his skill and enthusiasm. He talked to Keith about possibly producing, and Keith, groggy and amiable, agreed. By the end of a sunlit month at Redlands, Gram felt ready to go for broke.

Keith, who was between engagements with the Rolling Stones, suggested he and Anita head to Los Angeles with Gram. It would be a change of scene, with Gram acting as tour guide and host. Within a week Gram was touching down on California soil with his two friends in tow, all of them drunk as skunks on first-class cocktails, and ready to take on the world.

At LAX, they stumbled into a limo. Their driver was Phil Kaufman, a thickly muscled, slightly haggard-looking man with a drooping salt-and-pepper mustache and a hard glint in his eye. Phil Kaufman was a former Hollywood stuntman and an ex con, whose years of tough living had disguised a surprisingly soft heart.

He had been hooked up at the last minute with the limo job,

asked by a friend to ferry around some famous people in exchange for a bit of cash and the possibility of future employment. He took one look at his passengers and knew they would need a nanny.

Keith's eyes were half-open, a silk scarf wrapped like a turban around his head. Anita was giggling. Gram, who was only half-conscious, settled down into the cushioned calfskin of the limo's backseat and gave cryptic directions, then winked at Phil and asked Anita to mix him a whiskey and water. The adventure had begun.

Gram's first few weeks back home were mildly victorious. He had arrived in America just in time for the national release of *Sweetheart of the Rodeo*, which was receiving a smattering of positive reviews. That combined with Anita and Keith's presence helped buoy his ego and keep hope afloat.

Meanwhile, the Byrds were swallowing a bitter pill. The South African tour had been a catastrophe—a logistical nightmare, a financial disaster, and a political misstep. Hillman and McGuinn arrived home with tensions running high between them and bank accounts substantially depleted. Furthermore, Hillman's marriage was wearing precariously thin. The combination of business and personal troubles took an overwhelming emotional toll on him, and finally—feeling exhausted, disheartened, angry, and creatively lost—he quit the band he had started four years earlier, leaving McGuinn to his own devices.

The *Sweetheart* album, despite its initial critical acclaim, found little love with Byrds fans and stalled somewhere in the far reaches of the charts. It was the band's worst-selling album to date. Gram, however, tried to protect himself behind a wall of rationalizations: if the album had been what they had wanted it to be, if Hazelwood had not played his hand, and if the label had truly trusted them, *Sweetheart* would have been successful.

In the end, it didn't matter much anyway. Gram had been with the Byrds for five short months, done his best to make his mark, and moved on. He was busy preparing the foundation for his second act, anyway, recruiting players for his new band. He and Etheridge auditioned a variety of players, but when the grapevine reported Chris

Hillman's departure from the Byrds, Gram gathered up his gumption and went to his friend, flashing his lopsided, mischievous, undeniable grin and asking Hillman flat out, "Come and play with me?"

The water that had flowed under the bridge between them flowed fast. Despite the fact that Gram had let him down, Chris, much to his own surprise, said yes. Within a few days, the two were making music together again, sharing hand-rolled cigarettes and writing songs as if nothing at all had happened. The rift had healed, and with it, Hillman began to heal as well.

Nancy by this time had retreated to Santa Barbara with Polly. Sudden bachelors, Gram and Chris decided to move in together, renting a house on DeSoto Avenue in Reseda, which was north of the Hollywood Hills in the stretch of Valley flatlands that was not much more than concrete and auto dealerships. By this time Gram had come up with a name for the group, borrowing the turn of phrase from his old friend Ian Dunlop, who had knack for unforgettable wordplay.

After his exit from the International Submarine Band, Dunlop had brought together a loose group of musicians for occasional club dates and parties. The Flying Burrito Brothers seemed the perfect handle to Gram, surreal enough to be touched with psychedelia but with a kind of earthiness too. The word "brothers" lent the band name the down-home family feel he was looking for. He co-opted the name, and soon he and Hillman had dubbed their new digs Burrito Manor and had started spending their days on the back patio writing songs and their evenings staggering through Valley dives.

Both Gram and Chris felt as if they had been set free from the artistic responsibilities of their past and from their romantic entanglements. They were still young, still hungry, and Burrito Manor was a gleeful haven for a return to adolescence, a return to drunken dawns, one-night stands, and complete immersion in their music.

Etheridge, who slept on the couch most nights, would wake up and make coffee while Gram worked out melodies on the piano. There was new excitement, a sense of rebirth and revitalization.

Gram and Burritos. PHOTO BY ANDEE COHEN NATHANSON.

Gram was incredibly happy to have saved his friendship with Hillman, ecstatic to be playing across the room from him again. The two had something between them that was special, and they knew it, knew it and were anxious to take it to vinyl.

The Valley was, literally and figuratively, miles away from the LA scene. The rugged ridge of mountains along its south side closed out the city and formed a kind of psychic wall against whatever pressure and pretense might be found downtown. For Gram, it felt like home. The clubs that clung to the curbs of the street housed a much different breed of both performer and audience member.

Gram getting mellow. PHOTO BY ANDEE COHEN NATHANSON.

You didn't go to the Valley to get famous, you simply went there to play, to play the music you loved for people who nursed their beers and their day-to-day worries. Highways 5 and 101 cut through the middle of the stucco sprawl, pointing an asphalt arrow toward Bakersfield and San Francisco, and bringing down real working-class cowboys from out in the Central Valley.

These were the people Gram wanted to impress, the hard sun-leathered farmers and field hands, the ranchers, the guys who rode horses and grew rhubarb and could spot a fake at a mile's distance. He knew if he could continue to try out his new songs while sitting in with local bands, then he had a chance of proving his mettle, of bringing his music to these people who normally would never give him the time of day.

The rest of the world may have been marching in the streets and making free love, but at Burrito Manor it might as well have been 1955. George Jones rose up from the stereo speakers in the front room, singing out heartache and hard country living. The grass

My Morning Jacket Interview
Interview by Jessica Hundley

Jim James is the lead vocalist and songwriter for Louisville, Kentucky's, My Morning Jacket. Part rock, part soul, part roots music, My Morning Jacket has won a devoted fan base that includes the likes of Bright Eyes and Neil Young.

Q: When did you first hear Gram and what was that experience like?

A: A lot of people have asked me that lately. I remember being with an early girlfriend, a first girlfriend, and she had a mixed tape and we went on a road trip out West. We had never been out West before, and Gram's version of "Do Right Woman" came on. I had never heard that song before, by Aretha or any-body's version. I just heard it and I couldn't believe what it was because it sounds so amazing and the vocal performance is so amazing. Then I went out and got all I could of Gram and the Burrito Brothers and stuff like that. It always represents to me, fun and travel, because when we first started touring, when we first got the band together, we'd drive out in our crappy van, we'd just keep on going and going and the Burrito Brothers was one of the things that we'd put on that everybody loved lis-tening to. We all had very different tastes, but we could agree on the Burrito Brothers every time.

Q: Do you have a favorite Gram song?

A: My favorites are the sad ones, "Dark End of the Street" and "Still Feeling Blue." I like "Still Feeling Blue" because it's really upbeat and peppy but the lyrics are so sad. "Hot Burrito #1" is probably one of my favorite songs of all time.

Q: Do you feel like some of that music has seeped into what you're doing yourself with My Morning Jacket?

A: People say it does, and I think it has. I always get weird with people saying influences and stuff because I think everything that is powerful couldn't *not* be an influence. People whose voices and whose spirits are so powerful, it's really impossible not to get influenced by them. The thing that I liked most about him is that he had to do everything. I think people label Gram Parsons as the "Father of Alt/Country," but I think that is kind of a stupid nametag. To me, I think that there is a ton of stuff going on in there, like R&B, country, all sorts of things. I always want to think of that when we make records because I always want to be different, to try different things.

Q: I think he's more of an inspiration to musicians in that he is an example of being influenced by whatever really moves you.

A: He was so lucky in his time, too, because nothing had been done before. Nowadays the world is so crammed and people are doing so much and there's just so much to break through to try and invent a new thing. It gets tougher and tougher. We have to try and keep crawling and keep channeling, to make new, exciting things. I think a lot of people are doing that but I think it's tough because all the masters are always shoved in our face all the time, but it's just like . . . yeah they're great but there are people making music today, too. I feel like as artists today all we can do is learn from the past, be inspired by it, but try not to replicate it.

grew tall in the tiny backyard, and Gram and Chris carved out their own rough-and-tumble reality.

They had both bought motorcycles, Gram's a speedy BSA, and the two played hard-ass, riding their bikes up into the canyons and down to the sea, the ocean waiting just across the westward mountains. They wrote a cocky, swaggering song about their love for the open road called "Wheels," its lyrics reflecting the confidence they were feeling, the invincibility.

> *We're not afraid to ride*
> *We're not afraid to die*
> *So come on, wheels, take me home today*
> *Come on, wheels, take this boy away*

They played incessantly, refining the sound they had started on *Sweetheart*, Etheridge adding his own warmth, everyone contributing his own take to the mix of boogie-woogie, gospel, soul, and the occasional kick of rock 'n' roll. Songs poured out of them, shit-kicking guitar jams, tearjerker ballads, lyrically brilliant numbers like "Hot Burrito #1" and "#2," and even a stray protest song like "My Uncle," which was spawned by the arrival of a letter for Gram with a governmental seal, a signal that the draft might be coming for him any day.

It was easy, sitting on the overgrown back porch, playing folk songs to shut out the chaos that was the late sixties. Girls, scattered around the house like wilted and forgotten flowers, provided a distraction as well. Meanwhile the LA scene was beginning to make its way out to Burrito Manor, led by Hillman's occasional paramour Pamela Des Barres, a fragile, thin-hipped beauty from a band called the GTOs, an all-girl novelty act masterminded by Frank Zappa.

The GTO ladies, pretty young women with sweet temperaments and quick wits, were all avowed groupies. Pamela had dated a long line of actors and musicians before she got to Hillman, and she knew enough about men to know that Burrito Manor needed a

John Doe Interview
Interview by Jessica Hundley

John Doe is former bassist/vocalist for legendary LA punk band X. He is now a successful solo artist, as well as talented character actor, appearing in such films as *Boogie Nights* and *Salvador*.

Q: Why don't we start with when you first heard Gram's music and where you were at in your own life at that time?

A: I guess I heard the Byrds' *Sweetheart of the Rodeo* first but didn't really think of it as anything more then just this band, the Byrds, which I liked. I think the first time I really became aware of him as an individual songwriter was through Miss Mercy of the GTO's. I was just about to start working on my first solo record and she said "Now you ought to do stuff like Gram Parsons," and I was like, "Who the hell is Gram Parsons?" Of course I didn't take her advice, I just did what I did, but that was the first time.

Q: When was this?

A: It was '88, '87, maybe something like that. I was already doing country stuff. We had done the Knitters record, which was X's country alter-ego. My first reaction to Gram's music was that it confused me because it wasn't country but it wasn't rock. It was almost like the Eagles but it didn't suck. I don't feel as though I am part of the cult of Gram Parsons, but after listening to these songs over and over, I fell in love. I don't think he walked on water and I don't think that he completely changed music, but he's really talented and took a lot of chances. I think he was the first person to take hippie culture and country culture and put them together. He had a lot of help, too, with the Byrds and the Flying Burrito Brothers and Crosby, Stills and Nash and all that sort of movement towards that, but he was certainly instrumental. My theory is that Gram Parsons was part of the first wave after an extreme catharsis in music, which I would say psychedelic music was. Anything prior to Jimi Hendrix and Love and the Doors and Janis Joplin is that era and with Gram, here's the new era. After that explosion dies down then there's a resurgence of country influence. And it's happening again. It happened with Uncle Tupelo after Nirvana and it happened right after the punk rock explosion. So, after this big upheaval, people seem to want to have something more comforting. He was part of that.

Q: Is that what you feel his music is—comforting?

A: Oh yeah. I mean, that doesn't mean that it isn't challenging.

Q: Well, I think there's something about his music being sort of pure and direct and uncomplicated by histrionics and production.

A: Well, there is a huge backlash right now to the pop juggernaut which has taken over all music. A lot of people are recording differently in reaction. They're doing the vocals live because it's about capturing the moment, not trying to piece together a moment and have it be fake.

Q: What are some of your favorite Gram songs?

A: "Hot Burrito #2" and "We'll Sweep Out the Ashes."

Q: Why?

A: Because I think if anything, Gram Parsons lyrically is tied to doing wrong and regretting it. He wrote about fire and heartbreak, knowing that you're doing the wrong thing but being sort of in a classic tragedy. Being unable to change it. I love "Hot Burrito #2" just for the music. I just love the sound of it, it sounds like a Big Star song, like a weird combination of rock/pop music. I don't really understand the lyrics. The only thing I can figure out is he's writing about this guy who is just a bad person. You know—"why did you love me even though I was sneaking in at night after getting all fucked up. It's your problem that I'm a fuck-up!" It's just so terrific to take that point of view, such unmitigated crap. It's like, "What? You're the guy that's sneaking in! You're the guy that's fucked up!" I relate to that. Not that I always do that, but I can definitely relate to that. A lot of the songs I write are about the difficulty of relationships. I relate to Gram in that way. He was always screwing up and always regretting it.

Pamela Des Barres. PHOTO BY TOM WILKES.

lady's touch. She and fellow GTO Miss Mercy would arrive with groceries and fix hot meals while the boys exhausted themselves over keyboards and guitars.

They would listen to the music as it evolved, providing feedback and encouragement. Pamela and Gram had known each other since his arrival in LA, and she was close friends with Nancy and was a godmother to Polly. Pamela provided the kind of mothering Gram needed at the Manor, a gentle femininity to offset the cool and cocky masculinity of the Burrito boys. The two had a solid platonic friendship, a rare find in the midst of a raging sexual revolution. Pamela watched over Gram, and over Nancy and Polly as well, often acting as mediator when relations became particularly strained.

Nancy was dividing her time between Santa Barbara and a room at Brandon De Wilde's Topanga ranch so she could be nearer to Gram. The gorgeous wooded canyon just north of Los Angles had become a favorite flower-power enclave, and hippies were buying up old ranchlands and playing farmer on acres of garden and orchard plots. From Reseda it was only a half an hour's drive to the ranch, and Gram was there often playing with Polly and visiting with Brandon and his wife Susan, whose home had become an impromptu commune. Nancy and Polly and quite a few other strays, including former Sub Band drummer Mickey Gauvin, all resided under the roof.

One heat-blasted Valley afternoon, Gram slipped into his Jaguar and drove out onto the freeway, seeking the cool shade and silence of Topanga. When he got to the De Wilde's, the sun was shooting bright clear bullets, blowing out the past week's storm clouds and welcoming in the fall. He pulled up and spotted Polly playing in the backyard. Nancy was sitting nearby, smiling and brushing her long dark hair. He stood in the driveway a moment and watched them, the wind moving through the pines. Polly laughed suddenly, and her high child's giggle shook open Gram's heart.

Suddenly, all the music and women and debauched Manor living seemed silly, seemed thin and false, and Gram felt himself split open wide, missing Nancy and his daughter with a desperation that shocked him with its potency. Before he knew it, he was walking quickly toward them. He had made it nearly to the end of the drive when a door to the house opened, and Mickey Gauvin walked out into the yard wearing his ever-present sunglasses. Mickey greeted Nancy by laying his hand on her shoulder, a gesture that may have been merely friendly, but to Gram seemed tender and intimate, even proprietary.

Gram's ribs squeezed tight, and a red, swelling anger took hold of him. He headed straight for Nancy and found himself on his

Burrito Brothers.
ALL PHOTOS BY JIM McCRARY.

knees, looking up at her face, at the porcelain doll's skin and the liquid eyes, his daughter clinging to the long lace folds of her dress.

"I'd like you to be my wife."

The words were out before he could stop them, hanging like bright lights in the air between the two. There was a soft pleading look in Nancy's eyes, a look that said she still loved him but that she didn't believe him, not for a minute. Gram proposed again, firmer, back straighter, and Nancy could do nothing but nod.

Too much had happened since Sweetzer for anything to be like it had been. Gram's life had moved too fast while Nancy's had been anchored by their only child. But Nancy still nodded, crying silently, nodded at the young boy who kneeled in front of her, mouth dry, eyes burning. Gram drove back down to Reseda in a kind of daze, too shocked to fully comprehend what he had done.

While Nancy waited for a wedding date, Gram dug himself in deeper with the Burritos, their music becoming infinitely more sophisticated and layered, Hillman gaining confidence, and Etheridge lending a pop framework and keeping the others from straying too far into obscurity. By fall they were ready to begin taking their demo to labels. Doors opened easily with Hillman on board, and a few offers were put on the table before the Burritos finally decided to sign with Jerry Moss and Herb Alpert's A&M.

A&M had been primarily a jazz label, but they were now ready to explore rock 'n' roll. They heard something in the Burrito sound that seemed innocuous enough, and Alpert, a successful musician himself, saw clearly that the boys had mastered their craft. The months of continuous playing and experimentation at the Manor had produced three tight musicians. Hillman was delving deep into traditional bluegrass, and Gram's fingers rarely left the keys, practice adding a relaxed ease to his already impressive piano playing. There was singing, too, Gram's voice hitting the right notes and clinging to them, cracking at the perfect moment.

By this time, the boundaries that had constricted commercial radio were being continually pushed, and rock was evolving at a steady pace. Creedence Clearwater Revival had recently produced two hit singles, "Proud Mary" and "Bad Moon Rising," hitting a nerve with a sound that spoke of river baptisms and southern meeting halls. The Stones had just released "Honky Tonk Women," their music getting grittier by the minute. Stephen Stills had written "Suite: Judy Blue Eyes" for Judy Collins, and Led Zeppelin had come roaring onto the scene with the epic stoner-rock anthem "Dazed and Confused." The Burritos sounded like nothing else on the charts, but it was just this sort of incongruity that A&M hoped would make them a perfect fit.

Installed in the label's new studios, Gram and his friends settled in to record, still writing new songs as they went along. As usual, sessions were fueled by whiskey on the rocks and fat, hand-rolled joints. Occasionally, a pile of cocaine would grace the shiny black top of the baby grand. Pamela and Miss Mercy would show up once in a while to sing backup or dance and cheer from the corner of the room.

Between Burrito songs there were a few country soul classics, too. "Do Right Woman" and "Dark End of the Street" were both born out of the famous Muscle Shoals Studios, a hotbed for the new country-inflected R&B. The folks at Muscle Shoals had already displayed some of the same love for mixing and matching that the Burritos were striving for. There, in Alabama, the color lines had been crossed, and white country songwriters had handed over hits to vocalists like Percy Sledge and Aretha Franklin. The result was some of the finest music of the decade, songs steeped in the spiritual. Gram loved the music coming out of Muscle Shoals and saw that the same match could be made between country and rock 'n' roll.

Looking to build a true country spine for their songs, Chris and Gram set about snagging a pedal steel player, someone who could add that sweet and lonely sound to the mix. Sneeky Pete Kleinow, a local musician and part-time animator was chosen for the job. Halfway through the session and still without a drummer, Gram called up Jon Corneal and convinced him to head back to LA.

With his old friends by his side in the studio, Gram felt loose and positive. It seemed he had found the appropriate partners, the kind of musicians who could manifest the music that floated in his head. He stayed at the piano, hovering over the keys, pausing now and then to guzzle a cold beer or snort a long line of cocaine. Sober moments were rare, and most of the album was made in a decadent glee or a slow syrupy haze.

Late one afternoon toward the end of the session, Gram stood up from the keyboard and grinned. "Come on boys," he said, eyes like glass, "We're going to spend some of Herb Alpert's money."

Within an hour the Burritos were at Nudie's Rodeo Tailors being outfitted for custom stage costumes. Hillman's was midnight blue, with a blood-orange flaming sun on the back, silk lapels, and a colorful embroidered peacock on the front. Chris Etheridge chose white with yellow and red roses, Sneeky Pete, the animator and pedal steel man, selected black graced with a soaring pterodactyl.

Gram's costume was the most intricate and consciously symbolic. There were emerald-green marijuana leaves curled across the front, a scattering of intricately embroidered prescription pills, vamping girls, and exquisitely detailed roses. On the back was a cross, huge and blood red, sequined and rhinestoned and sending off sparks. It was Gram's nod to his hope, his spirituality, and also to his own sacrifices, the wounds he had endured to be redeemed. Before leaving, Gram ordered Nudie to start on a wedding dress as well, and he sent word to Nancy to set the ceremony for January 31, 1969.

For the cover photo of the upcoming album, A&M art director Tom Wilkes decided on the Mojave as a backdrop. The Burritos were blinding in their sunlit suits, the landscape of the California desert rising dry and rugged all around, the perfect contrast between the barren and the luxurious. Wilkes was actually a neighbor and frequent guest at Burrito Manor, a good friend of Chris's, and someone who was instrumental in bringing the band to the label. He knew what the Burritos were up to and had a clear vision for their look. The moon-crater stretch of desert added an element of the space-age and the celestial, and the Burritos posed like cowboy astronauts, all rhinestones and color against the burnt-out browns.

That chilly fall of 1968, Wilkes, the band, and a few stunning women who were to serve as models and company all piled into several vans and headed out to Pear Blossom, an hour north of the city in a scorching corner of the Mojave. Gram looked out the back window as the van sped north. It wasn't long before the bacterial spread of LA suburb gave way to jagged rock peaks and boulder-lined valleys.

The palms gave way to water-starved pines, then Joshua trees, those alien-looking plants that grew in scattered groups along the highway, their trunks lined with angry spines and their branches thrust up to the sky. The early settlers had named them after the prophet Joshua, arms lifted to God. Gram had never seen anything like it, the spread of rock and cactus and the hunched spine of white-tipped mountains in the distance.

As they set up for the shoot, Gram, dressed in his white Nudie, the cross flashing in the afternoon glare, went ambling off into the scrub, drawn forward by some strange charge in the air. He walked for a few minutes until the photo crew looked small enough to fit into his palm, until the Burritos were only bright spots on the horizon, until the girls' long hair was fanning in the wind.

There was a noise out there, a low yet persistent hum that seemed to vibrate in Gram's belly. The space rolled out and around him, and he was suddenly aware of how he might look from high above, a white diamond speck in a sea of yellows. By the time the sun had sunk over the teeth of the mountaintops, Gram knew he needed to come out to the desert again. There was something there that calmed him, that made him feel wiped clean.

Gram spent the next few months staying as sober as he could, making business arrangements for the Burritos, and visiting Nancy and Polly. He was doing his best, trying to live straight, trying to follow the path that felt right, but there was something stopping him.

He craved that freedom he'd felt in the desert, and as the day of his wedding approached, his feet grew colder. He felt trapped suddenly, searching for breath. He knew he had stepped into something

Devendra Banhart Interview
Interview by Shirley Halperin

Devendra Banhart is a world traveler, gypsy philosopher, and
one of the finest in the new age of mystical folkies. Raised in
Texas and Venezuela, and educated in San Francisco, Banhart
mixes poetic lyrical musings, whimsy, and a voice like a broken
angel to create his own brand of psychedelic/folk/rock magic.

Q: What was your initial reaction to Gram's music?

A: People call it cosmic country, but for me I never saw the
cosmic side at first. I only saw the side that was absolute love
for country music, because for me it's pretty much straight-up
country music, it's not like it's psychedelic, except for the
sounds, like pedal steel, lap steel can make those really beautiful,
kind of astral, star blinking in the sky, kind of sounds. But the
lyrics are beautiful, pretty much standard, really poetic, and
beautiful, down-in-the-dirt love stories. Those are really beautiful and to me, really classic country songs. They had style, and
of course in the country scene it wasn't accepted to be talking
about smoking weed or anything like that, or being stoned.
He had his weed leaves sewn into his Nudie and he looked
good. He looked beautiful, so beautiful. I think in every picture,
he's such a badass heartthrob. He really had a beautiful, real
California vibe. I think everyone thinks of country as a mid-
America, but Gram had this whole California style. You imagine
him playing out in the redwoods.

Q: What were some of the first songs of his that you heard and
were drawn to?

A: The Burrito Brothers' version of "Dark End of the Street" is
so amazing. They're like the Band in some ways. All the hippies
are around and Gram is making this cosmic country music,
bringing in all this sunshine and the Band brings in the dirt, the
grit. My favorite Gram stuff is the gentler stuff, "Brass Buttons,"
or that song "Oh my land, is like a wild goose"—"Song For
You," "Hickory Wind." I heard Gram because there was a band

called Mover out in San Francisco and every year they would put on a show called "Sleepless Nights," a Gram Parsons tribute every year. It was before I was playing music and so I always knew Gram's name. But I mean, I got into Gene Clark before I got into Gram. Then one day I was like, "enough is enough, I'm going to go out and buy Grievous Angel," and I really flipped when I heard all the beautiful ballads. The standard country stuff, it all kind of washed over me. I really enjoyed it, but it was formulaic in the way a lot of country is, but the ballads seemed to really come from him. The other music, they're playing the music they love, but those gentle songs, he's singing his soul out. He's singing his songs, his experiences. Beautiful sunshine soul, white soul music and it really freaked me out and I felt some connection to it, I guess. But so much of his music is secondary to him, to his image and his vibe, that's right there next to the music. It's not that it outshines the music, but it's so essential to the music, his entire being is part of it. He and his music are part of one harmonious being, perfectly balanced.

Q: What touches you most about his music?

A: I dig his sunshine, gypsy punk, moving statue, golden man/woman vibe. I think when people think of Gram they think of the Mojave Desert and the redwoods and all that California feel, the canyons and the tumbleweed. Those are the places where Gram's spirit dwells.

he wasn't prepared for, something that frightened him more than anything, more than the stage, more than standing in front of a thousand faces all waiting for him to sing.

That December, on Polly's birthday, Gram drove up to Santa Barbara and took the girls out to dinner, smiling and soothing and doing his best not to reveal the crack that had begun to shoot through his committed veneer. He decided to go back to the city that night. Making up some excuse, he kissed Nancy goodbye and headed down the highway.

The road followed the ocean, moving south along the shore, the lights of distant oil rigs glowing like fairy islands. Gram pushed the pedal on the Jaguar. He opened the windows wide and smelled the salt, felt the pavement beneath the wheels, and knew he was not going to marry Nancy, not in January—not ever.

The wedding dress would sit, untouched and unpaid for, in Nudie Cohen's window, and Gram would pull himself in reverse, extricating himself from his relationship by gently avoiding it. It was a tactic he'd learned from his mother, to pull out, to ignore, to pretend a thing wasn't there if it was something you didn't want to see. He knew in his heart this was weak, and he was ashamed, but he did it nonetheless, burying his doubts in the business of making the Burritos famous.

Chris and Gram devised a method to spread word of the new band, managing to convince A&M to fund a multi-city train tour, a trip through the interior by old-time rail. It was a brilliant plan, the perfect way to avoid airplanes and airport security and hole up, instead, in a luxury train car fully stocked with drugs and guitars. It was also the perfect way for Gram to forget about what he'd done to Nancy.

At first the label was hesitant, but Gram was a fine salesman, wooing the moneymen with promises that the trip would be beneficial to all. One day, in early February 1969, the band finally boarded the Super Chief at Union Station in downtown LA, Gram clutching a guitar case full of whiskey bottles and an enormous steamer trunk of Nudie suits. Brandon and Pamela were there to wave goodbye. The Burritos settled in to the train car, everyone half in the bag already, the journey not even started.

By this time Jon Corneal had opted out of the tour and had been replaced by another drummer, one-time Byrds alum, Michael Clarke. The rest of the Burritos crew consisted of Michael Vosse, a young A&M assistant enlisted as symbolic chaperone, and Phil Kaufman who was there to manage the tour. Phil, who had been Gram's hire, was fresh from his tenure overseeing the Rolling Stones. He had become more than capable at hiding illicit substances, manhandling hotel clerks, and sweet-talking the authorities.

By the time the train finally lurched out of the station, the Burritos and their friends were soaring like kites and deep into a game of high-stakes poker. The game continued—with brief respites for the popping of pills, the refilling of whiskey glasses, and the snorting of cocaine—across the entire country.

The Burritos stopped occasionally to play a haphazard show or make a quick radio appearance, always certain to book the best rooms at the finest hotels, running up a hefty tab on A&M's dime. The playing became secondary to the experience, the great forward thrust of the train on the tracks, the giddy, bright white high of cocaine and uppers, the cards in your hand, and a girl, never the same one, by your side. The women flashed in an out of the scene, a parade of willowy hippie chicks with ironed hair and children's faces, girls backstage, girls sprawled over hotel-room beds, girls gazing wistfully out train windows.

In Chicago, the band wreaked havoc at the Biltmore. In Detroit they wandered through crumbled-down alleyways, searching out authentic blues and jazz dives, wandering in with their Nudie flash and their white skin and ingratiating themselves, Gram's ego swollen enough with cocaine to allow him to sit in with nimble-fingered old timers. In Boston the crew visited Gram's old friend Jet and played with some success at a local club.

A blinding New England blizzard handicapped the next leg of the journey, an important New York date booked for label bigwigs, celebs, and selected press. With most of the band snowbound in Massachusetts, the show was a fiasco, and the A&M higher-ups were shocked when the Burritos checked themselves into the Gramercy Park Hotel and took up a brief residency, entertaining friends and friends of friends and living the high life, treating themselves like royalty or sheiks.

In Philadelphia the party continued, the band gobbling up a bag of magic mushrooms and floating on stage wearing silk turbans and an air of mystical remove. By the time the Burritos sailed back into port, they had spent a massive amount of A&M's money, had destroyed an immense amount of brain cells, and had left a trail of broken hearts and infuriated hotel managers in their wake.

And the album had not even been released yet.

Back in LA, Hillman settled into Burrito Manor II, taking up residency in the wooded seclusion of Beverly Glen, a high-end retreat in the hills of Bel Air. The party continued in high gear, the second Manor the scene of continuing debauchery and the occasional moment of brilliant music-making.

Gram spent much of his time holed up in the guest room with his notebooks, scribbling down scattered thoughts and scraps of lyrics, waking up dazed and aching, a strange girl sleeping at his side, and the sun coming through the windows like a blade.

After the weeks on the train and in the hothouse atmosphere of the Manor, Gram decided to waste some of his trust-fund cash on a room at the Chateau Marmont. The hotel was a looming French Normandy palace that hovered over the eastern tip of Sunset Boulevard. The Chateau had been a Hollywood stalwart since the silent-screen days, and it was full of myth and wandering ghosts, tattered carpets, and thick stucco walls that drowned out the sound of the street below.

There was a scattering of bungalows crouched around a small pool, a palm-shaded courtyard, a bar that served killer margaritas, and a dusty, haunted lobby with a grand piano. The corner suites were mini-apartments with polished floors and a legacy of celebrity secrecy. The Chateau was part hideout and part clubhouse, with an

Michael Vosse Interview
Interview by Jessica Hundley

**Michael Vosse was a young assistant at A&M Records when he
first met Gram. He was assigned by the label to accompany
the Flying Burrito Brothers on their infamous cross-country
train tour.**

Q: When did you first meet Gram?

A: I met him through Chris Etheridge and I know it was a social
gathering, hanging out. I think it was at a bar out in Topanga. It
was like a little bar, coffee shop, dive. I worked for the then-
president of A&M as his assistant and I had no idea what my job
was supposed to be. I liked Gram, but he could be a real pain in
the ass. It depends on what was going on, you know? If he wasn't
too drunk or stoned you could have really great conversations
about music with him because he was really in love with country
music. Most people I knew could tell you a lot about folk ori-
gins, many rock and roll bands had come out of folk at that
point in the sixties and Beatles influence and all that, but
country . . . So Gram was quite personable and gregarious
talking about music and, yes, he would try to convert you and
show you things and play you records. When he was really
fucked up he was impossible and I got tired of that part because
I got exposed more and more of that part outside of work. But
he could be very charming, too.

Q: Can you tell me about the Burritos tour?

A: That tour was insane. And they had me in charge, a total
rookie, who didn't know what we were supposed to accomplish.
They were crazy, running up huge tabs. They stayed at all these
great hotels on tour. In Chicago, the hotel had some fabulous
restaurant attached to it. That was a big deal for them because
the restaurant had room service. As soon as they got there they
found out the place had lemon soufflé and when I came back
from dinner they had ordered all the lemon soufflés they could
get. They had them everywhere. In the refrigerator . . . they had

them on the countertops because they were so afraid that they wouldn't get enough. Then the other thing in Chicago was Gram wanted to go to the Playboy Mansion. I think they probably all did but he made the most noise about it. So the Chicago label people set up for us to go to the Playboy Mansion and it was a total disaster. We got there and were greeted with as little enthusiasm as possible. Oh man, somebody came to the door and it was like the housemother or whatever, she was just withering. Everybody in the band was probably kinda fucked up and she was not pleased. So all of a sudden we were in this entrée area with no place to go and nobody would help us. They just kind of left us there. And this one girl said, "Oh I suppose you want to see the grotto." So they took us down and there's no one around. So we were kind of left to our own devices and we'd been there for about twenty minutes and nothing had happened and really the whole thing was, well, let's just say the hard-on was over right away. So Gram strolled over to the grand piano in the living room. He sat down and very quietly began to play something pretty and all of a sudden these two girls popped out and were all like, "Hi, who are you?" But then, down the stairs comes this woman again and she says in an irritated voice that this noise would have to stop. And that was it. It was pretty deflating.

Q: From Chicago the band took the train to Boston?

A: Yes. I know most of the gigs on the tour were not very good. And I know that Boston was the most fun because we went to see Gram's friend Jet. He was still living on Harvard Square. He was so nice that things calmed down, going to his place. We went there and it was all snowing and it was all nice and warm. What a sweet person. In Boston, Gram was pretty happy, I think, because we were back where Harvard was and this time he wasn't the guy who didn't do too well, even though he had been back there with the Submarine Band, I'm sure, but he kinda had a confident walk. He was fun there and he wasn't so fucked up. Gram and Etheridge would go anywhere for music. When we were in Detroit, the three of us went to some completely black club in the roughest part of town, after hours, and they played good music there. I think those two did more when they were out and about in strange towns because they had to look and find out what was going on. They were all happy on that tour. Most of the shows were great and there were a lot of kids there who liked the music. The band was always happy to meet anyone who liked them. You could tell that just thrilled Gram and not in an egotistical way. He was just happy people were connecting with what the band was trying to do. That whole experience, as nuts as it was, made him believe, I think, really believe, in what he was doing.

Andee and Gram. PHOTO COURTESY OF ANDEE COHEN NATHANSON.

"anything goes" management policy and an intensely private feel. It was populated by beautiful actresses, haggard rock stars, pale-faced screenwriters, and various Hollywood hoi polloi.

Gram shared a room with Tony Foutz, a young actor, writer, and filmmaker. Foutz was in the midst of directing his debut, an LSD-tinged sci-fi epic that he was shooting in fits and starts in the Joshua Tree desert, about ninety miles west of the Marmont. The movie was a classic psychedelic mishmash, with outer-space aliens, futuristic sex sequences, and a total lack of traditional cinematic narrative. Joshua Tree was the perfect spot for the endeavor, a scantily populated stretch of glacier-hewn boulders and empty sky, just a two-hour drive from Los Angeles but a million miles away in spirit.

Foutz enlisted Gram, along with Gram's friend Michelle Phillips of the Mamas and the Papas, and photographer/artist Andee Cohen also enlisted any able-bodied hippie who happened to wander into the Chateau. Weekends were spent burning up rolls

Andee Cohen Nathanson Interview
Interview by Jessica Hundley

A writer, photographer, and world traveler, Andee Cohen Nathanson starred with Gram in *Saturation 70*, Tony Foutz's environmental desert movie. She shared in numerous Joshua Tree adventures and recorded, for posterity, some of the most intimate and revealing portraits of her friend.

Q: When did you first meet Gram?

A: You know how your friends are really your family? He was my cousin from the South. We would listen to George Jones, Merle Haggard—all the great ones. Somehow all of us, film people and music people, knew each other. Gram fit right in, in both worlds. He was just so real, so down to earth, that he was able to feel comfortable almost anywhere. We'd just sit there all night listening to music. My place was like a salon in a way, with lots of artists converging there. We were reacting to the old paradigm, shifting into the new. Worlds were being destroyed and reborn on a daily basis—and music seemed to give us a means of processing all of it. I felt that in my work as well, with photography—and now, looking back, I can see so many things in one image, captured in time. The same with the music—it just brings you immediately "there."

Q: Was it difficult when he died?

A: The heavy drugs—time has proven they win and one rarely does. There was no reaching him, it was like watching someone in quicksand—you can throw them a rope—but if the guy is stuck you're going to lose that battle. Once someone's a part of your life you never really lose them. Someone said we're all one big compost heap, all recycled atoms, and so we carry each other—in subtle and sometimes not-so-subtle ways. "I am also a You." So great to know his magic is still coming across and being shared with others. May it always be so.

"Here Today," a letter to Gram from Miss Andee:

We, the curious, recognizing greatness, on the path to enlightenment, mending our broken hearts, were forged out of the pain of the civil rights movement, the Vietnam War (and ending it at any cost), Martin Luther King Jr.'s and Bobby Kennedy's assassinations, the Chicago convention (our dear friend Michael Cooper bringing back firsthand accounts and pictures).

I had been gone for years, living in England and Rome, so all this was new to me too—what's happened to our country, to our world? We were being tumbled in the giant shaker of time—we were so young, what did we know?

Finding our center without one cell phone, iPod, fax machine, or even voicemail, we gathered round the turntables and "hung out." None of us believed these to be random events—there was something much greater going on. We pored over the books of Stonehenge and the Great Pyramid—they left messages for us here, but what does it all mean?

Can you love country music and be metaphysical? Can you be part Elvis, part George Jones—a guy who plays after-hours clubs in the City of Industry and is looking for the light? You were . . . ! How can somebody be so beautiful and so sad—how can somebody hold all that inside of him? Even when you were smiling, it was there in your ancient hands.

You used to pick up crazy recordings from the swap meet and we'd listen to real people in the booths singing their songs and we'd laugh 'til morning—then there was Stax Records. I drove all the way to Memphis to hang out with Steve Cropper, then onto Waycross—that was a trip. You influenced me as an artist, encouraged me to photograph the people of this land. . . .

Then there was Delany and Bonnie and the Main Street band—and we rocked like never before—that little club where they played in the valley—the roof blew off of that place. We went insane on more than one occasion—J. J. Cale playing such hot guitar with his back to the folks at the tables, Leon Russell melting the keys on the piano. I seem to remember you jumping up on that stage as well. You brought everybody down to that club, brought them all together. You weren't threatened as an artist—good was good.

Denny Cordell arrived with Joe Cocker and suddenly we were all thrown together one wild weekend at the Joshua Tree Inn.

There was a little trailer out back underneath the vault of stars. At one point during the night, I saw it rocking wildly back and forth. When I opened the door, everybody was singing and swaying 'til they almost turned that thing over.

One big beautiful jam session resulting in an amazing tour—"Mad Dogs & Englishmen, Limeys & Okies (and you)"—but you jumped off the bus the first day, right when it was pulling out of the A&M parking lot. The lone wolf had to go.

When I look back at my photos of you, I find my clothes, at least my favorite shirts from "Hung on You," antique goodies, too, from London—it wasn't easy getting them back.

I hear you drifted around and I believe it, too. I guess we stayed so close because we were all part of the same extended family, living at the Chateau and my place on Alfred Street—life was a village then.

I remember one night in the studio—there were a bunch of us: you, Bonnie, Delany, Carl Radle, Leon, and other amazing people—all singing "Will the Circle Be Unbroken." It struck me to the soul.

All the pain of the world was going to transform through this pillar of light—this holy spirit of gospel, country, and soul—everything was going to be alright—it always was alright and always would be if we had each other, believed in the power of "The Lord" (whatever that meant to you).

They say, on the other side, that you discover there are only two truths: Love and Light. I know you got that, baby—and you're looking on, watching us trying to figure it all out.

Gram and Andee, 1970. PHOTO COURTESY OF ANDEE COHEN NATHANSON.

On the set of *Saturation 70*.
ALL PHOTO COURTESY OF TOM WILKES.

of Super 16 stock, ingesting hallucinogens, and staring into black desert night.

The Burrito's debut, *The Gilded Palace of Sin* was finally ready for the public in April of 1969. The Burritos stood on the cover, legs wide and faces grim. Inside the sleeve were eleven songs that embodied, completely, Gram's ideas of what music should be. They were all solid, unforgettable numbers, with highlights including the melancholy "Juanita" and "Sin City," the latter of which Chris and Gram had penned one haggard early morning, nursing hangovers and various feelings of guilt.

"This old town is filled with sin," they warned on "Sin City." "It'll swallow you in . . ."

The reaction to the record was generally positive, particularly from the music critics, who saw the band's point and did their best to translate the message for the public. Things were looking good, both professionally and personally. Within a few months of high living at the Chateau, Gram had invited a new girlfriend to move in, another beautiful young girl who he had met through mutual friends. Linda Lawrence was twenty-two years old, stunning, and British, she had been a former lover to the Rolling Stones' Brian Jones and had been employed as a nanny for Mary Travers of Peter, Paul & Mary.

When she first began to fall in love with Gram, she had already lived in London and New York, had wandered the world with Julian, her young son by Jones, reliant upon the goodwill of friends who (luckily for her) happened to be in high places. She moved into a private bungalow with Gram soon after they met, Gram suddenly serving as father and husband.

That summer was long and dry and dreamlike. Gram spent his weekends in the sun-seared landscape of Joshua Tree and his weekdays drinking by the pool or making love in the sweltering bungalow. Everything seemed strange, clouded, and wonderful to Gram, a fantasy fulfilled.

Meanwhile, the Burritos did another quick tour and, on a whim, recorded an ill-fated single, "Train Song," a traditional travel song

Jay Farrar Interview
Interview by Jessica Hundley

Jay Farrar fronted the legendary alt-country act Uncle Tupelo, a band he cofounded with Wilco's Jeff Tweedy. Since Tupelo's split, Farrar has gone on to a successful solo career that has included work with Gillian Welch and the Flaming Lips, and he founded the band Son Volt.

Q: When were you first introduced to Gram's music?

A: I first heard Gram when I was twenty-one years old and I think at that point I was coming to terms with a lot of the music my parents listened to, folk and country music. Hearing Gram Parsons do his work with the Flying Burrito Brothers and the Byrds kind of brought a rock sensibility to country music and kind of elevated it. The rebellious spirit I think is what you kind of notice as soon as you pick up *The Gilded Palace of Sin*, which is the one I got to know. The pot leaf on the Nudie suit, like "Whoa, what's going on here!" When I heard the music it just spoke to me.

Q: In what way?

A: I guess there was an air of familiarity to it. I had heard the Everly Brothers before so there was that element to it. The pedal steel of Sneeky Pete was kind of a highlight for me because it was kind of out there, you know? The effects on it, I hadn't heard it in a country context before.

Q: What are your favorite songs?

A: "Christine's Tune" and "Drug Store Truck Drivin' Man" are two of my favorites. Those are two songs I have done in one form or another over the years. I actually played "Drug Store Truck Drivin' Man" with a different incarnation of Uncle Tupelo. I also sang when the Jayhawks played that song. "Christine's Tune" was always a song I wanted to do. I messed around with it before but never had the chance to do it.

Q: How long have you been making your own music?

A: I think at the point when I first heard Gram I maybe had been making music about a year, just getting started writing songs when I was twenty-one. I had maybe written a couple songs earlier than that but I wasn't really confident yet. So yeah, it was right about at the same time I started feeling comfortable writing songs.

Q: Do you feel like that influenced what you were doing?

A: I didn't start wearing Nudie Suits, but I did really appreciate a lot of the lyrics on the Burrito Brothers and Byrds stuff. I felt it was topical singing protest songs about Vietnam and singing about earthquakes and songs about how California's going to wash away and things like that. Putting that in a country music song, I thought was really cool. Gram was a catalyst for a lot of amazing music that came after him.

they had written in the midst of a cocaine blitz. It lost its appeal, however, in tattered, half-assed production. The single was the first sign that the band's cohesiveness was beginning to fray, with Hillman holed up at the Manor and Gram wandering the desert with glassy eyes.

There were fewer give-and-take sessions together, and live shows were ragged and too loose, audiences becoming scant, impatient with the Burritos' lack of professionalism. By the end of the summer, things seemed to have gone slightly haywire, a dark, swelling paranoia taking over. Vietnam was a bloodbath, and in the black heat of August, LA found itself ripped open by the brutality of the Manson murders.

There had already been trouble brewing—acid-burnt teenagers, homeless hippies on the Strip, the darker side of the counterculture exploration rearing its ugly, drug-addled head. To the north, in the deceptive safety of the hills, the Manson cult, with its longhaired girls with heart-shaped faces; cocky, barrel-chested cowboy types; and Charlie himself, had integrated themselves into the homes of the Hollywood elite. To grow its membership, the cult relied on the open-mindedness of the times and handouts and favors from people like Dennis Wilson and record producer Terry Melcher.

Manson had dreams of rock 'n' roll stardom and a wild look in his eye. In LA he was one of many, but his entourage of free-loving women and his supply of good dope had been enough to open several high-profile doors. Gram's friend Phil Kaufman had had a more intimate experience with Manson, having met him in jail while Phil was serving time for marijuana possession.

There was only one degree of separation between Gram and the kids at Spahn Ranch. They had partied under the same roofs, had smoked the same grass and eyed the same women. The grotesque, brutal murders terrified and saddened Gram in a way that he found hard to verbalize. He had been battling his own demons, drowning the persistent ghosts of his past in any drug he could get his hands on—cocaine, tequila shots, and an occasional hit of smack. Heroin was becoming more alluring by the minute. Dulled, deadened, his

Ben Lee Interview
Interview by Jessica Hundley

As founder of Australian indie-rock band Noise Addict, Ben Lee was a teen sensation in the early 1990s. He has since gone on to weave intelligent, witty lyrics with acoustic guitar poignancy in a successful, always-evolving, solo career.

Q: Well, why don't you tell us about the first time you heard Gram's music, and where you were in your own life at that time.

A: I got to know his music through Evan Dando of the Lemonheads, who was just a complete champion of Gram Parsons's music. I think he turned on a lot of people. We were hanging out a lot when I was a teenager. Particularly it was that song "$1000 Wedding." There was something about that song that was like it had no era attached to it. I couldn't understand, the song was completely perplexing, as a student of pop "craftsmanship" I was so befuddled by it. It took a narrative position, it was completely original, it was empathetic, it could get everybody involved. And so much folk and country music was stuff that was storytelling. It's like linear. It's so trapped in its own, I don't know whether its geographic or emotional state. And I think that's where a lot of the prejudices of country music come from. It does seem often imprisoned by its own perspective. And there was something about that song, it just had complete compassion for everybody involved in the story. Let alone the fact that you couldn't tell exactly what the story was. It was sort of an abstract tale being told. The song just really deeply affected me. From there I went on to explore his records. As a fourteen-, fifteen-year-old, country music was not something my peers were into. That was definitely something that was all my own. It was really weird. People try and be experimental and quirky in their music. For me, when someone just speaks with complete humanity, it's completely original every time. That's what it was for me about that song. It was so human. He's singing about himself in third person. Again, hearing that now it's like, what an ability to step outside of his own limitations. So often people get caught up in their own perspectives. The ability to look at yourself with that much objectivity. It's incredible.

Q: Do you have any other favorites? Are there certain songs that move you particularly?

A: It's not particular songs, it's more like moments. There's one that really captured my imagination. I remember doing a drawing and using some of his lyrics as a text. It was that "Twenty thousand roads up and down . . ." Yeah, that's a stunning song. That was the record I got into because of "$1000 Wedding." I was talking to my guitar player about this yesterday and we started talking about the "Mythology of Cool" and what it means when people get mythologized especially when they die tragically. And we started talking about Gram in the same terms as people talk about James Dean. It's so easy to look at Gram as this personification of cool. But in the same ways with James Dean, if you go back to those films and watch them, they're so vulnerable. They're not cool at all. But playing it cool was about emotional detachment. And there's nothing cool about James Dean. There's nothing cool about Gram Parsons. These are people that were raw. Really exposed. And that to me is like when you see all these artists that when they come out they appropriate just the aesthetics, they don't take the emotional content. Then they're just dealing with a culture of cool. They're not dealing with what's making that work, like "Oh I'm culturally valuable." These things get so bastardized. Like looking at James Dean and just seeing a leather jacket. That's not what made these artists valuable.

Q: I think that Gram has this cosmic cowboy thing and interesting masculinity, too. For him to be vulnerable like he was really takes a certain amount of . . . balls, you know?

A: And it requires so much femininity. It is the strongest male thing someone can do—to reveal that tenderness in them. It's so rare in an artist. There are a lot of artists that connect with that side of themselves. You hear those Curtis Mayfields who just open up and shine in that way. It's special.

Q: What was it that first compelled you to make music?

A: I think compel is a good word and the thing about compulsion is it's completely mysterious. There's no rhyme or reason to it. And I think that's why when you talk to people who do something creative with their life they often use words like destiny and fate and calling because it was in me. I've got it in me. It was in my family. My great uncle was the court violinist for Czar Nicholas in Russia. Maybe it's biological or something. But it was this inherent sort of naïve belief I had so young that the power of song actually meant something. It wasn't entertainment. It could be, but that wasn't what it was about. It was this totally transformative act. And it was just something I believed in. That's the whole thing about discovering songwriters like Gram Parsons or Dylan or whoever if you go through your compulsory studies as a songwriter, you realize that to really get to that level takes a huge amount of faith. It's all about the invisible world, it's all about vibration. It's not about doing a picture that you can look at. It's about energy and it requires a huge leap into the unknown every time you want to make music. For me, it was being pulled into the most seductive thing in the world.

Q: I'm guessing that you still believe in the way that you did that?

A: I believe more than ever that when an artist distills down their faith into a piece of work it has a vibratory power that stays in that piece of work, that that power remains and that nothing can happen to it. That's why Gram's work still has that resonance, that power to it.

creativity paralyzed, Gram found himself forcing ideas to the surface, struggling to find music beneath the deep blanket of sedation in which he had wrapped himself.

Meetings with Hillman were sporadic and inevitably frustrating. Etheridge, tired of the lack of direction and sobriety, dropped out of the band, leaving Gram and Chris to push forward with the second Burritos album by themselves. Gram did his best to focus, writing "$1000 Wedding." A wistful commiseration with Nancy, the song was about a girl abandoned at the altar, and Gram sang it with real heartache in his voice.

> but where are the flowers for my baby
> I'd even like to see her mean old mama
> and why ain't there a funeral, if you're gonna act that way
> I hate to tell you how he acted when the news arrived
> he took some friends out drinking and it's lucky they survived
> well, he told them everything there was to tell there along the way
> and he felt so bad when he saw the traces
> of old lies still on their faces

A&M helped the pair put together a team of backing musicians for their second album, a group that included Michael Clarke on drums and Bernie Leadon joining in on guitar and vocals. Gram tried to stay clearheaded enough to get the job done, but his efforts were foiled by the arrival of Keith Richards and the Rolling Stones, who had come to LA to begin sessions for *Let It Bleed*.

With Keith in town again, Gram felt himself falter. He missed practices, forgot about them entirely, and spent all his spare time with the Stones, picking up where he and Keith had left off months before. The days became a blur of parties and late, lazy afternoons spent listening to his country music singles, sitting cross-legged in the Chateau bungalow, drapes closing out the searing daylight. He lived in a constant blue dusk, the evenings bright with possibilities, the Stones the talk of the town, Gram along for the wild ride.

Gram amd Bernie Leadon. COURTESY OF PAUL SURRATT.

He led them his own way as well. One cool afternoon he drove Marianne Faithful, Anita, and Keith to his new hideout, the Joshua Tree Inn, a tiny motel just outside of Joshua Tree National Park. Armed with a pocketful of pills and a few hits of acid, the foursome hiked out to Cap Rock, a natural stone formation at the center of the park. The sky was full of flashes, meteors, spaceships, and the moon was swollen. By dawn they were back at the hotel, frazzled and wild-eyed, the chill waters of the courtyard pool washing away the desert dust.

Back in LA, Gram gave himself halfheartedly over to recording, already bored with what he had started and too lost in his outside recreations to truly care. Chris tried his best to hold up his end of the deal, however, and there were days when the pair laid down some brilliant, heartfelt material. When Gram's twenty-third birthday rolled around, the Burritos were well into recording their second album, *Burrito Deluxe*.

Brian Reitzell Interview
Interview by Mark Olsen

As the drummer for LA's seminal Redd Kross, and later for acts such as Beck and Air, Brian Reitzell has recently emerged as one of the most innovative and imaginative music supervisors of the new Hollywood. In charge of the soundtracks to films such as *Friday Night Lights*, Reitzell has also worked intimately with director Sofia Coppola since her *Virgin Suicides* debut. He continues to be responsible for writing and overseeing the scores to her subsequent films, including her Academy Award–winning feature *Lost in Translation*.

Q: Can you tell me a little about when were your first introduced to Gram's music?

A: When I was a kid, between probably eight and ten years old, I lived on a commune in Redwood City, California. And every weekend, we would go to a biker place out in the woods, it was all picnic tables and peanuts and motorcycles. That was the first time I ever heard Gram Parsons. It was very much a part of the place where I lived.

Q: That seems like the perfect setting. If you were to score that setting, you could easily have used Gram Parsons's records to do it.

A: I know. I mean, the most popular record in our house was *Goat's Head Soup* by the Rolling Stones. We lived in this huge house in Redwood City, not far from Neil Young's place. There was a guy who lived in the garage and all he did was fix motorcycles for the Hells Angels. And so music was everywhere, that sort of subversive sound of the Rolling Stones and Gram Parsons.

Q: Did it strike you as good music at the time, when you were a kid? Or did you hear it later in life and like it then?

A: My mother always played good music my whole life. I remember "Hearts on Fire," and I remember there was something about his voice that was kind of sweet. I think kids can recognize that. It's friendly music, on the surface, at least. You have to grow up a bit to realize how dark some of the stuff is, but as a kid, I remember those melodies and I remember the slide guitar because I had never heard slide guitar before.

Q: Are there certain songs you have a specific connection to?

A: Oh yeah. "$1000 Wedding." It's such a great song, such a great story. I remember the first time I ever heard that song. I was on a road trip and I only had a few cassettes and that was on a mix that a friend of mine from New York had made. I had one of those tape players where you could press rewind and it would go to the beginning of the song. And I would play that song three or four times in a row. It is such a tragic song. He was a very good storyteller and you can listen to that song and see the whole film in your head. I also love "Brass Buttons," for the same reasons. For me, the thing about those songs was that the stories were so good that it painted this picture in your head. And the way he would sing with Emmylou Harris, the way their voices would work together, was so crazy. The way they harmonized together. Amazing.

Q: Gram keeps coming back around in a way. What do you think keeps him relevant?

A: I think in part because the things he sings about are things that will never go away. I think in part it's the production of his albums, too. They sound so good, especially in a day and age where we make records that sound like they were made on hard disc, which they were. But you put on Gram's records and there is soul, there's playing, they sound great. You put on those records and you're in the room with those guys, you're having a beer with them. And the themes he explored, the stories, the heartache, that's just universal stuff.

The Stones had arranged for a party in Gram's honor that was to be held at Stephen Stills's house, a birthday celebration that quickly became the hottest invite in town. Gram was flattered, thrilled, floating high on a mix of uppers and tequila and his quickly evolving brotherhood with Keith Richards, the two of them having holed up the week before in the desert, writing songs on guitars and passing out next to each other on the motel's polyester bedspread.

It was after midnight when Gram arrived at Stills's house. The party was in high gear, and the crowd of faces flickering in the candlelight sang "Happy Birthday," loud and off-key. In the midst of the celebration, Gram noticed a fragile, pale young girl in the doorway, the lamplight from the kitchen framing her slender figure, making her look as if she were glowing from the inside, filled with a delicate yellow light.

He smiled at her hungrily, and she lowered her head, shook it slightly, then threw her chin up and faced him. The last chorus of "Happy Birthday" rang through the room, and Gram took a breath, made a wish, blew out his candles, and headed straight for the girl in the doorway.

Gretchen Burrell was only sixteen years old, bird-boned, with white blonde hair, a tiny upturned nose, wide eyes, and high cheekbones. A few weeks after Gram's birthday, Linda Lawrence left the Chateau bungalow in tears, and Gretchen moved in, bringing a few suitcases and some pots and pans from her parents' kitchen. She had been raised in the wealthy suburb of Newport Beach. Her father was Larry Burrell, a popular TV news anchorman. Gram somehow charmed her folks into letting her live with him, and the two settled into something like domestic bliss, save for the fact that Burrell was barely legal, and Gram was continuously stoned.

But the pair looked good together, Gretchen whip thin, Gram slightly bloated from all the self-abuse but still the feathery-haired cowboy angel, long-legged with a cockeyed grin that had helped extricate him from more than a few tense moments. Gram knew he was hard to resist, and he relied on his charm to smooth the worn nerves of the Burritos crew and to keep himself firmly entrenched with the Rolling Stones.

When Gram did show up for the final days of the Burritos recording sessions, fine music was still emerging from his partnership with Chris. The Stones gave the group permission to record "Wild Horses," which they had written not long before while staying in Muscle Shoals. Gram sang his heart out on the Burritos' version, doing his best to play the song with real tenderness. There were a few standards on the album as well, but the highlights remained Chris and Gram's original compositions "Older Guys" and "High Fashion Queen," no matter how sloppily or drunkenly Gram sometimes executed them during recording sessions.

Things chugged along in a numb, vaguely pleasant way, with Gram recording in the dark and smoky studio and nursing hangovers in front of the Chateau pool. Gram was doing his damnedest to ignore his growing dependence on drugs and alcohol and his abandonment of Nancy and Polly, whose lives he was fading out of already. During those times he did see them, he was just a specter bearing infusions of cash and strained emotion. Gram watched as his daughter grew, saw his face in hers, and was hit with the truth of his own selfishness. Instead of reaching out, however, he retreated, into drugs, into music, into his relationship with Gretchen.

Not long after Burrell had been installed in the bungalow, Gram got wind that the Rolling Stones were organizing a free-for-all blowout at a northern California racetrack, a show that would serve as a fitting finale to the 1960s, an all-star jam with no admission charge, rock 'n' roll as it was meant to be, for the fans. Gram called up Keith and begged to be part of the event. Wheeling and dealing, he secured the Burritos an opening slot in the show.

On December 12, 1969, he found himself caught tight in the swell of an enormous traffic jam, an eternity of VW Buses and tricked-out hotrods, all headed toward the Altamont Speedway, drivers and passengers all looking forward to a day of debauchery,

The Beachwood Sparks
Interview by Jessica Hundley

Comprised of veterans of such revered indie-rock bands as the Lilys, Further, and the Tyde, the Beachwood Sparks are new generation California cosmic-rock at its very finest. Farmer Dave is cofounder and singer/songwriter, Aaron Sperske keeps the beat.

Q: What was it in Gram's music that influenced your own music?

Aaron Sperske: Much like the Band, Gram's music touched a deeper part of my connection to music in the twentieth-century form. "There's the blues and the rest is zippee-de-do-dah," I believe is his quote, and it's really true when you get down to it, "we all know oblah dee oblah dah but can you tell me how you feel" is another way of puttin' it (thanks, George). Gram's sense of style was immense as well. Who else could take country (a hawkish redneck thing) and turn it into a vibe the kids of the day could feel and boogie to? Let alone, with a few others, create what would be the status quo in pop till the late '70s? You always have the seminal vanguard, and the cash cow that follows far behind (à la the Eagles) in any musical movement going back as far as I can tell.

Q: What are your favorite songs of Gram's?

AS: His two songs that really kill me are "Hot Burrito #1" and "#2." That's the essence of Gram to me. What makes Gram relevant now is the same as then, real soulful stuff that cuts to the bone, same as Dylan or whoever moves you to tears and joy.

Q: When did you first hear his music?

AS: My first exposure to Gram was in the Stones' *Gimme Shelter*. It's the only part of the film where Frisbees are flyin', bubbles are blowin', and sisters are smilin'. The rest is dismal. If he could stand in front of that crowd and cause that to go down he was touched by an angel. And their take on "Six Days" was the inspiration for the first Beachwood Sparks song I wrote. I've been changed by a group of writers, to really feel and listen, and Gram is among them—Dylan, the Band, and Gram.

Q: What first drew you to Gram's music?

Farmer Dave: My family has been around in California for six generations, so I always grew up with this sense of a "Mythical West" which may have existed, and may continue to exist. You have the coastlines and natural wonders of mountain, sea, and desert mixed with the larger-than-life human-made excitement; the Gold Rush, Spanish, Mexican, and Native American past, Hollywood, Disney, surfing, skateboarding, and car culture . . . and then, there's the sound. All that southern California pop music of the '60s: the Beach Boys and Phil Spector, the Byrds, Buffalo Springfield, Love, the Seeds, Neil Young, and all the canyon music and country-rock of the '70s. All my life, these elements seemed to still be hovering around in the ether here. My dad and his buddies had lived through an era of southern California that seemed pretty amazing, and pretty much bygone . . . but not totally. We don't have miles of orange groves or pristine coast anymore, yet a certain spirit prevails. In college in the mid-1990s, I was a DJ on KXLU FM at Loyola Marymount University. Most of us there started off playing contemporary bands, mostly alternative, earlier punk, the early, really scary form of emo that was coming out (like the Gravity Records stuff from San Diego—Angel Hair, Heroin, Mohinder, etc.), and a lot of music from England, like Creation Records releases (My Bloody Valentine, Primal Scream, Slowdive) . . . plus Spacemen 3, Spiritualized, Denim, or Aphex Twin. I made some good friends up there who were genuinely into buying and listening to records . . . and when you go digging for records, you come across all different types of music, and you can afford to be adventurous, because vinyl can be really inexpensive (with a little luck). So some of us DJs started getting into and buying a lot more different kinds of music from the '60s . . . I remember my then-future bandmate, Chris Gunst, and I were up there in the control booth really getting excited listening to "What's Happening?"

by the Byrds from the *Fifth Dimension* album. It just sounded fresh and new. A lot of us were playing more and of this older music mixed in with the new stuff. We had a big love of the Byrds, especially *Notorious Byrd Brothers* . . . they've been kind of a gateway band appreciated by all different kinds of other groups around the world over the last forty years. And we were always meeting more of the record listening community: people at the radio stations, people in bands, people working at the shops . . . straight-up music lovers. That was a great way to cross-pollinate, get together, listen to and learn about more music—obscure, contemporary, old, new, and otherwise. Well, discovering Gram Parsons and the Burrito Brothers is a short ride away for Byrds fans. And in the grand scheme of things, the Flying Burrito Brothers' music felt very natural, like it was already in the air. It had a very complementary feeling to the music we already liked, like another branch of the same tree.

Q: What first drew you in?

FD: It might have had something to do with the "cosmic" elements of the music (Mother Nature, the Universe, Joshua Tree, getting high, etc.) but Gram and his band, themselves, also felt familiar. And tied with that was the universality of the traditional elements of the sound. Everybody can relate to good country songs. They resonate to your core. It was soulful, honest, emotional, and fun—great music! Pretty soon, on several afternoon rock shows up at the radio station, you'd start to hear "Hot Burrito #2" mixed in to the same set with My Bloody Valentine, Sonic Youth, Orange Juice, Unwound, Further, Nina Simone, Dinosaur Jr. There was some debate about it among the DJs at the time, but it felt natural to us, and just as defiant or "underground" as anything else that was being played, and you certainly couldn't hear the Flying Burrito Brothers on any mainstream radio station!

Q: How do you think Gram ended up affecting your own music?

FD: Around the time I was leaving college, I became interested in the sound of the slide guitar. My dad had bought me an old six-stringed lap steel named "Bessie" at Lark in the Morning up in Mendocino, and I was learning to play it. So Sneeky Pete Kleinow, with his fuzz/delay pedaled approach to the instrument, was one of my favorite musicians right off the bat. When I'd hear the way his notes bounced and flew all around the band and Gram Parsons's voice in "Dark End of the Street," I'd feel like I was in a hot tub after having some good tequila. I ended up joining up with the fellows and starting Beachwood Sparks. Gram Parsons and his legacy were a cornerstone foundation of our style at the start, and we wore it on our sleeves, literally, with the vintage western shirts, long hair, and recreational habits. Over time, I think we increasingly developed a unique voice in our sound and style, and walked our own path, but we always held a deep love for music of the West Coast and America beyond, and viewed it as our spiritual base, the Byrds, Neil Young, Gram Parsons and the Burritos, the Band, Bob Dylan, the Louvin Brothers, and a lot more. Sometimes, we encountered a bit of backlash to being modern Gram Parsons appreciators, that we were being retro or throwbacks with our look and sound. I always felt that critique was shortsighted. It seems people can get so fixated on defining (and confining) musical ideas, looking at different movements and their influence as these short little mini-eras within decades. Or they judge a musical style's development by the few years when that certain style is popular and sells the most in the marketplace, then it's on to the next.

Q: Do you feel like Gram's music remains influential?

FD: Gram Parsons was and is an enduring musical force. And he's like a tributary, or a stream, coming from a place all his own, but part of a larger musical tradition. Much like the different schools of thought about style and form in Chinese martial arts, or the different movements in art and painting. Parsons has his own rich musical vein lying in wait for any music appreciator to discover. As for musicians keeping the spirit of Gram's music alive, anybody who has a love for it and wants to continue the tradition can do so, all you have to do is be yourself, and hopefully add something new and positive to it!

with no intervention from the Man. Instead of hired security, the Grateful Dead, who were also booked to play, had suggested the Hells Angels as authority. The Stones consented, and the notorious biker gang was handed over crowd control duties for the day.

Impatient in the backseat of the Burritos van, Gram heard a motorcycle moving in from behind, and he immediately opened the back door. He saluted the rest of the band and flagged down the bike, catching a quick ride between the stagnant rows of traffic.

It was cold, and the wind bit through the thin skin of his Nudie jacket, whipping his silk scarf across his cheeks. As he found his way to the stage, soundmen were doing checks, their voices floating above a huge shivering mass of people, all huddled together against the icy breeze, sharing joints and hits from communal whiskey bottles. The Stones were holed up in a trailer, enjoying the company of an array of young groupies. Keith was slumped in a corner with a glazed eye.

The sky was a pale eggshell blue, and the sound from the amplifiers drifted out and immediately dissipated in the air. It was impossible to hear at any sort of distance, and the stage was low to the ground and close to the faces in the front row. Gram wandered to the side of the barricades and watched the audience. He looked at the leaden palm of sky above and felt a jittery, anxious pull in his stomach, too much speed and a touch of stage fright maybe, but something seemed not quite in tune.

The Burritos went on first, playing to the largest crowd they had ever faced and feeling good about it. The audience seemed more or less content, applauding lightly, some people hooting with glee. The Hells Angels loomed in front of the stage and shot vicious looks at anyone who dared to come too close. Keith and Mick watched from backstage. Everything was going smoothly; the Burritos were as tight as they could be, given the fact that they had barely rehearsed and were more than a little wasted. When the band had played their last song, Gram shouted a warm "thank you" into the mike and took a long last look at the throng of people heaving in the weak sunlight.

Tim Burgess Interview
Interview by Jessica Hundley

Debuting in the late 1980s as front man for Manchester, England, sensations the Charlatans UK, Tim Burgess helped to instigate a definitive movement of neo-psychedelic Brit-pop. Now residing in Los Angeles, Burgess continues with a much-acclaimed solo career.

Q: Do you remember when you first heard Gram?

A: I was living in Camden, England, and I think what I first heard was a sort of greatest-hits kind of LP. That was it really. I guess I was instantly attracted to "Wild Horses" because of the Rolling Stones and you know everything started just to grow on me. Probably I was initially drawn to the more upbeat ones—like "Burrito #2" got me instantly and from then on it was slowly but surely. I just got into it.

Q: What do you think it is about his music that attracted you particularly?

A: Well, I was never really into country music, before I heard him. Obviously a million people would have never gotten into listening to country music if it wasn't for Gram. It was just the vibe really, just the overall vibe and the seriousness of it, I suppose.

Q: Do you feel that his music is still resonant? Does it sound contemporary to you?

A: Definitely. I mean I never have a problem with old stuff sounding contemporary. I think if it's good, it's timeless, like a Stones record or a John Lennon record, really.

Q: Do you have some favorite songs?

A: I like "Love Hurts" a lot and I like "Juanita." I'm just looking at the anthology now and it's quite brilliant. "$1000 Wedding" of course, I think that's a favorite to quite a lot of people. I don't think you can get much heavier, really, than that song.

Q: Do you think Gram's music has affected your own music in any way?

A: I would like to think so. I guess old songs, if you can appreciate them, you know you're not too far off really, that sound ends up in the music you're making. And with Gram, I did go through an obsession, bought all the records, listened to him incessantly.

I had my photograph taken at Joshua Tree. Someone took a photograph and I don't usually believe in stuff like this, but there was definitely what looked like someone playing guitar in the background. In a way, he's still here. I think his spirit is still around, in music and in the feel of things.

The Stones came on much later, in the midst of an ink black night, their fans impatient. Dirty, speed-tainted hits of LSD had made the rounds earlier in the evening, and most of the kids were wild-eyed with grinding jaws. The presence of the Stones was secondary to the saber slice of spotlights in the dark and the taste of iron in the air.

By the first song, there were scuffles, shouts, and bodies pushing violently against bodies. The Stones stopped playing and begged for some peace, Mick doing his best to tame the crowd with soothing words. Gram watched from behind the barricades with Michelle Phillips, gazing on the scene with a growing fear. The crowd smelled of sweat and anger and something darker, something black and unstoppable.

Suddenly, midway through the Stones set, something gave way and went wrong. There was a fight, the flash of knives, the kids white-faced and gape-mouthed, a girl screaming. Gram grabbed Michelle by the hand and led her toward the back. Keith unplugged his guitar and followed. The group stumbled toward a helicopter that sat hunched on the grass, crouching like an insect and tearing the air to pieces. The rest of the Rolling Stones were close behind, holding onto guitars and blinking out the dust. Gram and Michelle were the last to climb aboard, immediately lifted high above the chaos below.

By the end of the night, four kids were dead. One had drowned in a nearby lake, two were the victims of hit-and-runs, and the last, a young black man, had died on the trampled ground, just in front of the Rolling Stones' stage, blood seeping from Hells Angels' buck knive wounds in his gut, in his throat, and one through the red flesh of his heart.

Later, in a suite at San Francisco's Huntington Hotel, what happened—the deaths, the violence—hit home. Pamela Des Barres and Michelle were sitting with their pretty heads in their hands and the Stones were scattered and silent. Gram sipped a bourbon and stared out at the city, his mind reeling, the silence in the room an impossible weight to lift. He tasted something sour and bitter

Pamela Des Barres Interview
Interview by Jessica Hundley

Pamela Des Barres was "Pamela Miller" when she first met Gram in early 1968. A member of the Frank Zappa–masterminded girl group the GTO's, Des Barres was an integral part of the Los Angeles scene, a musician, dancer, and devoted supporter of some of the finest acts to emerge in the late sixties. Des Barres would later go on to document her memories of that time in her best-selling book *I'm with the Band*.

Q: Tell me about the first time you met Gram.

A: I believe it was the *Yellow Submarine* premiere and the GTO's had arrived in a big Hudson Hornet painted yellow like a submarine. We saw this guy and he had a red Nudie suit on, with yellow submarines—we had thought we went all out, but that suit was amazing. So my friend Miss Mercy and I, who was also in the GTO's, just went up and made his acquaintance because we were so impressed. He said he was Gram Parsons and he was new in town. We went just gah-gah over this guy. So soon after he joined the Byrds, I saw him at this club, I think it was called the Kaleidoscope at the time, it was called so many different things, but I saw him play there and I loved it. I thought, "Wow, this is interesting music!" I'd never even considered listening to country music at that point. I was only nineteen years old. I was in love with Chris Hillman, I had been in love with him for years, from the time of the early Byrds, I guess I was sixteen when I first fell in love with him. I was not dating him yet or anything but you know, I was flirting with him and seeing him around and talking at the clubs and all that. And that night he was out with Gram and introduced me to Gram. Gram and I, we just sort of hit it off instantly. He actually took me out on dates, he took me out on three different dates. This is while he and Nancy were separated, you know, they went back and forth, and I didn't even know about Nancy at this point. He was taking me to little restaurants and driving around in his Thunderbird and I was just so smitten I was like "Oh my God, what's going on!" Soon after that Nancy came back into the picture. Then I met Polly, so I refocused on Chris and he and I had an off and on years-long relationship beginning right about at that point. So I started taking care of Polly, that was such an honor, I was so thrilled and honored that Gram would entrust me with her. He brought Nancy up to Hollywood off and on and whenever Nancy would come with Polly, I would be the babysitter, so it was really wonderful. The first time I met Polly she was walking and had these gigantic eyes, sort of had a vibe, you know? I had never been into kids but I had recently been this acting governess for the Zappas, so I had really started understanding little toddlers and stuff, so it was good timing for Polly.

Q: Do you have any particular memories from this time?

A: Gram used to take Mercy and me out, driving around in his Thunderbird and he used to get us so high. He had the best pot in the world because of his inheritance money and all of that. He had the best of everything. But he never let the girls snort coke, he was really old-fashioned, at least in those days. At that time, it was '68 or '69, the Burritos were happening. We were very separate, the girls. At the house, when the guys were playing poker in one room, we would be in another room with Polly, hanging out, and they would do what they were doing and we were not invited. Pot was okay, though. That was in the Burrito Manor, the one up in Nichols Canyon. Gram and I got very tight as friends because I was around all the time to be with Chris or Polly, or he was hanging out with just Mercy and me. I was in full-fledged regalia when I started hanging out with them and slowly I started adding bits of cowboy stuff just like when Gram hooked up with Keith and kept adding the Keith stuff. I started adding cowgirl stuff to my crazy feathered getups, I must have looked so bizarre. I had long cowgirl dresses on with clown makeup, you know, that kind of stuff. I went every Monday night to the Palomino. The Burritos played every Monday night and I never missed a show even when Chris and I were on the outs and he had other girls there and everything, because I loved Gram so much, too. I didn't wanna miss a single show because it was my favorite band ever.

Q: You've known a lot of bands. The Burritos were your all-time favorite?

A: People always ask me "Who was my favorite band?" They think I'm going to say Hendrix or Zeppelin, but no, it was always the Flying Burrito Brothers, because I was so moved by Gram. He was the most moving, emotional singer I have ever seen. He put it all into his music, even if there was just a handful of people in the audience, he just delivered. It was just inspiring, it made you want to do something great yourself and that's what great art is. I just danced and danced and twirled and spun around and was in some universe with him. And Gram was always great to me. There was never a time that I felt ever once slighted by him and in that world, sometimes you could be ignored easily, there is so much going on, but he never did that with me. In fact, the night I finally went home with Mick Jagger, from the stage Gram saw what was going on because the Stones were in the audience. It was at the Corral Club and all the Stones went to the show and the feeling in the air was just crackling. Mick came up to me, I was on the dance floor with Mercy in a black velvet dress, and he came up and wanted to meet me and he kissed my hand and everything. Gram was watching and he said from the stage "Miss Pamela is a beauty, but she's tenderhearted," like he was warning Mick, "You better not fuck with her!" It was great. He was such a sweetheart. He was just the sweetest person, just a brilliant guy, one of my favorite people. I just treasure my friendship with him.

Q: He was gentle?

A: He was, but he had an edge to him though. You weren't quite sure sometimes where he was going to go with something and that made him more exciting. But he was basically just sweet, just a sweet, sweet guy. And way before his time, people are still trying to catch up with him. And some people are, I think some people are catching up with him finally. It's taken this long but there are some really good cosmic American musicians out there, picking up where he left off and I think part of the reason

his spirit has hung around so long was for that purpose. I think
he wanted to make sure the music he started really got off the
ground. Certain bands through the years have made a mark but
I think, finally, I think it's becoming much more largely embraced.
And I think a lot more people are drawn to his music, a lot of
young people are drawn to his music.

Q: Why do you think he has such resonance today?

A: Well, he's hard to deny. He was so hip because he was taking
his Nudies and his southern consciousness and drawing some
Keith Richards into it and it was just the perfect rock and roll
look. Those people are still trying to do it. And he made
amazing music. I went to many Burrito sessions, I got to sing on
"Hippie Boy," Mercy and I, and you can hear Mercy just cater-
wauling in the background. We were just there a lot. We were
there when they did "Wild Horses" with Leon Russell and it
was literally just Chris and Gram and Leon and me and Mercy.
We knew that we were sitting in this historical tub of greatness.
Locked in this small dark room with these people, it was just so
otherworldly. Just the knowledge that "this is eternal," whatever
was going on there, no one would ever forget. Being a part of
that was so . . . it's indescribable really. I was aware of the magic
in the moments that I was with him, that's why I kept all of these
copious diaries. I wish I could have recalled exact conversations.
I do remember once when we were looking at his hands. His
hands were just the longest fingers I had ever seen and they were
so elegant, the way he used them . . . they were just
exquisite, they almost had a mind of their own. One time in the
studio, he came to watch the GTO's when we were in the
studio, too, and they wanted to play on the thing and Frank said
no and we were like, "Are you guys crazy?" But anyway, that day
he played the piano for Miss Andee, my roommate and I. He
took us in this tiny little room and just played the piano for us
for ages, singing these songs, and he just looked at his hands that
day and said, "I don't know where they came from. Sometimes
I expect to look down and see stitches around my wrists."

Q: How was he as a father?

A: He was a great dad from what I could see. He was very hands-on and loving and adoring and attentive—when he was around. He was very into Polly when she was there with him. He would put her on his shoulders, you know, just mess with her. He was very tactile. He was someone you could hug and grab ahold of and he was not at all "cool" like some guys were, still coming from that era. A lot of men hadn't yet gotten soft enough, but he was very warm.

Q: You were there that day when they went off on the train tour?

A: I saw them off. It was some wild new event that Gram wanted to go through with. I've seen some of the films from that time. Those were his tragic coke days. Of course I was already doing it too at this time, even though he didn't give it to me. I was going out with Brandon De Wilde, who was a very good friend of theirs, very influential. His influence on the music was very profound. He was my boyfriend at that point because Chris and I were going back and forth. Gram called me a lot during that train trip. He would call me in the middle of the night and just sing to me and just talk and I would be just laying in bed listening to him. I remember I would feel so good the next day. I loved him so much. Gram was someone who was very in the moment. He was a very immediate, "living in the now" kind of person. Always just looking one step ahead musically, kind of putting the right things together. I didn't hang out with him when he got real wrecked. When I was spending a lot of time with him, he was really not all that messed up yet. I continued to see him and hang out into the early stages of the Fallen Angels because I remember going to Phil Kaufman's room, watching him rehearse with Emmylou and stuff like that. But I didn't see him much after he hooked up with Gretchen and was sequestered in the Chateau Marmont. Mercy saw him then, and he was high as a kite. I just didn't want to be around that or see him do that, because it was upsetting to me. Last time I saw him—I wrote about it in my book, too-was at the Troubadour and he was using a telephone right there when you walked in and he was on there trying to reach his dealer. There was just chaos inside him, I could just feel it. He just was off and on, not in that good of shape and it really upset me to see him like that. I like to remember Gram as he was when I first met him, in that crazy suit, just looking beautiful and electric and full of magic.

Gram, Little Avis, and Bob Parsons. PHOTO BY ANDEE COHEN NATHANSON.

in the back of his throat and knew, with unalterable certainty, that what had happened that night would affect everything, would, like the Manson murders, the race riots, the acid casualties strewn across the Strip, shake them all awake from the sweet dream that had been the 1960s.

He thought about the boy dying in the dirt that night, about his mother wasting away in a hospital bed, his father with the cold pistol to his head. Death had been shadowing Gram since childhood, hovering over everything, and Gram knew it was drawing closer, the two of them intertwined—brothers.

Gram in contemplation. PHOTO BY ANDEE COHEN NATHANSON.

Hour of Darkness/ Time of Need

THE LAST DAYS, 1971–1973

NEW YEAR'S CAME and went, a new decade limping in, everything uncertain. *Burrito Deluxe* was released and immediately panned, and at home at the Chateau Marmont, no amount of money or drugs could cloak the fact that Gram was losing his hold. His interest in the Burritos was fading, and his relationship with Gretchen was strained, his days fading away in a drunken blur, music lying stagnant inside him, the piano accumulating dust.

Back in New Orleans, his sister was having her own troubles. He opened letters from her with a black dread, anxious to know if she was okay but terrified at how helpless he was to save her. She had become pregnant far too young and was now bouncing in and out of dubious mental institutions, sinking under the weight of memories and the cruel pressures of her present. Bob Parsons cared for her in the only way he knew how, with a baffled concern and a blank check, sending her off to be poked and probed by a series of psychiatrists and physicians.

Gram wrote her long rambling letters in which he pleaded for her recovery and boasted of his accomplishments, hoping to brace her and give her hope and heart. Some days, when Gretchen was shrilling and screaming, everything seemed wound too tight, and he would climb on his new motorcycle, a Harley he had tricked out in buckskin and fringe with trust-fund cash, and he would head out of town, wind pulling at his hair, dust in is eyes.

Once in a while he would leave the bike and take the sleek white Jaguar instead, driving the long black strip of pavement to Joshua Tree. He would go alone, forgo the Inn for the park, building a small fire in the dry sand and emptying his flask while the sun appeared over the lip of the world, dawn breaking like glass.

In the city there were the usual rounds of parties in the hills and along the Strip, everything tempered nicely by a stash of prescription pills provided by a dentist in Watts. Gram bought only the best—stimulants, cocaine, uppers, downers, huge bags of mushrooms. Meanwhile, the Burritos were beginning to dissipate, the rift between Gram and Chris a mile wide, Hillman trying to put his life back together as Gram was trying to tear his own apart.

Gram's bout of self-destruction came to a head one late afternoon in the spring of 1970. On a whim, he decided to pay a visit to his friend John Phillips. They shared a drink and Gram impulsively suggested a motorcycle excursion. Before John could answer, Gram was placing the nearest girl on the back of his bike and heading down the drive. John followed on his own cycle, the riders zooming through the exclusive streets of Brentwood and Bel Air, moving fast through quiet neighborhoods, engines roaring and spitting smoke.

Gram had been riding since he was a kid, having owned a succession of bikes, from scooters to the BSA, but the Harley was huge, long, and mean, and it had a busted front fender that Gram had recently jury-rigged with a coat hanger. The girl on the back, a singer whose name he couldn't quite remember, was holding on for dear life, her thin, warm arms wrapped tight around his waist. He had given her his helmet, and the air felt cool against his cheeks as he pushed the bike faster down the open stretch of pavement.

It was only a second later, it seemed, that the girl's arms were gone from around his chest. He was on the bike one moment, and then he was floating a few feet above the ground, spinning, crashing, the fender torn to pieces, the front tire rolling ahead, beckoning him, the girl on the ground crying. Then there was a shattering, blinding, incredible crack of pain, and that was all.

When Gram awoke in the hospital, it was night. He heard the soft whispers of nurses walking the hall in rubber-soled shoes, the slow click and beep of machines, and someone coughing. Gretchen was asleep in a chair by his bed, looking like a child. Gram sighed and felt a knife thrust in his ribs. His face felt huge, and his heartbeat pulsed through the flesh of his cheeks.

It was a month or more—he stopped counting the days—before he walked into daylight again. During the weeks of healing, the windows read the slow passage of days, the nurses were hushed and quiet, and everything was muffled by the cotton-candy gauze of painkillers, the morphine drip.

But finally, miraculously, he was himself again, battered, broken, but alive, walking and talking, and the music was still there too, but by then Gram's attachment to the Burritos had evaporated. At a local show in the Valley a few weeks after Gram's recovery, things came to a drunken, sad end. Gram was too wasted to remember the set list; something sour in him didn't care, and he deliberately fucked up, making a fool of Chris, his bandmates, and most of all himself.

Later, backstage, he stood swaying in front of his old friend Chris Hillman, who was red-faced and furious, his words indecipherable; Gram was too lost, too far gone to bother listening. He closed his eyes and opened them again to see Chris clutching Gram's guitar, swinging it high in the air and bringing it down hard on the chipped tile of the dressing room floor. Gram saw the body crack, the strings bend, the neck hang morbidly, and the rosewood splinter. Hillman immediately looked sorry and immensely sad, but he turned around and closed the door, and with that, Gram and the Burritos were finished.

It wasn't long, however, before Gram found another musical cohort. Terry Melcher was another rich kid and a consummate self-abuser, a record producer who had come onto the scene fast and hard, producing several hit records in his early twenties, including the Byrds version of "Mr. Tambourine Man." Melcher and Gram were drug buddies first, but music had its place as well, and it wasn't long before they were trying out various numbers at Melcher's home studio, Gram slumped over the piano, Melcher swaying by the boards.

There were days when Gram couldn't be bothered to find his way home, when he would wake up flung over an easy chair or find himself cotton-mouthed on Melcher's floor. Gretchen put up with it, in part because she adored Gram and forgave him most everything, and in part because she was distracted by her own burgeoning success, a plum role in Roger Vadim's movie *All the Pretty Maids* and an impressive spread in *Playboy*.

Gram, when he bothered to notice, was less than pleased by Gretchen's evolving career. It went directly against his southern upbringing to have his woman strutting around barely dressed in front of other men. Eventually, he roused himself from his stupor long enough to forbid her to take any more jobs. For a brief moment, he kept a close eye on her, clinging tight to the thin fabric of their relationship.

On his good days, when his head didn't feel soft or swollen, Gram did his best to woo record-label contacts, bragging about the magical sessions at Melcher's, insisting that with Terry as his producer, nothing could go wrong. Jerry Moss at A&M was understandably leery of Gram, knew his reputation and his habits, but he finally gave in and signed him on again.

Moss saw talent there, real talent lurking beneath the glazed eyes, the slur, and the posturing. Another impressive roster of musicians was rounded up for the sessions. Gram, with his remaining charm, his money, and enough respect for his writing and playing, continued to draw great artists to his projects. Old collaborators like Clarence White and Earl Ball showed up at Melcher's studio, as did a young Ry Cooder and singer Merry Clayton.

Somehow, the group managed to record ten songs, but from the get-go the sessions were a disaster. Melcher passed out at the mixing board. Gram was falling-down drunk and even puked into the concert piano. Moss got wind of the mayhem a few weeks in and cancelled the contract, taking the tapes with him. With the end of the album came an end, more or less, of Gram and Terry's friendship, each blaming the other's excess, their words turning bitter. Eventually Melcher pointed toward the door.

Through the winter of 1970, Gram spent much of his time in half-sleep with his shades drawn. The only visitors were strangers with dubious medical credentials, men who doled out pills of all colors to help Gram dull the pain. He had had a seizure not long after the Melcher debacle. His muscles had gone tight, and his eyes rolled up into his head. The episode shook him and Gretchen both. It was uncertain what had caused it, brain damage from the accident or possibly the continued drug abuse. Gram took whatever the doctors gave him, so long as it made him forget.

When he was not completely sedated, he drifted through the city, still appearing at all the right places in all the right clothes. He pretended not to notice that he had failed, that he was on a losing streak of his own devising, that the list of his failures included not only the last album and his friendship with Melcher, but also the end of his relationship with Chris and the slow loss of his connection to Nancy and Polly.

He played here and there, when he was sober enough, adding vocals or keyboards to a few friends' projects, playing piano for his old friend Fred Neil, even singing harmony on a track off the new album from the latest incarnation of the Byrds. By spring he was ready to start fresh, convinced that if he could walk away from the messes he had made, at least for a little while, then he would be capable of cleaning some of them up. In March of 1971, he and Gretchen decided to pack their things and take off for England, hoping to return, somehow, with a slate wiped clean by time and distance.

The couple arrived in London just in time for a Rolling Stones tour, immediately accepting an invitation to hop aboard the bus and take an impromptu trip through England. The Stones were weary, burnt out from too many years on the road and too much

Gram in England.

water under the bridge. They had grown accustomed to having an entourage, a trail of pretty, pleasant people who followed them wherever they went and added some equilibrium, a buffer between band members when things got tense.

Gram was a welcome addition to an already motley crew. He knew the right moments for an injection of wry humor, and he consciously tried to be as polite and cheerful as possible, a balm to the frayed nerves of a traveling rock band. The gloomy, nondescript coal-mining towns of northern England were booked for most of the tour, and Gram watched the landscape through the smoked glass of the bus window, seeing kids playing soccer in dirt lots and men with blackened faces leaving the mines. At night he drank thick brown ales with ruddy-cheeked locals in dank antique pubs.

With the constant company of other people, both he and Gretchen behaved, managing to get along, for once, smoothly and easily. Gram would wake up in strange hotels, factory smokestacks looming outside the windowpanes, the bed small and the room narrow, and he would watch Gretchen sleep. She looked like a doll, all milky skin and yellow hair.

On the long drives between cities, he would wander to the back of the bus to play cards or pick George Jones songs on Keith's guitar. Sometimes he would slump down low and shoot junk with Keith and Anita, who were by then full-blown addicts. Gram himself was not far behind. Smack suited him perfectly; it was just the right drug to fill all those empty spaces, to dull the pain and paranoia, to bathe him in water-warm comfort, in a wash of feathery heat, and then provide a welcome amnesia, everything hovering and hopeful.

By midsummer the Stones' recording contract was pointing towards a session, and the band decided to relocate to the South of France to make the next album. It would be the perfect spot to simultaneously evade the English tax collectors and live like kings. In the interim Keith headed out to Redlands, inviting Gram and Gretchen to join him in a self-imposed detox.

Worried that drug connections would be few and far between at their new French digs, Gram and Keith surmised that it might be a good idea to dry out for a spell. The two couples holed up in the sprawling stone house, attempting to kick with the help of a nurse recommended by none other than Beat novelist and career junkie William Burroughs. Gram and Keith took the "cure," attempting to resist a bad habit with the help of medical science and frequent infusions of fine music.

The nurse prescribed a plethora of legal prescription drugs, and evenings were spent floating, picking out Merle Haggard numbers on an old piano in the parlor. Days were spent shifting uncomfortably on the red velvet chaise lounges, scratching at an itch that seemed to sit just under the skin. Gram was forced to admit that the drug had taken hold of him and that he was helpless. Too many hours without a fix, and he would feel an anxious tug, an impatience gripping at him, making him short-tempered and frantic for the first time in his life. The lackadaisical, easy-living cowboy was beginning to slip away under the weight of the leaden nod, the dreamy liquid daze that would descend with the first hit of smack.

The move to Nellcote in mid-July did very little to help with the mutual drying out. Almost right away the group found a French supplier, a nearby drug dealer appearing with a seemingly endless supply of sugary, pale pink heroin. Dubbed "cotton candy," the drug was ever-present, arriving almost as soon as the group of friends and hangers-on had settled into the sprawling villa.

Nellcote had a decadent beauty reminiscent of French nobility. There were Persian carpets, echoing hallways, enormous rooms with parquet floors, and glass doors that opened out to the cool breeze of the veranda. The piano was promptly moved from the ballroom to one of these balconies, placed to take advantage of the shade and air, the house itself stifling and stuffy, hundreds of years of dust and old silks simmering in the torpid French summer.

The Stones set up a studio in the dank basement, and recording sessions were impromptu affairs, the band and an assortment of crack studio musicians descending the rickety staircase to engage in both meandering jams and tight, strutting, staggeringly competent rock numbers. Gram was a fixture, his presence integrated into the creative atmosphere of the house, the imaginative free-for-all that infused the lazy, high-noon air with an electric charge.

He was far too well mannered to push his ideas on his new friends, but it was obvious that Keith's playing, tunings, and singing style were all affected by Gram's proximity. Keith's music had been influenced by Gram, by the intensity of their friendship, by the long nights the two had spent together in England, Burroughs's nurse watching over them as Gram showed Keith the chords to Haggard's "Sing Me Back Home" and J. Ripley's "Your Angel Steps Out of Heaven."

At Nellcote, Gram would lay dozing on the thick cushioned couch they had pushed out by the piano, drifting into daydreams, the sun burning the skin at the tip of his nose, dusting gold into his long, lank hair. He was getting heavier, doughier, and softer by the day. He'd wake sometimes with a taste of blood in his mouth and find the pink skin of his gums lightly bleeding. This was somehow not at all troublesome; the whole house was floating on a cotton candy cloud, everyone dosed and dazed.

Once in a great while, Gram would veer dangerously close to sobriety, and there would be a bitter jolt of panic, the painful realization that he was watching other people, more famous, more important people doing what he was supposed to be doing. But the allure of the situation, of being part of something as epic as the Rolling Stones recording *Exile on Main Street*, was a seduction he could not resist.

He pushed any doubts he had, any pride he had, quickly away, avoiding the truth quite neatly with a few glasses of tequila or another snort of candy-colored smack. Gretchen, meanwhile, was alternately bored and furious. Anita Pallenberg, the uncontested woman of the house, had finally made her feelings clear about the wispy blond California girl wandering her hallways. There were catfights and quiet battles for control, and the rare bond of sisterhood against the little-boy antics of the men.

Gretchen wanted out of Nellcote within a week or two of arriving, but Gram ignored her, focusing instead on his long, still slender fingers on the yellowed ivory keys of the old piano, or on the satiny orange sunsets that ducked under the veranda railings. There were too many one-sided fights, Gretchen wired high while Gram smiled in mild amusement or closed his eyes and dreamed her away.

Within a few weeks, even the cavernous villa began to seem too close for comfort. Tensions were pulled taut as the drug supply began to run low, and the Stones began to feel the strain of playing host. Anita was sick of mothering, of setting a dinner table for haggard, blank-eyed boys and strangers. Keith tried to keep things cool but saw clearly that his guests had overstayed their welcome.

Gram was too lost to notice the vicious looks burning the air between the women, the muttered complaints of Mick, and the subtle evasion of Keith, who did his best to avoid the coming

Al Perkins Interview
Interview by Polly Parsons

Undoubtedly one of the greatest pedal steel players of all time, Al Perkins has played with everyone from Emmylou Harris to Crosby, Stills and Nash to the Rolling Stones. He contributed his talents to Gram's last two solo albums, *GP* and *Grievous Angel*

Q: When did you first meet Gram?

A: I guess it was in Georgia or Alabama, might have been Alabama, with Chris Hillman and Rick Roberts. He came and sat in at a show. I think we were playing at a university, you know like a small university in the auditorium. He sat in and I noticed him looking over once in a while and grinning and after [the show] he said, "Well you know if you had been our steel player we'd still have this group going." He was talking about the Burrito Brothers. That was a good compliment, I remember that. And then it wasn't too far after that, it was about the time he was hanging with Keith Richards and those guys, and I went on to do the Manassas thing. I remember we went down to see the Stones play at the coliseum, which is kind of like a rodeo. Shortly after that they called me to do the record *Exile on Main Street*, and I think it is because of your dad, you know, talking to them about me. Not long after that Gram was starting the Fallen Angels, so he was traveling quite a bit in and out of town and he usually stayed at Chateau Marmont. Whenever he was in town, I was out of town, so we didn't see each other a whole lot after that. But then he called to do the second album. He had most of the Elvis guys, playing, you know, plus or minus one or two. We had a ball.

Q: When was the last time you saw Gram?

A: I saw him a couple of times after we finished recording. I remember that because I think they were showing me the album cover, I think it had Emmylou and him on a motorcycle. He was living with Phil I think on Chandler, and I moved down the road. I remember going over there a couple of times, you know, after the recordings and stuff. And then, I think at that time, let's see that would have been '74 . . . '73. That was the last time, but I remember him like I just saw him yesterday. He made an impact, you know?

confrontation. It was the Rolling Stones' assistant who finally cleaned house, letting Gram and Gretchen know that it was time they were on their way, out of Nellcote, out of France, back to the torn scraps of their life together.

Gram saw the situation suddenly, the sharp-edged truth of it. Keith, his friend, his brother in old vinyl, in Baptist-hall piano chords and high-quality heroin, was, as politely as possible, throwing Gram out of the house. The fact knocked his ego aside, left him feeling hollow and foolish. Finally, Gram saw that the space had grown small in the last weeks, that Keith had his own band and his own troubles, and that perhaps Gram should be facing some of his own.

He packed up his guitar, his Nudie suits, and his frail, thin-boned girl, and he did his best to keep his integrity intact, calling upon the southern gentleman inside, the gracious Gram that was waiting under the surface, just below the skin of the belligerent drunk and the useless junkie. He put on his silk-mannered, well-educated face and did his damnedest to dissolve the tension, to smooth over the edges of an uncomfortable situation. When he said his goodbye, he kept his back as straight as he could and walked out the door as if it had been his idea to go in the first place.

The only trouble was that he and Gretchen had no place to go.

After boarding a ferry to London and making a few frantic phone calls, the two had money at least, and they soon found a cold-water flat. Then, in a flash of inspiration, Gram remembered that Ian Dunlop, his old Submarine bandmate, the man with the knack for names, had moved back to England. Last Gram had heard, he was living somewhere out in the green hinterlands, playing out a Farmer Joe fantasy on a few acres of fertile ground.

Dunlop and his wife welcomed Gram and Gretchen with open arms. Their hospitality came just in time. The Dunlops lived in a bucolic setting—a country cottage with good land, organic vegetables, and homemade wines. They spent their nights at the local village pub or played guitars by the cottage fireplace, waking up to berries and fresh cream in the morning.

Dunlop was still in love with music, still playing with a few locals, a farmer up the road with an accordion, a kid in the village with an old drum set. Gram and Gretchen, for the first time in too long, felt a quiet descend on their frazzled, high-strung hearts. The food, the fresh air, and the Dunlops' own solid bond soothed something that had shattered inside them. Gram, without much remorse, watched the last of his drug supply dwindle until there was nothing left except a few sticky buds in a ceramic cookie jar and Ian's syrupy pear wines.

He found himself writing again, scribbling down bits of lyrics, stray lines of poetry, and scraps of dreams in his spiral-bound notebook. His guitar was with him everywhere. He would bring it on the long walks he'd take with Gretchen, the two of them packing up homemade bread and jam and setting off over the brilliant green hills. Before anything could sour, the couple said a gracious goodbye to the Dunlops, Gram having tracked down another old acquaintance, Rick Grech. Grech had been part of the hugely successful band Blind Faith and had met Gram through the rock 'n' roll grapevine.

Grech lived in another picture-perfect English village on a small farm surrounded by a spread of beautiful land. He and Gram found themselves instantly compatible, particularly musically, playing guitar and banjo in the wide-open fields behind Rick's cottage, fingerpicking honky-tonk numbers, sipping ale, smoking, and falling deep into music again.

There were late afternoon idylls—Rick sprawled in the grass taking a catnap, the girls picking flowers, Gram cotton-headed from the last joint, rubber-boned and relaxed, picking out old Louvin Brothers songs on his guitar. It was on one of these lazy days that Gram decided, with the concrete insistence of the best epiphanies, that he would go back to LA—this time as a solo artist.

He would enlist Rick in the endeavor, fly him over as a good-luck charm. He'd woo the finest musicians and make it clear that he was steering the ship, and he would finally make the music that poured from his heart without any interference from other egos.

Everything was simple, suddenly, and in the haze of the late summer afternoon, the decision seemed final and undeniable.

He would make his first solo album with the help of professionals and a few old friends. He would settled down in LA and focus, and (he was watching Gretchen now, small and laughing, her hair like a halo, a spray of violets in her hands) he would marry Gretchen and be a good husband to her and a good father to Polly, start everything again clean and fresh.

By the time he and his friends returned to the house, night was coming on fast, bringing with it a gray mist and the threat of rain. Gram remained determined. He called Bob Parsons and little Avril, the only family he had left, and told him he was getting married, getting hitched as soon as possible and that he wanted his stepfather, who he knew was a consummate host, to organize everything.

Gretchen was thrilled at the proposal but wary. She knew Gram's history, his manic moods, his bad habits, knew he had asked Nancy the same question not too long ago and had then gone back on his offer. Gretchen knew that if the marriage were actually going to happen, it would have to happen soon, before Gram's whims took him away from her again.

By now, autumn was approaching England, bringing cold air, drenching downpours, and mud. The couple said their goodbyes to Grech, Gram promising to send for him as soon as things were settled in LA. After a brief stay back in London in another cold-water flat, the city's streets soaked, the whole town smelling of wet brick and blanketed with fog, Bob Parsons sent word that he and Gram's sister Avis were ready. They had planned a small ceremony in New Orleans for September, everything in place for Gram and Gretchen's arrival.

On the flight back to America, Gram woke up from a long, restless dream and looked down at white clouds shifting below, forming valleys and mountains, strange and lovely landscapes of mist and floating water. His mouth tasted sour, his eyes itched, and there were tight cramps in his legs. Gretchen was sleeping beside him, breathing softly, her face slack. Soaring high above the Atlantic, Gram realized clearly that things were moving forward now, and he was powerless to stop them, his life like some swift-moving river, Gram caught breathless in the fast-moving current.

His stepfather was the same as he remembered, slightly worn maybe, but with the same slick suits and playboy style, pinkie rings and brilliantined hair. Little Avis, however, had become woefully thin, looking like a branch about to snap, eyes pleading, lips cracked. Bob, in his own way, loved her, loved Gram, wanted them to be happy, wanted to please and charm them the way he did most anyone else he set his mind to seducing.

He threw an enormous, lavish party for Gram and Gretchen, a wedding banquet and all-night celebration, a guest list comprising business associates, men from the club, and various New Orleans elite. Gram had asked his old Harvard cohort, Jet Thomas, to preside over the ceremony.

Jet agreed, reluctant and more than a little concerned about Gram's state of mind, trying to disguise a growing panic when he arrived in New Orleans and saw the bloat in Gram's face, saw how young Gretchen was, how the shadows had carved hollows under the couple's eyes.

Jet was Gram's only real friend to attend the ceremony. The rest were a crowd of gawkers, all strangers save for a few Snivelys up from Florida who looked on disapprovingly. Little Avis, with wet eyes, clung to her brother's arm as if she were drowning, and Gretchen herself was dazed and uncertain.

Gram was drunk for most of the ceremony. He had grown a thin mustache, and his hair hung down to his shoulders, brushing against his polyester tuxedo jacket. He went to the bathroom sometime during the night, looked in the mirror and barely recognized himself. Where were his friends? Where were Chris Hillman, Paul Surratt, and Jim Stafford? Why was he in Bob Parson's house, a place he had studiously avoided, dressed like a big-band leader with a gold ring on his finger and bride who was not yet twenty-one? He saw Polly's small round face, his mother's

The Thrills
Interview by Jessica Hundley

Hailing from Dublin, Ireland, the Thrills make irresistible country/psychedelic pop music that is undeniably influenced by Gram and his contemporaries. Padraic McMahon is the group's guitarist, bassist, and official "Gram fanatic."

Q: Do you remember the first time you heard Gram?

A: I remember very vividly that I heard "Song For You" in Dublin. A band was playing that song, doing that cover and I remember thinking, "What the hell is this?" I asked the singer afterwards and he told me, "It's Gram Parsons." I knew that Gram had been in the Byrds, but I didn't know that he had done his own thing too. I heard that song and that was it. I listen to that music all the time. It's great road music, especially Burrito Brothers; all of those songs are road songs. It's really good truckin' on, movin' on, old time music. It's great when the band is touring. His lyrics are all about melancholy—travel and returning home.

Q: What do you think it was about that song?

A: I think with Gram's music in general, it's the whole sound of it, the guitar work, the piano, Hillman is so good. And Gram's voice, it's not even that good, on a technical level it's quite flawed, you know? But it has that nice inflection, it sounds as if he'd had his heart broken. It's a really characteristic voice. It was the music and the players who played it. He surrounded himself with such great musicians and he kind of fed off it. Then when he met Emmylou, it all came together. They suited each other so well. She's such a great harmonist.

Q: What are some of your favorite songs?

A: "The Last Horse" is a good example of how Gram would harmonize on his own. The last part he does a simple two-part harmony with himself and the hairs on the back of your neck stand up. "Streets of Baltimore," "Juanita"—I don't know, there's just too many. I go through different phases where I listen to different periods of him, Byrds, Burritos, and then the Fallen Angels. Gram's version of "Wild Horses" I think blows the socks off the Stones' version. It has a different soul, a depth to it that the Stones didn't quite catch. It's interesting, I don't know where it came from, but in the last few years there's been a real resurgence in interest in Gram. I think there's something in his music that has such resonance, that it's still affecting music today. With his death, the way he lived his life, he's such a mythical kind of figure. He looked cool all the time. He was an absolutely amazing rock star. His whole look, the voice, he was the whole package.

sad smile, and he slumped down and pressed his cheek against the cold tile of the bathroom floor.

The next day Gram called Chris Hillman, who was touring with the latest incarnation of the Burritos, and told him the news. It had been a long time since they'd had a civil discourse, and Hillman was missing Gram despite himself. Gram told him about the wedding, about the plans for the solo album, about getting clean again in Ian Dunlop's cottage, and playing music in the freshly mown fields behind Rick's. Chris found himself shot through with pity and forgiveness, and before he knew what he was doing, he had invited Gram up the coast to join in on a few dates for old times' sake and to check out a young girl singer who had just blown his mind in DC.

Gram was there within days, his new bewildered bride in tow. He was his old self, save for the extra pounds and his slightly dazed demeanor. Still, Chris was shattered by the change in Gram's appearance, the loose rolls of fat around the waistband of his Nudie suit, the double chin, the wispy mustache giving him the look of a used car salesman or undercover cop, a sleazy shadow of hair across his upper lip and something hard in his eyes that had never been there before, something almost cruel.

But Gram could still talk a good game, still had those beautiful hands, those fingers made for the piano keys, and Chris wanted to help as best he could, lend a hand without getting in too far himself. He told Gram about the singer he had seen a few nights before, a woman with a voice like honey and white gold. Gram took heed and tracked the girl down, managing to set up an impromptu meeting. A day later he was hopping a train from Baltimore to DC, Gretchen by his side, slightly suspicious about the trip, about another woman drawing Gram to her with such obvious magnetism.

On the way down, Gram was jittery, nervous with expectation. He had always wanted a partner for vocal harmonies, a female voice to match his own, to trade off with on a chorus and instill real passion in the lyrics of his love songs. He knew Chris Hillman wasn't easily impressed, knew that whatever happened this women was certain to be something special.

Emmylou Harris was only twenty-five years old that fall of 1971, but she had already lived her share of struggle, a single mom trying hard to make a living out of late-night club dates and week-long East Coast tours. She had a clear head and no time for fast acts. She had no idea who Gram was or what he wanted, but she had been charmed by his gentleness on the phone and by his child-like enthusiasm.

Gram arrived at a club called Clyde's in the Georgetown neighborhood of DC just a few hours before Emmylou was set to go on. He only needed a few moments to pass between them to know there was something there. She was beautiful, with dark hair, pale skin, and soft eyes that were both inquisitive and intelligent. Even her speaking voice was lovely, honeyed, and full.

Gretchen looked on helplessly as Gram and Emmylou made their way to the tiny dressing room to work on a few songs together. In the smoky back hall, amid the pervading smell of stale beer and cigarettes, Gram took out his guitar and hit a chord, and the two of them were off, voices intertwined like lovers, everything coming together in one crystalline moment. Gram and Emmylou had been destined to sing together, each possessing a voice that made the other's complete. By the end of the night, Gram was buzzing with excitement over the way Emmylou held his notes aloft, the way she followed his trail, reading his eyes and knowing, innately, whether to travel up a note or down.

Near dawn Emmylou drove the young couple back to Baltimore, Gram chattering in the front seat, promising to send for Emmylou, to bring her out to LA to make an album, to tour the world. All the while Gretchen sat in the back, feeling smaller by the minute. At the hotel Gram grabbed Emmylou impulsively, hugged her tightly, then looked at her dead on. They were going to make great music together; he could feel it. They were going to change each other, and there was no stopping it now. He promised a plane ticket in a few weeks' time and blew her a gentle kiss goodbye.

Emmylou Harris Interview
Interview by Nigel Williamson
Reprinted with permission of *Uncut* magazine

Emmylou Harris was Gram's protégée, his muse, his intimate friend and vibrant creative partner. Together they sang some of his finest tunes. Since Gram's death, Emmylou has proven herself an incredible musician in her own right, one of country music's very finest.

Q: Do you remember when you first met Gram?

A: It was in Washington, DC, in October 1971. Chris Hillman and Rick Roberts from the Burritos had heard me sing in this little club there. Then they went up to Baltimore. Gram showed up and told them he wanted to find a girl to sing real traditional country duets and they told him about me. The next day he called me.

Q: Did you know anything about him when he rang?

A: I was a jaded twenty-five-year-old single mother struggling to raise her daughter and playing three or four shows a night and I was lucky to make $100 a week. So no, I had no idea who he was. He said, "Why don't you come up to Baltimore?" I said, "You got to be crazy," and suggested he take the train down to me. That's what he did, and he came to my gig.

Q: Was the chemistry instant?

A: We worked up some stuff between my sets sitting on the beer kegs down in the basement. I can't remember what the song was. But it sounded good and we went back to a friend's house afterwards and played a bit more. But I didn't really hear the uniqueness in Gram's voice until later. I went on the Fallen Angels tour with him because it was an opportunity. But Gram was drinking and I was a little wary of him. I kept my distance. He was an incredibly kind and generous person, but I wasn't exactly sure what was going on. I was still a folk singer who dabbled in country. I didn't quite get it.

Q: So when did you get it?

A: When he turned me on to the Louvin Brothers. We worked up one of their songs, "Angels Rejoiced," and somebody taped the show on a cassette and I was listening to it. For the first time I heard what Gram was doing on the harmony part. All of a sudden, my ears shifted into a different gear. It was also the time our version of "Love Hurts" was coming together. There was definitely something happening between us on that song. We were delving deeper and I was starting to sing differently. Gram never told me what or how to sing. But just duetting with him was teaching me. . . . He was an innovator and he came up with something completely different. He was the first person who brought rock poetry to country music.

Q: Then he invited you to sing on his first solo album?

A: I got a round-trip ticket to LA in the mail from him. I didn't think the album was going to happen. But I thought, "Well, okay, I'm going to get on the plane just for the adventure." They took me to the Château Marmont and Rick Grech and Gram were there. They offered me $500 to do the whole album. That was a whole lot of money to someone who was struggling to make $100 a week. I remember making the record but not really the details. It was, "This is 'Sin City.' Sing now."

Q: Did you recognize his self-destructive tendencies?

A: I knew his history of drug addiction. But in my naïveté I thought Gram was indestructible. It was like a student-teacher relationship because I was learning so much and he seemed so vital and such a wealth of inspiration. I couldn't imagine anything was going to happen to him. I look back now and it amazes me how blind I was. I had never been around anyone with a serious addiction, so I just didn't see the dangers. It didn't seem to me that people around him were worried. He was getting off on the exercise of singing duets because we were making a pretty extraordinary sound together. There was something beautiful happening and he was on fire with the music. So all I could see was a future for us working together. I thought he was on the road to recovery. But I realize now if someone has an addiction the danger is always going to be there. It's the hole in the road you don't see until it is too late.

Q: How did you feel after his death?

A: It was like someone had chopped off my arm. There was a part of me that was missing. I cared for him so much and I had never lost anyone in my life who was young and who was a friend. One day somebody is in the world and the next day they are gone. It's as if the ground has opened and swallowed them up. . . . There was no way to go through the grieving process of a funeral. I was back East with my family and everyone else was in LA. There wasn't going to be a ceremony there, because the body had to go to New Orleans in order for the stepfamily to get control of his money. It was made clear to me that I wasn't welcome at the funeral, so I was completely cut off from everything. I didn't know how to grieve.

Q: So what did you do?

A: First, I drove to Virginia Beach to see Gram's sister, whom I'd never met. Then I drove to see Jet Thomas, who was Gram's counselor at Harvard. I had to find a way to connect. But the way I really dealt with Gram's death was to throw myself into my work. I furiously got a band together, worked up all these songs, found a gig, and I guess I haven't stopped since.

Emmylou. PHOTO BY TOM WILKES.

Gram and Gretchen's arrival back in Los Angeles was quiet, the two hunkering down in the old Marmont bungalow and doing their best to keep a low profile. Gram was wary of getting sucked back into the flow of parties, of drinking and drugging, of getting pulled under again before he'd had a chance to swim to shore.

He would wake up as early as he could, limiting his vices to pot and tequila. He devoted himself to songwriting and the difficult task of finding someone to help make his intentions manifest. Gram had burned a lot of bridges, and he knew it. He had burned them with A&M, with various local players, and with more than a few friends.

He still had some tricks up his sleeve, however, still had his bond with Hillman and his link with Keith, who sent word that Gram could use his name to woo record-label higher-ups. And Gram still had his trust fund, too, the Snively fortune dwindling but still formidable, more than enough for Gram to pay his own way, no matter what direction that way might lead.

Convinced that much of the failure in his past had been due to the lack of a solid foundation and remembering the advantages of a clear-headed manager like Buddy Freeman, Gram decided he needed a businessman first, someone who knew the music industry but still had some taste of his own.

Eddie Tickner had been at the fringes of Gram's career for some time, a savvy moneyman who had managed an early incarnation of the Byrds, nursing the band through some financial scrapes and woes. Gram got him on the phone, mentioned Keith as a willing producer and collaborator, and Tickner was hooked, despite Gram's rep as a drunk and consummate bullshit artist.

Tickner knew Gram was a risk, but he also knew that not much came from playing it safe, and he took on Gram as a potentially lucrative client. Together, the two made the label rounds, Gram the charismatic talent, Tickner the straight man. With Keith Richards giving his blessing, it wasn't long before they found a taker, Mo Ostin at Reprise, who was in the process of starting Warner Brothers' first country division and was hungry for acts.

Norah Jones Interview
Interview by Jessica Hundley

Daughter of Indian music legend Ravi Shankar, Norah Jones's amazing singing voice and her jazz/soul/country blend of songwriting have earned her numerous Grammys and a slew of critical accolades. Over the course of her career thus far, she has performed alongside Ray Charles, Willie Nelson, and Keith Richards.

Q: When did you first hear Gram's music?

A: Probably about five years ago when I moved to New York. I had a lot of gaps in my music knowledge. I'm from Texas where you'd think I would have heard it, but I didn't really listen to a lot of that music growing up. I listened only to jazz until I moved to New York and that was pretty much it. In New York, I made a few friends who turned me onto Gram Parsons and all that kind of stuff. It really opened me up, it was a whole other world of music that I'd known nothing about. I think it helped to broaden my tastes, because it was so different than what I'd been listening to, what I'd been raised on. I learned a lot of the songs and eventually I started doing Gram's songs "Sleepless Nights" and "She" in my shows.

Q: Why did you choose those particular songs?

A: Because they were great songs and they seemed to fit into our set well. I have a country band at home called the Little Willies with my friend Richard Julian and he sings "Streets of Baltimore." I actually sing harmony on it. I know those songs really well, they're amazing to sing. Gram wrote so many really beautiful and intricate harmonies, it's perfect music for a vocalist. I usually play "She" just on piano and there's really something gorgeous about that song. It can make your hair stand on end.

Gram auditioned for Ostin, inviting him to the Chateau and banging out a few of his own songs on piano in the hotel lobby, plying the exec with margaritas and frequent mentions of his good pal in the Rolling Stones. Ostin was certainly no sucker; Gram was obviously a dedicated self-abuser, you could tell that with one look, but he was also a smart kid who loved music, who had the respect of the Rolling Stones. And if Keith Richards believed in Gram, who was Ostin to argue? By the end of the evening, they had penned a deal.

Keith was first on a wish-list of producers, but a close second was Gram's longtime idol Merle Haggard, who had been grinding out shit-kickin', pure-blooded country hits from his outpost in Bakersfield for years now, hitting big with tracks like "Sing Me Back Home" and the hilarious anti-hippie rant "Okie from Muskogee."

While Keith was caught tight in Rolling Stones commitments, family troubles, and his own self-indulgences, Merle was easy to access, having recently begun taking on clients at his personal studio just up the freeway. Tickner and Ostin pulled a series of strings and set up a meeting between Gram and his hero, sending Gretchen and Gram up north for a few days to do a trial run with Haggard.

What might have been a catastrophe was an unexpected good time. Haggard, who had no patience for longhaired kids playing at cowboy, fell, at least slightly, for Gram's formidable charm. Merle was impressed with Gram's knowledge of country music, with his manners, with his pretty little wife who kept herself quiet, and with those Snively fingers that really could play the hell out of the studio's baby grand. Gram may have been just a little boy, gone puffy with drugs and drink, but Haggard softened when he witnessed Gram's love for music and was willing, in some sweet place in his hardened honky-tonk heart, to give the kid a chance.

Gram was elated. He called Emmylou, Rick, Chris, everyone who might remotely care, to tell them the good news. Merle Haggard, the original outlaw, had agreed to produce Gram's record, had given Gram a final and undeniable seal of approval. Things, at long last, seemed hopeful, a darkness and dread lifting. Gram was

Phil Kaufman Interview #1
Interview by Jessica Hundley

Former convict, stuntman, and "executive nanny" to the stars, Phil Kaufman first met Gram while giving the Rolling Stones a ride home from LAX in 1969. Over the next few years he would serve as tour manager, advice giver, and, ultimately, protector, extricating Gram from more than a few tight jams and providing shelter through the various emotional storms that plagued Gram's final years.

Q: Do you remember how you first met Gram?

A: I got a call from a friend of mine who told me that the Rolling Stones were coming to LA. They were just finishing an album and they needed someone to look after them, you know, do things like driving them around, answering the phones, doing security. That's how I got into it. My first day in the music business, I came home with a car and all this money and my girlfriend thought I was going back to prison. That was how it all started. Gram had flown in with Keith Richards and Anita Pallenberg. When I first met him I thought he was a pain in the ass. It was a typically hot LA day and when they flew in, when I picked them up with Mick and Marianne with a limo, Gram said he was staying at a friend's. He asked me to take him there and I was pissed. I wanted to hang out with the big guys, you know? I didn't want to hang out with this guy with crushed velour pants and sissy scarves. And then on the way there he borrowed twenty bucks from me for a six-pack.

Q: How did he end up charming you?

A: He would show up to hang out with the Stones and I realized quickly that he wasn't just some loser groupie, he was their equal. Gram introduced us all to country music. We went and bought thousands of dollars worth of records and then we'd go up to the house and Gram would tell us to put on a certain record and a certain track and he would go, "Now, that's Buck Owens and that's George Jones and that guitar player is—whoever." And

Keith would listen to the licks and Mick would listen to the lyrics and we did that for several days. I got inundated in country music until I was up to my chaps in it. Then I took a liking to him and we became friends. Then Gram called and asked if I would be his road manager. I didn't know what the hell that was. You have to realize, today a tour manager has email, he has a cell phone, and he has a fax machine and a credit card. Then, a road manager has a roll of quarters and a yellow legal pad and a pencil—if he was lucky. You learn your trade on the job, there's no Remedial Road-Managing 101. Most of the guys were frustrated musicians themselves, and they figured they'd make more money as roadies than they ever would as musicians. It was kind of a natural progression.

Q: You were the road manager for the Burritos' infamous train tour.

A: Yes. I learned right away that they required a lot of assistance. It was the kind of thing where they would need wheelchairs at airports, that sort of thing. It was like being a housemother. We always say "Remember the sixties, when drugs were our friends?" It was very naïve, but that's what we thought. We thought we could handle it. Drugs were everywhere. And the dumb died young.

going to be given a real chance to show what he could do, to spill out all the music he had been storing inside himself all along.

But before things could move forward, they went sour. After a long and bitter denouement, Haggard's marriage to Bonnie Owens went south, Owens kicking him out of their lux Bakersfield home, Haggard digging himself into a cheap room at the Holiday Inn and throwing away the key. No one could rouse him for weeks. Haggard opened the door only for the liquor-store deliveryman, soaking up booze like a dry towel. He was impossible to reach, impossible to reason with, let alone work with.

Gram's potential producer was suddenly buried deep in a depression that didn't look as if it was going to lift for some time. The news hit Gram with a blunt, openhanded blow. Once again things had stalled, and he blamed everyone and everything around him, another chance blown, another door closed.

He and Gretchen were at each other's throats, Phil Kaufman finally stepping in to separate them, moving Gram into the Roosevelt Hotel in Hollywood and guarding the door against bottles of Jack Daniels and stray hits of smack. Gram paced the room, furious, miserable, alternately kicking the wall and leaning against it in paralyzed self-pity.

Rick Grech got the news in England and told Gram to come and see him again, hoping another infusion of outdoor jamming and an early English spring could heal the wounds. Gram agreed, flying back over the Atlantic in May of 1972, another year already begun and nothing to show for it.

Grech realized almost as soon as Gram arrived that there would be no taking care of him. They played together, did the same things they had done the previous summer, but there was less feeling in it. Gram was hollowed out by disappointment and the heroin he was using again. The needle was in his arm more often than the guitar was in his hands.

The other musicians Grech had gathered around, all hoping to take a stab at recording the magic that had occured the year before, saw the inevitable. One member of the group, Sam Hutt, was a medical doctor turned rock 'n' roller. Hutt had met Gram before and liked him enough to tell him the truth. Gram had to get it together, and they could all forget about recording until Gram decided to take the good doctor's advice.

Not long after landing in England, Gram found himself on a plane again, heading west and feeling foolish, his pride hurt just enough to make him stubborn. He didn't sleep. Instead, he threw his drugs down the toilet somewhere over the Atlantic, looked out over the patchwork fields of the American Midwest, and gazed down at the brown wound of the Southwest deserts. By the time he touched down in LA, another idea was born, another rush of hope and adrenaline running through his veins.

The next morning, fresh from his first night of clean-blooded sleep since longer than he could remember, Gram called up Eddie Tickner and told him his plans. He was going to produce the record himself, and he was going to hire the best band in the land to play with him as studio support, Elvis's backing lineup, and he would use his Snively trust fund as the lure.

It didn't take long for things to fall into place. Tickner was smart with money, and Gram had more than enough of it to spare. Drummer Ronnie Tutt, legendary pianist Glen D. Hardin, and guitarist James Burton had been playing with Elvis for years, but all were studio musicians for hire and were more than ready to try something new if the price was right.

As the contracts were cleared, Gram sent word to Grech to get his ass to California, and he called up Emmylou. It had now been nearly a year since that night in DC, but everything about their time together was still fresh in his mind. He told her that a ticket was in the mail. A few weeks later, word came that the band had agreed to the terms and were ready to record as soon as their touring contract with Elvis was up.

Tickner, anxious to get things off on the right foot, arranged for Rick (who had just arrived from England) and Gram to head out to meet the players during the last weeks of the King's Vegas run. A few debauched days later, Gram arrived back at the Chateau

Bright Eyes Interview
Interview by Jessica Hundley

Adored by fans and critics alike, Conor Oberst, a.k.a. Bright Eyes, has founded an immensely successful record label, produced several incredible albums, and wowed audiences around the world with his blend of folk and distortion, raw emotion and unforgettable lyrical intensity. Enlisting a bevy of fine vocalists to accompany him on his 2004 release *I'm Wide Awake, It's Morning*, Oberst held the Parsons torch aloft, infusing his songs with country rock twang and pairing his own distinct voice with that of Gram's dear friend, Emmylou Harris.

Q: What made you decide to ask Emmylou Harris to sing with you on your *I'm Wide Awake, It's Morning* album?

A: I had a wish list, I was looking for a particular sound, something that would really bring the songs to another level. She was my first choice. I've always loved her singing. I knew her stuff and I loved the way she sang with Gram, the way the two voices worked together. So I managed to get some of my music to her and she agreed. I couldn't believe it. She came to the studio and she was just such an angel, you know? And when she started singing—my words, my songs—I kind of had to go out into the hallway, it was so overwhelming. I had to go take a deep breath and get it together. After that it was easy. She told me we had a "nice blend." Knowing the other people she's sung with, that was a huge compliment.

Q: It's interesting because in a lot of ways your voice is reminiscent of Gram's. It has that same crack and ache in it.

A: God, he's got a beautiful voice. So many beautiful songs too. It's kind of amazing that he wrote so much in so little time.

Q: Part of that ache and that beauty came from his sadness. It's nice to see that tradition carried on, but without that self-destructiveness.

A: Yeah, I feel pretty good. I'd say I've got my chin above the water.

with a good feeling in his gut and the start of a new song in his head, a giddy, rambunctious travel song titled "Ooh Las Vegas."

By the time Emmylou arrived, bringing along not much more than some clothes and her guitar, things at the bungalow had kicked into high gear. It was summer, and the bougainvillea was bright and blooming, the pool was filled with starlets in tiny bikinis, and aging actors sipped cognacs in the courtyard. Gram invited everyone to stay as long as they liked, and there was an endless, blurred cycle of rehearsals, songwriting, singing, drinking, dope smoking, and good vibes.

With Gram's energy up and his outlook better than ever, it seemed only fitting that tragedy would strike. On July 6, Brandon De Wilde died in a car accident on his way to a film shoot. It was harsh news for Gram. Brandon had given Gram the key to the city, initiated his LA experience. He had been responsible, in large part, for everything important in Gram's life, including Nancy and little Polly.

Gram's grief lifted slightly when he and Gretchen found a pretty little house in the sanctuary of Laurel Canyon, a wood cottage perched not far from the mountaintop and the intersection of Mulholland and Laurel. The party continued in the living room there and out into the terraced backyard, the music coming from everywhere. Despite De Wilde's death, Gram was happier than he had been since England the year before. New songs were evolving, and old songs were injected with new life, transformed by Emmylou's harmonies and the stellar playing of Grech and Elvis's boys.

The band booked sessions at Wally Heider studios for September, the group ready to lay down on vinyl everything they had been brewing up together. But just a few days before the recording was about to begin, Grech doubled over at the breakfast table, the victim of a massive kidney stone. While he healed in an LA hospital room, Gram and the band went on without him, unable to stop the momentum despite the loss of a favorite bandmate.

Emmylou kept things balanced, adding both her incredible voice and a much-needed equilibrium to the proceedings, a woman's soft touch to what might have been a boys' club brawl. Burton, Hardin, and Tutt were Nashville-hardened veterans of countless sessions with Elvis himself and a number of other country and rock 'n' roll legends. Around Emmylou, however, they softened, didn't think to pull rank. They were just happy to be taking direction from Gram, happy to be playing his songs, which were familiar but just deviant enough to be pleasingly rebellious.

Grech's illness finally subsided toward the end of the scheduled recording time. He came by the studio, frail and enthusiastic, adding enough of himself to the final mix to feel a part of it. Gram finished the last tracks increasingly optimistic, thrilled at the performance from his hired hands, and incredibly excited by the collaboration with Emmylou. The sound of their two voices together could cut you clean through.

The relationship between Gram and his new backup singer had, however, put a strain on his new marriage. Gretchen was not at all happy that her husband was spending the bulk of his time in an intense creative give-and-take with another woman. On visits to the studio, she would watch the two of them singing together, see clearly the connection between them, and no amount of protesting from Gram could subdue the blossoming of a green and poisonous envy.

Almost as soon as the album was finished, Gram lapsed back into debauchery, music-making his only defense against his addictions, his pride the thin barrier that had kept him relatively sober in front of Burton and the boys. Once they had all departed for another tour with Elvis, Gram fell back into his old bad behavior, unable to stop the momentum once it began.

At a Christmas party at Chris Hillman's, years of strain finally snapped the last weakened link between Gram and his friend. Gram was drunk, too drunk, belligerent, and condescending, his upper-class breeding showing an ugly side. He made snooty comments and showed an unbridled arrogance, insecurity and tact vanishing with every glass.

By midnight Gram was intolerable, loud, and swaying. Chris

Willie Nelson Interview
Interview by Shirley Halperin

Songwriter, movie star, country music legend, and Original Outlaw, Willie Nelson is perhaps one of the best-loved musicians of the past half-century. By introducing long hair and wild times to staid country tradition, Nelson helped to usher in the age of the Outlaw, a new style of Americana that matched hard-time lyrics with a hard-living ethos.

Q: Are you a Gram fan?

A: Very much so, yes.

Q: Can you tell me a little bit about what you like about his music and did you guys know each other? Did you ever cross paths?

A: Not that I know of. Emmylou and I are great friends, we've known each other for years. I know that she had that connection there and we've talked about it a little bit. But I've heard his songs and his music and he was incredible.

Q: He died before the Outlaw scene really broke, but do you think he should be included in that scene? And do you think his music has an influence on what's happening today?

A: I think you can hear a lot of his sound in the music you hear today. A lot of what you're hearing today, it reminds me a lot of Gram Parsons's stuff. His music was a real link between country, rock 'n' roll, blues, that whole thing.

Q: Would you consider him an "original outlaw," along with you and Waylon?

A: Oh yeah. Absolutely. No problem there. I didn't know him personally, but I knew a lot of the people who did know him. I know the Mangler, Phil Kaufman, who managed Emmylou for a long time. Phil was the one who stole Gram's body.

Q: Do you have any favorite songs?

A: I like all of them. I actually was thinking of doing some songs of his, going into the studio, bringing down Emmylou and covering some songs off his albums. I'd really like to do that, next time I'm in the studio. But yeah, he was an outlaw, alright. No doubt about it.

had finally had enough. Grabbing his former bandmate by the collar, Hillman opened the door and threw Gram forcefully out of the party, closing the door in his face and effectively writing him out of his life.

The humiliation of the incident and the truth of Gram's own sloppy indiscretions burned him to the core. He came to the bitter realization that he was becoming his mother, drowning out reality with midmorning cocktails, becoming stupid and clumsy, and embarrassing everyone with his helplessness. He tried his best to wait until the afternoon before his first tequila, tried to keep some sort of control, still refusing to completely admit that liquor was destroying him in the same way it had destroyed other members of his family.

He stayed sober for his visits to Polly, trying his best to watch his daughter's growth attentively, to watch her go from infant to child with a clear head, to commit every moment to memory. She was five now and beautiful, with Gram's full cheeks and sweet smile.

When the new album, entitled *GP*, was finally released in January 1973, Mo Ostin was impressed enough with what Gram had produced in the studio to agree to a national tour. Rehearsals began at Phil Kaufman's ramshackle house in the Valley, Gram gathering Rick and Emmylou and a backup crew for the traveling band. In the late afternoon, Phil would make enormous pots of chili to feed everyone, the band playing far into the evening, neighbors complaining, and Gram feeling content.

Slowly the group was beginning to gel enough to impress themselves and the label, which sprang for an old tour bus, emblazoned with the group's new name, a moniker born of all-night jams and early-morning regrets. "The Fallen Angels" were ready to depart by early spring, the whole motley crew sent off in style with a huge, clamorous gathering at Kaufman's, the bus allowing barely enough room for equipment, the roadies, and Gretchen, who would be damned if she was going let Gram and Emmylou spend even a minute alone.

The bus lurched out of town, belching exhaust. A fender-bender in a motel parking lot the first night of the tour set the tone for the rest of the journey. The trip was a rambling, ill-organized affair, Gram barely able to play through what had been nearly a week-long drunk. But as the miles rolled by, the Angels got tighter and tighter, Gram sobering up as they traveled farther east, and each show was a bit better than the last.

When they weren't playing, the band was joining Gram in a daily round of drugs and alcohol. Emmylou, the only clean one in the bunch, watched the chaos with a bewildered and maternal eye. When Gram bothered, he and Gretchen would battle over some misunderstanding or other, upsetting hotel managers and their bandmates with the violence and bitterness of their disputes.

It was high drama and rock debauchery, but Gram was having a ball despite everything and was determined to make it to New York and win over at least a few new fans. By the time they hit the Atlantic coast, he'd done just that, seduced a trail of wide-eyed kids in towns across the country, he and Emmylou finding a sweet groove and sticking with it, blending their voices into moments of undeniable magic and bone-shiver beauty.

Here and there the kids heard the message he was spreading. Slowly but surely there would be starry-eyed boys and girls in the front rows and waiting backstage with gifts and gushing admiration. In Boston a young poet named Tom Brown presented Gram with a poem he had written in his honor, a liquid-eyed portrait of Gram that spawned a melancholy observation on the "truckers and the kickers and the cowboy angels."

Gram was flattered and touched, immediately setting the lyrics to music, writing a song with Emmylou that would eventually bear the poem's title, "Grievous Angel." In New York, Gram and Emmylou charmed the hosts of various radio shows and played a string of nights at Max's Kansas City. Their opening act for the residency was from New Jersey, a band called the Quacky Duck that included Tony Bennett's son, Danny, and David Mansfield, who would go on to play with Dylan.

Fallen Angels interview.
ALL PHOTOS BY
KIM GOTTLEIB-WALKER.

OOOH – LAS VEGAS ~~Out of me~~ Sure gonna make a wreck
I said oooh Las Vegas sure gonna make a wreck
~~out of me~~
~~Everytime~~

OOOH LAS VEGAS – Ain't no place for a poor boy like
me — (Repeat) –
Everytime I hit ~~the~~ your crystal city — ~~your~~
you're ~~sure~~ gonna make a wreck out of me –

① 1st time I lose I drink whiskey –
2nd time " " " " gin –
3rd time " " " " anything 'cause
I think that I'm gonna win –

Ⓧ Ooh Las Vegas Please don't drag me
beneath your marble floor
I said ooh Las Vegas — not the first
time that you've bounced me out your
door –
~~& think~~ you think that I'm a loser –
& you know that I'll be comin' back for more –

② Queen of Spades is a friend of mine
Queen of Hearts is a bitch
One day when I make up my mind
I know they'll make me rich

(Back to top –)

Pages of Gram's journal, 1972.
COURTESY OF JEFF GOLD /
www.recordmecca.com.

SNA
Fold
SNAPS

(or – who stole the brandy?)

"Royal Jelly"

Love medicine
the only important thing is
what the bottle looks like...
could marry...hallelujah...
brothers + sisters too much time to
But it takes too much time
and
When I'm 200 yrs. old
I must be careful
I can't tell you
How ugly I'll be then
200 yrs old from now — 200 yrs. from
magician   now.
I'll be a magician

TA·TA·TA·TA !

And I can't find
out in what hotel I'm
dying...

makes sense

>OO

③ ① THE
      2 SNAPS THROUGH. JUST
      ONE SIDE

      THE 2 LEVI BUTTONS TROUGH
      ENTIRE JOB.

SNAPS

"RED VELVET"

Purple Pillows Paisley Sheets + A RED VELVET

BED SPREAD — Kitchen's filthy — BEER FOR

BREAKFAST — HARDER TIMES AHEAD!

Smokin' cigaretts for My TENNESEE

My DEAR OLD HOME — HOPE THEY KEEP

IT — ? FARMS + (SWEET) MEMORIES. — NICE PLACE

ALL YEAR ROUND — (SORT OF LIKE ENGLAND)?   TALK +
                                            (DRIFTING)
A tall SAD COUNTRY SINGER WAS PRAYIN' FOR TA' DAY,

WHEN PEACE WOULD COME SO EVERYONE'D BE LIVING

HIS OWN WAY / Still it WAS an old man who told
who raised me from a kid
who taught me the real truth — a good old friend of mine

who I knew in my youth.
this old man understood

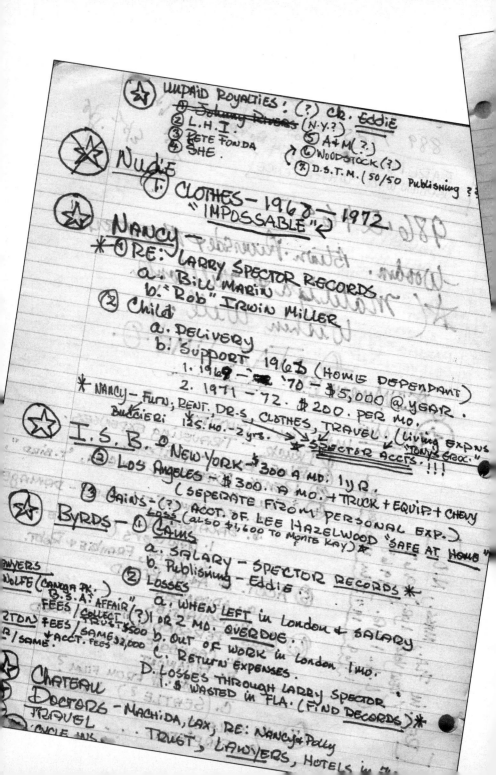

(☆) UNPAID ROYALTIES: (?) Ch. Eddie
① ~~Johnny Rivers~~ (N.Y.?) ⑤ A+M (?)
② L.H.I.
③ PETE FONDA ⑥ WOODSTOCK (?)
④ SHE. ⑦ D.S.T.M. (50/50 Publishing ?)

(✳) NUDE
① CLOTHES — 1968 — 1972
"IMPOSSABLE"?

(☆) NANCY —
*① RE: LARRY SPECTOR RECORDS
   a. BILL MARIN
   b. "ROB" IRWIN MILLER
② Child
   a. DELIVERY
   b. SUPPORT 1968 (HOME DEPENDANT)
      1. 1969 — '70 — $5,000 @ YEAR.
      2. 1971 — 72. $200. PER MO.
* NANCY — FURN, RENT. DR.s, CLOTHES, TRAVEL. (LIVING EXPNS
   BUTCIERI ½5. MO. - 2 yrs. → ⟶ "TONY'S GROC."
                          * SPECTOR ACCTS. !!!

(☆) I.S.B. ① NEW YORK - $300 A MO. 1 YR.
② LOS ANGELES — $300. A MO. + TRUCK + EQUIP + CHEVY
③ GAINS - (?) (SEPERATE FROM PERSONAL EXP.)
   LOSS (also $1,600 to MONTE KAY) *
(☆) BYRDS — ① GAINS   ⟵ ACCT. OF LEE HAZELWOOD "SAFE AT HOME"
   a. SALARY — SPECTOR RECORDS *
   b. PUBLISHING — EDDIE
② LOSSES
   a. WHEN LEFT in London + SALARY
      1 OR 2 MO. OVERDUE.
   b. OUT OF WORK in London 1 MO.
   c. RETURN EXPENSES.
   D. LOSSES THROUGH LARRY SPECTOR
      $ WASTED in FLA. (FIND RECORDS) *

LAWYERS
WOLFE (CANOGA PK.)
"B.S.A. AFFAIR" (?)
FEES / COLLECT
2TDN) FEES / TRUST $500
R / SAME.   + ACCT. FEES $2,000
           SAME $32,000

(☆) CHATEAU
DOCTORS - MACHIDA, LAX, RE: NANCY + POLLY
TRAVEL . . . TRUST, LAWYERS, HOTELS in ~
CYCLE INS.

A VAGUE
2-DIMENSIONAL **PART ①**
SYNOPSIS
ON THE BEGINNING OF.....

FROM A SCRIPT TITLED SIMPLY:

SEE PEARLBUCK

HIGH FIGURE
TIME-CONTROL   } HE ACHIEVES THE WISH
ART - LEGEND   } ≯ THE SPACE-TIME FREAK ~
≯ THE ~~ONE~~ "MAN"   } ≯ THIS COULD HAPPEN TO ANYONE !!

A.   ACTS
     I. SEE ≯ FEEL TING
        IMAGINATIONS
    II. PEODLE ≯ LIFE (BASICS)
        PERIOD ≯ GOVT.
   III. BASICS CHANGE ~ FAITH
        FREE SPIRITS - MAGIC

B. TIME SHIFT - DREAM O.D. ≟ THE HUMP "CRYING WOMAN"
   I. THE CLIFF ~ THE MONASTARY
  II. GRASS GROWS ~ CAVES EXPLORED
 III. FINALLY LOVE ≯ 2 children

C. SECRET PLAN - DANGER FROM REVOLUTION
                 ≯ OCCASIONAL TROOPS ETC (Hong Kong ?)

1. HUGE BUNDLE OF GRASS so ROTTEN
2. CAUGHT COMING UP CLIFF.
   SCARED SHITLESS (FARMERS VS. IMPERIAL HORSEMEN) bu
   THEY ESCAPE DOWN THE GREAT CLIFF.
   HIS FRIEND SHOT - HE TAKES FAMILY BACK UP TO
   VILLAGE - CREATS PULLY ≯ ROPE DEVICE TO MAKE
   QUICK DECENTS ≯ CARRY MATERIAL TO
   COMPLETE MONASTARY ≯ CHAPEL ABOVE THE
   HIGHST WATER LINE ONTHE GREAT CLIFF STILL HANGIN
   THOUSANDS OF FEET BELOW THE EDGE - INVISABLE FROM THE

Elvis Costello Interview
Interview by Polly Parsons

Elvis Costello has been making great music for the past twenty-five years, from his amazing collaborations with his band, the Attractions, to his more recent partnerships with Burt Bacharach, Paul McCartney, and with his wife, jazz great Diana Krall. A much beloved singer-songwriter, Costello's unique sound has inspired an astounding list of performers to cover his work, including George Jones, Chet Baker, Johnny Cash, Roy Orbison, and No Doubt. Elvis Costello and the Attractions were inducted into the Rock and Roll Hall of Fame in 2003.

A: Can you tell me the evolution of how you found Gram?

Q: I started out like everybody started out, playing different kinds of music that they loved. I grew up with all the mixture of music of the 1960s. Like most people my age at the time, the Beatles were a very big thing and then all of the music that came out in America. We got it sometimes a few weeks later than they got it in America, but eventually it filtered over obviously. Every group that came over was compared to the Beatles and so were the Byrds. I was very smitten with that band, with the sound they made, and I followed the group as they changed and evolved. When Gram joined the Byrds I didn't know completely what it was but there was a sudden change that had come over the group. And at first, you know, like anybody who had liked a group and then they changed, you're sort of a bit startled. Bear in mind that country music was pretty obscure to people growing up in England. Country records that tended to make the charts were somewhat novelties, even Johnny Cash's songs. They weren't always the really great songs that I got to know later. So when I first heard Gram singing and the influence it had on the Byrds' direction at that point—it was to take a deep breath and "What's all this music? Who's this Merle Haggard?" I then fell in love with that *Rodeo* record. So naturally when he left the group, the Burritos was the next thing, I had to hear that and so it went on and while I was making my first steps to playing music, I would listen to all these records. I didn't have a big collection of records, but I had some of the records I had grown up with, the ones that had a big impact on me, a lot of them were American records. So there was *The Gilded Palace of Sin* and things like that that gave me a different sense of the history of the music than just what was in the charts. I carried along with that way of thinking the next couple of years. I tried to learn off everybody that I listened to and I came to London in 1972 and by now I was playing in groups and we listened to a pretty wide range of music. We liked country music. We didn't get it firsthand, but rather as others had interpreted it. That made it hipper to us because we didn't really get what was great about some of the originals at first, you know? With Gram it was twofold. You've got a really great songwriter and song interpreter. He's got a sense of the continuity of the history, but he's trying to do something original with it.

Q: I think there are parallels between you and my father and how incredibly unapologetic you are about influences and how strong your commitment is to the music you love. Last night I was listening to your album *Almost Blue* and it was an extremely cathartic moment for me because I've heard it many, many times before but I heard it last night as sort of an answering call to *GP* and the *Grievous Angel*. It felt very personal to me from you.

A: That's a great compliment because what happened with that album was listening over and over to your dad's music, particularly to *Gilded Palace of Sin*. I loved the songs off that. I remember one of my favorite records growing up was *I Never Loved a Man the Way I Love You*, the album. Now that's the album that contained "Do Right Woman," and I also liked Percy Sledge, who had done "Dark End of the Street," and suddenly to hear somebody now who's mixing up the music, like your father? I think of somebody who I'm sure your father would have admired is Dan Penn, who is one of the great unsung heroes of American music because he is writing exactly where country and soul meet, you know? He wrote "Dark End of the Street," he wrote "Do Right Woman," and I imagine that was very inspiring to Gram, because you always try to imagine how he got to the place he was. And in the same way as I love Dan Penn songs, so it came that I started to think that maybe I could write something that has all the music that I love, all that stuff in it. Not every song that I wrote lives that out but some of it does. I remember going to a secondhand record store that dealt with a lot of import records. Like I said there wasn't a lot of American music playing on the radio. Disc jockeys would seek it out and buy all the copies that would come into the country and they were expensive. Consequently because they were expensive, they were like currency. People would absorb them then they would sell them. There I was going through this stack of records, I was looking though this big rack of records and some of them weren't in sleeves and there it was, *GP*. I'd heard about it but I'd never seen it. You couldn't get it in England and there it was! I had it in its original sleeve, with the gatefold with the semi-truck picture and everything. I couldn't believe it, it was in good condition, a brand new LP and I took it home and put it on and of course it was different. There was more of a self-conscious, sad feeling, like the flip side of *Gilded Palace of Sin*. This was a lot more straight ahead, this was very legit sounding, it sounded really legit. It took a moment to get used to it, "oh this is the guy that changed the Byrds." I'm starting to pick up who these players are, now he's gone and got himself a real band. Not that the Burritos weren't a real band, but he's gone and got the guys off the albums he likes. It was amazing.

Q: And you were making your own music at this time?

A: I had a band and it wasn't very good, but we did what music we loved. We took our musical cues from the Band, the Burritos. It was our homegrown version of that. I have to credit your father for inspiring that curiosity in this music, because we didn't get the opportunity to hear the best of it and by the time I went to America for the first time in 1970, I was plundering every record store I could get. By then I want every George Jones record I can get my hands on. I want everything. You could pick them up for nothing. They were really cheap and I would come home with a suitcase of every kind of music, R&B, country, blues, jazz, and there were so many riches there, everything to learn. My musical education tripled or quintupled in about four or five years, up until I recorded the album, *Almost Blue*, which was the most advert expression of the love of another style of music, because I didn't even bother to write the songs, I just did other people's. I did "Hot Burrito #1" and I called it "I'm Your Toy" because, taking it outside of the context of it being performed by the Burritos, it seemed to be too beautiful a song to have that title. It needed to have a title that would communicate to everybody, so I took the liberty of renaming it because I thought the song deserved it. I recorded *Almost Blue* because I was in an impasse in my emotional life that I don't suppose I had the honesty to get at in my own words. So I used other people's words to get at how I was feeling.

Q: Is that what you identify with, with my father, the honesty?

A: Yes. The theme of shame and guilt which runs through so much of country music was especially strong in my life. I think most of the people that I value in music try to do the very best with whatever their idea is at that moment. And that can be their focus and their curiosity and their passion for different threads of music as they interweave and offer us new possibilities all the time. That changes all the time too, because a new experience broadens it and you live a little but longer and understand. So I listen to *Almost Blue* now and think how young I was. I was only twenty-five when I recorded that record. I sounded much bolder-headed than I actually was.

Q: If Gram Parsons was sitting right here, what would you guys talk about?

A: I generally find that when somebody's got a sense of the history of music, you usually start talking about those great old records. I think that, with somebody like your father, who came out of a lot of that old music and then made something of his own, it was quite different and didn't fit in as well, it didn't fit in with what Nashville wanted to be. You could only hope that you could have a conversation about all the great records that you loved, all the little sidetracks that make it rich. And that's including appreciating the people that, I think his example taught me that, you shouldn't be skeptical about. People who are thoroughly in the mainstream of their time, not today's music scene but the music scene of the 1960s. You weren't necessarily looking for everybody to be, what they called "counterculture." Your father was the guide that opened a whole bunch of people up to the beauty in that stuff and it's why I am driving around now in Los Angeles with "No Reason To Quit" by Merle Haggard on my car stereo, because I wouldn't have even known how good Merle Haggard was, you know, if I hadn't looked beyond some of the clichéd ideas we had in England. That was the really cool thing. There were other people who took up the thread of this love of music and did other things with it. There are other people, there are other artists, but it's the first person that does it that you have to credit the most. It's the boldness and the vividness of the idea and also to use it as the foundation for writing some really beautiful songs. They're very timeless, Gram's songs. I remember it was 1982, I had very nice things happen to me, because just in the same way I got turned on to this trail of music, I would have people come up to me and say "Thank you for turning me on to so-and-so"—as if I was somehow responsible for those records being made, simply because I had covered one of the songs that had mattered a lot and inspired curiosity in other people. You know, there's always a flame being kept for your father's music, somebody's always digging it. It's great music in that it's young, in that there's something that's timeless. The lessons in it, the freedom and the boldness of it. Your father's records will always sound great, they're never going to be dated. They're always going to sound like great records and they're never going to go out of style, for one thing because they were never "in style" in a trivial way. They were always pure and they were always honest and in the end, that's what truly lasts.

Quacky had been born of a shared enthusiasm for bands like Poco, Buffalo Springfield, and, particularly, Gram himself. The kids from Jersey were absolutely enamored of his music, seduced by the Sub Band, the Burrito Brothers, and Gram's work with the Byrds. They were breathless and thrilled to be sharing the bill with him, and the adoration did Gram good—made him feel that someone, somewhere had been listening.

By the time the band pulled back into LA, the relationship between Gram and Emmylou had solidified into mutual respect. The remaining months of 1972 were spent at the house in Laurel Canyon, working out new songs, sharing lyrics, and constructing complex, utterly lovely vocal harmonies.

Meanwhile, Gram realized that he was slowly drifting away from Gretchen. In an attempt to find some ballast in their thunderstorm of a relationship, he decided to take his stepfather up on an invitation for a sailing trip to the West Indies. The couple packed their bags and took off for the tropics in the early spring of 1973.

As soon as he and Gretchen boarded the boat, however, Gram realized his mistake. A weeklong trip with Bob Parsons, shut up together on a tiny yacht with little opportunity for escape or respite, was not necessarily one of his better ideas. He was still doing drugs frequently, not an easy feat with his stepdad watching every move. Gretchen was moody and, worse, not at all keen to spend time with Bob, who she found to be an insufferable sleazeball.

Things came to an ugly head one night after a bout of hard drinking on both Gram's and his stepfather's part. Some deeply buried guilt had been slowly simmering up to the surface, Bob talking of Gram's mother with bitter tears, Gram devastated at the mention of her name. He was embarrassed by Parsons's emotional remorse and his stepfather's confession that he felt he hadn't done enough to save her. He told Gram, tearfully, that he hadn't had the strength to stop her from drinking, had helped her even, smuggling in liquor bottles to the hospital and mixing up drinks when she had begged for them.

Gram and Gretchen returned with what was left of their relationship in tatters. They avoided each other, Gram spending his
days at Kaufman's house, sleeping in a shabby room above the
garage, staying in bed until the sun was low, getting up only to
make music and to drink. Kaufman did his best to keep the harder
drugs at bay, but there was a darkness in Gram that was spreading,
a feeling of desperation, and a sad empty space widening inside
him. However, by midsummer he'd written several new songs,
which were touched with a nostalgic melancholy, as if he were
deliberately pushing at the sore spots, refusing to allow his emotional wounds to scab and heal.

In July, Gram got news that Clarence White had been killed, hit
by a drunk driver, dead instantly, another friend gone before his
time. The funeral was packed and stifling; Gram stayed outside for
much of it, smoking on the church steps and pacing nervously.

At the graveside he felt sick in his guts and sad to the core.
Clarence had played guitar like no one else, had given everything
when he played, and some bastard had plowed him down and
grabbed him from his friends, his wife, and his kids. What was the
sense of it?

As the casket was lowered, Gram started to sing an old hymn.
After a moment, other voices joined in, bringing power to the
chorus. Clarence was put in the ground while the people he loved
sung for him, filled their lungs with their grief.

Later that night Gram sat on Kaufman's porch and wept into
his whiskey. He'd had enough of death, of dying, of the false
pageantry of funerals, the sad procession of mourners, everything
done to console the living without consideration for the desires of
the dead. Clarence would not have wanted all the pomp and cir-
cumstance. He would have wanted a song, and that was what
Gram had tried to give him.

Somewhere a police siren tore open the night. Gram poured
another glass and looked hard at Kaufman. He told him to make
him a promise, to swear that if Gram should die there would be
none of the bullshit. He didn't want a funeral, didn't want Bob

Jonathan Richman Interview
Interview by Christian Bruno

Jonathan Richman began his music career in the early 1970s with his band the Modern Lovers, whose sound foreshadowed the pop-punk era to come. Beloved by a dedicated fan base, Richman continues to make utterly imaginative music. He first met Gram when he was nineteen years old.

Q: You met Gram in southern California. How did you end up there, what year was it?

A: In 1972 Warner Brothers and A&M Records wanted to offer my band a chance to try out their studios, because they both were interested in our band.

Q: What was the band?

A: The Modern Lovers. And we also didn't have a manager at this time so they were trying to show us studios and they knew they would eventually rather deal with a manager than four twenty-one-year-old boys. I was only twenty, in fact. So they had several different people come out and one of them was Eddie Tickner, who managed Gram Parsons and later managed Etta James, and he had managed the Byrds. They had "Mr. Tambourine Man," so he was my favorite. The other guys weren't sure who they wanted. I was sure I wanted Eddie Tickner. And his right-hand man was Phil Kaufman, who was my favorite too.

Q: What was it about those two that you liked?

A: I just trusted them. And they were fun and I just liked the way they talked. Eddie Tickner, when we finally moved out the next year, in 1973, we still didn't have a manager but we signed with Warner and I still wanted Eddie Tickner to be our manager. But by this point I think the other three had determined they wanted someone else to be our manager. Anyway, we would all go over to Phil Kaufman's house all the time.

Q: What was it like there?

A: Phil Kaufman's house was out in Van Nuys. They had great parties. Phil Kaufman would cook up these giant ten-gallon pots of chili. And he loved parties and there would be everybody at these parties. These parties would have solid fifty to a hundred people. That was just the people, then there would be another twenty or thirty dogs. Great Danes and all kinds of different dogs. And Gram would be there since he lived in the back shed. So he was always there. And I got to meet Gram and talk to him. And one of the things that happened then was Warner Brothers was still looking for managers for us, so some management firm thought up a show, having us open for Tower of Power and Lean Michaels. It was 1973 at this place called the Swing Auditorium in San Bernardino. Friday night. It was really not our crowd. Which was fine with us because we were used to playing not our crowd. This was really, really not our crowd. Gram and Phil Kaufman and Eddie Tickner went along with us, helped us. If it weren't for Phil we wouldn't have gotten a sound check. But we went out and played and the audience truly didn't like us. The person who did like us was Gram Parsons who came back there and told us after-wards. He especially loved the fact that we gave the audience what they didn't want to hear. He loved stuff like that and he and I went out into the crowd afterwards, the big three-thousand-seat audi-torium, looking for people because people were throwing things and booing and stuff. We really weren't what they wanted and no one had heard our brand of crap before so I went out into the audience trying to see if anyone would say anything.

Q: What was that like for you, to meet Gram? Did you know about him before?

A: Yeah, we'd seen him play before. I liked his stuff. I liked him. I mean, he wasn't the legend in his own time, you know. That happened later. To me he was just a fun guy who played music. He was saying "Hey, Jonathan," he was a big fellow, over six feet, two hundred pounds, anyway he'd say, "You want to arm wrestle?" I'd go "Okay, sure." You know he'd say things like that. And, for the record, he would win. Anyway, we'd be sitting around while Gram was recording with the Fallen Angels, talking with James Burton and other musicians. Gram was lots of fun.

Q: Could you describe what he was like at the time? What he looked like and what his attitude was like?

A: He was big. This was about the last year of his life so he was twenty-six. He would play miniature golf. Phil would organize a miniature golf expedition and he could barely move sometimes he would be fucked up enough so that he could barely hit the little golf ball. And we laughed, we thought it was funny. I don't know what he thought of it himself. But his eyes were pretty well bloodshot. And he was a graceful person, but he moved slow.

Q: Graceful in what way, physically graceful?

A: Yeah, and a good lookin' guy. He would roar up in a car screeching to a halt at the gates and stuff like that. He was playing it up, you know. He knew he was fucking up and he was making a bit of a spectacle of it. But we loved him. And the parties at Phil's were amazing, just plain fun. I loved to eat, and there was lots of chili. And there was music, so I'd get to check out this southern California style of music that Gram and his friends would make. A lot of Fender amplifiers, good musicians. They would take us out to the desert to little bars and stuff like that. It was great fun.

Q: Did you find it troublesome to see him get so drunk and drugged up?

A: We were young, I don't think we understood what was happening really. I was thinking he was a little young to be acting that old.

Q: He seemed old?

A: Yeah, he seemed decrepit. And he was. As Phil Kaufman said it, his liver and his kidneys just said "Fuck you." That's what happens when you put every chemical possible, that anyone hands you, into your mouth or into your nose. I would play music with him once in a while.

Q: What was that like?

A: It would've been great if he wasn't shoving stuff up his nose as he was talking to you. So eventually, within ten minutes he already couldn't play anymore. But the first minute or two was amazing. If he'd have lived, he'd have sang on our record. He offered. We probably would've used him on one of our songs. And I offered to play guitar on his record. I knew enough not to offer my froggy singing voice. All I know is, Gram could really sing a sad song. And it was fun. He loved to play. At someone's birthday party he would be there with Emmylou Harris—they would just sing together, like they were pals. Whoever was around liked the music he did. It was good, and they'd sing. He and I would talk about guitars, he was always trying to get me to try out a Fender Telecaster for my sound. I said, "But Gram can you get that old rock and roll sound out of it. Do you think you can?" He said, "I know you can." I had been using a Stratocaster, but I wanted even clearer . . . that sound of surf Fender Jaguar kind of sound, so I was using a Jazzmaster. And it just seemed to have an older more '50s sound even than a Stratocaster somehow just for what I was looking for. And I would use really heavy gauge strings on it. I mean like fourteen for the E string and sixteen for the bass string, you know, and high action.

Q: He felt like the Telecaster could have been a better choice?

A: He was a Telecaster fan. I played one at a music store on his recommendation. It was just a little too distorted. The sound was too raspy for what I was going for. I wanted even more clarity. But Stratocasters, they're all good. He and I would just have little conversations. He recommended the Louvin Brothers to me. He said "You'll really like them." And I think he recommended them because they were honest and sincere, which are qualities that he told me about my own music.

Q: So he felt like there was some kind of honesty that was similar between you and them?

A: That's what he said. So I listened and they sure were good. He probably got me to listen to more country-western and bluegrass music, that's for sure. I became a fan of the Country Gentleman, the group that did "Fox on the Run." He got me thinking about different kinds of music than what I had been listening to before. One of the things that I like about Gram, is that he really wanted to play. He wanted to talk music and play. He would invite me back to his little cabin in the backyard of Phil Kaufman's house and we took out guitars and started playing. I liked that. He didn't waste time. He wanted to, you know, play.

Q: Did that seem unusual to you?

A: No, but it was a relief 'cause people were talking too much.

Q: People were talking business and about music, but not playing music?

A: Yeah, that and they were just talking too much, period. He just wanted to play.

Q: What was his little cabin behind Phil's house like?

A: I was only there a few times so I forget, and all I concentrated on was the guitar chords.

Q: What was your music like at the time?

A: I was starting to get tired of what we were doing. And maybe Gram Parsons had a bigger impact than I had been realizing, now that you mention it, because I was getting into acoustic sounds too. I was just starting to think like that. In fact I was thinking of stuff like Leadbelly and things like this. And I was getting tired of the sound that we had had a few years before. And Gram Parsons is a big player of acoustic instruments, as well as an admirer of the Fender Telecaster. I'm sure that got me thinking too. Because the music he recommended to me, the Louvin Brothers for example, was music made with acoustic instruments in an old-style way. And I liked that. Vocals up front, melody, no fancy twenty minute guitar solos. So, in a way it was a very good time for me to meet him. It might have had a bigger impact on what I did than what I realized until this very minute. Mainly I knew that I liked him and that there was a sad quality to his music, which I liked.

Q: Did he sort of embody that sadness, or did he just feel like he was able to express something in the music that might not have been on his person at that time?

A: Neither. It just felt sad. I didn't bother to figure out why. I had a teeny little influence on him. On the record with "Ooh Las Vegas, ain't no place for a poor boy like me . . ."—right after that last guitar solo by James Burton he was in the mixing lab putting it together and there was a pause necessary, as there is between all songs on a piece of vinyl, and he was saying "How long do you think that pause should be?" He said, "Let's listen." And so I listened, we both agreed, "How about one, two, three . . . there!" I said, "Sounds good to me."

Q: You had uncredited inspiration on the album.

A: Yeah, pacing.

Gram relaxing.
PHOTOS BY ANDEE
COHEN NATHANSON.

Parsons burying him in New Orleans, didn't want the coffin, the priest, or the regrets. What he wanted was to be taken out to the desert, to his beloved Joshua Tree. He wanted a funeral pyre in the warm desert night, a poet's farewell, ashes in the wind.

"I want to go out," Gram said, "in a cloud of dust."

Before August was out, another tragedy struck. A late-night cigarette or maybe the old stove's pilot light set off a burst of flame that took Gram and Gretchen's Laurel Canyon home. The fire burned up everything they had together—clothes, records, Gram's handwritten lyrics sheets, old recording tapes, everything eaten by flames.

The catastrophe marked the unofficial but final death of their marriage, Gram moving the few belongings he had left to Phil's house, filing for divorce, and giving orders to keep Gretchen at bay. In the midst of the chaos, he and the Angels had begun recording again, Gram taking on the role of producer and staying relatively sober, pouring all his worry and lament into the microphone.

Gram and the band had admirers, younger musicians who could clearly see what Gram was trying to do. The boys in Quacky Duck arrived in LA that summer to record an album and spent much of their time holed up with Gram in his tiny room above Phil's garage. Phil himself had started managing a band, the Modern Lovers. Its front man, Jonathan Richman, was only nineteen but hung out with Gram often, watching Angels rehearsals and sitting in on recording sessions.

The Angels were making great music, and Gram knew it, knew all the hurt was seeping out of him and into the songs, and he knew that that was a good thing, a useful catharsis. He and Emmylou were singing beautifully, as always, covering Bordeleaux and Felice Bryant's "Love Hurts" and Walter Egan and Tom Guidera's "Hearts on Fire."

The group laid down the most beautiful version yet of Gram's "Hickory Wind" and turned Tom Brown's poem into magic with "Return of the Grievous Angel." Gram wrote and recorded an original track in honor of Clarence White and Brandon DeWilde, a bittersweet hymnal to death and friendship, a song that eloquently stated what was inside Gram's own head. "In My Hour of Darkness" was, in a way, Gram's own plea for redemption, his own keen desire to keep a firm grip on his life.

> *In my hour of darkness*
> *In my time of need*
> *Oh, Lord grant me vision*
> *Oh, Lord grant me speed*

With Gretchen out of the picture, Gram began searching for a pretty shoulder to cry on, realizing, all too clearly, that he needed a woman to balance him. One afternoon, on a trip to a friend's casting office, he saw a photo of a girl on a desk, an actress maybe. She was gorgeous and young and somehow familiar. He asked for her name, and, within days, Margaret Fisher, his high school girl-friend turned free-love flower child, was being flown down from San Francisco for long, passionate weekends.

By the time the Angels had finished their second album, Gram was exhausted and hollow, but happy too. The experience had been liberating; it was as if all the sadness had been bled from him, the songs like leeches on the skin. He wrote a long letter to his sister, told her to hold on tight, to keep her head up, and to know that he was there for her.

He added that he was well, that he was making the finest music he had ever made, the music he had been hearing in his head since Waycross, since the hot afternoons in the parking lot of the box factory, Coon Dog smiling and smoking hand-rolled cigarettes while the workers played and his only son sang, high and clear. Gram decided to call the record *Sleepless Nights*, in part because he had put everything into it, had drained himself dry.

As fall drew closer, bringing in the dry, warm air from the desert, Gram finally felt ready to celebrate, celebrate everything—the album, the rediscovery of Margaret Fisher, Tom Brown's lyrics, Emmylou's voice, the sun in the sky, and the Santa Ana blowing in mischief.

David Eagle Interview
Interview by Jessica Hundley

In 1973, David Eagle was the road manager of the young New Jersey country rock band Quacky Duck. Enamored of Gram and his music, the group opened for the Fallen Angels in New York and went on to befriend Gram in the last year of his life.

Q: How did you first hear about Gram?

A: Gram and the Burrito Brothers and the Byrds at that time were the groups that we all looked up to. We were a young group, I was nineteen, our youngest member was sixteen, the oldest member of the group was twenty. I was not in the group, I was the road manager. The guys idolized these people like Gram. Then they got the opportunity to open for Gram at Max's Kansas City and I guess it was March of '73. I didn't know who Gram Parsons was at the time, but the guys were so ecstatic that they were getting to open for this guy that they idolized. We got to Max's after the Fallen Angels had already done their sound check. We loaded in, we did our sound check, and then we sat back, just hung out waiting to hear Gram. I remember when the Fallen Angels finally came on they opened up with "We'll Sweep out the Ashes" featuring Emmylou. And I'll never forget it. It's a noisy place, Kansas City, it's not generally a place where a folk singer could come and play. People were clanking dishware and cups and talking, not really paying attention even though they had come to see Gram Parsons. Then Emmylou does her solo and everything stops. I couldn't believe what was coming out of her mouth, it was like the voice of an angel. I'd never heard anything quite like it. It stopped everything in there. The waiters stopped, people stopped talking. There wasn't a sound except for the band playing and her singing. From that moment on everybody was paying attention to this band. We hung out with them from that time on. They were in New York only for a week, but Quacky Duck had a house that we all lived in with our girlfriends and friends, roadies. We invited Gram and the band and Emmylou over to our place. They came over one night for dinner. That's how we got to know Gram.

Q: What were your impressions of him on first meeting him?

A: This was his last year. He was a really nice person. We came out to LA in the summer of '73 to record an album and we would spend time with Gram. He was living above Phil Kaufman's garage. I guess his house had burnt down and Gretchen, his wife—they were either separated or divorced at the time—they weren't seeing each other. We went to visit him a few times in Phil's guesthouse. Our whole group went over and he was there and he had crappy furniture but a really nice stereo system and he had just finished recording his second album and he wanted to play it for us. We were just blown away, he played the test cut of the record, the record was not out yet. I think Poco had an album out at that time and they had on the album one of Gram's songs and he didn't know it. We had just bought the record from Tower, we had it with us and one of the guys said, "Did you know Richie Furay from Poco is singing your music?" We put it on and he cried. He was so moved by the fact that Richie Furay would sing his song and put it on his album, that he cried. He had been telling us a lot about how some of his music publishing had been ripped off by some unscrupulous people and he was warning us to make sure we protected our music publishing. He told us about the situation with Gretchen and why he was living in Phil's guesthouse. The only things he had left was his Jaguar, a white Jaguar, and his guitar and his stereo. That's basically all he had from his other house. So we would hang out with him. He was a very sad person and he was a very kind person. Being in rock 'n' roll, especially in that time period, was a lot about ego and about performing and always being on. Gram was not like that. He loved what he did. He loved music and he never threw his weight around as far as I could see. He was very unpretentious, very down to earth. I didn't sense any anger from him, even though he had things to be angry about. When he talked to our guys about protecting their music publishing and talked about losing his own, I never sensed he had anger toward the people who had wronged him. That was not his way. Maybe it was his country background. He was a gentle, kind person and perhaps whatever pain he had in his feelings manifested itself in his drinking. Because I remember maybe one time out of a dozen times I spent with him that he was not drunk. Ten in the morning, ten at night, it didn't matter and it was very sad. I remember, as a nineteen-year-old, thinking how sad that was. Here's this guy with tremendous talent, with a great gig, with great connections, you know, hanging out with the Rolling Stones and everybody else in the music business, but yet he was so self-destructive. But that's the only way he knew how to deal with it. The thing that struck me the most was that, despite the pain, despite the loss of his house and most of his possessions, his wife, despite all that, he still had somewhat of a positive, hopeful attitude. He still moved on without anger, at least from what I could see.

Q: But he seemed sad?

A: I think that he was going through a lot of pain. He was going through a divorce, and he had lost a lot. I think he died before the second album actually came out. That night he died, he was supposed to be coming over to our house. We were having a goodbye dinner because the very next day we were all leaving to record our album back in Massachusetts. The band was getting on a plane the next morning to fly there and me and one of our roadies were driving all of our equipment back in a twenty-foot truck. When Gram didn't show up at our house for dinner that night, we just thought he was off somewhere, you know, "that's Gram." The next morning I got up early and got in this truck that we loaded the night before and started driving back to Boston. I'll never forget, within a few hours we were listening to the radio and the announcement comes over that Gram Parsons was found dead and it just completely blew us away. We didn't have cell phones then, so we had to stop and call somebody. I tried calling Phil at that time and couldn't get ahold of him. I think the band was in the air so I couldn't get to them. So we were very concerned about what had happened. That's how we left California, with that news and that experience, after having a wonderful time with him during that summer and the previous spring and winter in New York. When the guys recorded the album they dedicated it to him and used to sing some of his songs in their live performances. He had a huge impact on us.

The guys in our group were diehard musicians. These were young guys who studied music and Quacky Duck, if you ever listen to it, they are a country-rock group. We used to call it "Good Time Rock and Roll." They used to do everything from traditional rock to hard rock to Beatles-type rock to country-rock. So when Gram countrified the Byrds, that was a big influence on the guys as they were growing up because they would listen to the Byrds, they would listen to the Burrito Brothers and to those kinds of groups. Gram Parsons that was a huge, huge thing for these guys. Even to this day, a lot of people don't know who he is or what kind of influence he had in a very short time. I've always likened him to Mozart. Mozart died when he was thirty-two. In that very short life of his, he wrote some of the greatest music in human history. Gram is like that, there is so much beautiful music that he either wrote or performed or influenced in some way. He helped to create a new kind of music that we take for granted now. He also sang other people's work and popularized it. Then to find someone like Emmylou, who carried on what he had started. A lot of people don't understand that we owe him a lot of gratitude.

He would be twenty-seven in a few months, and he finally felt he was becoming the man he had always intended to be. With that sweet optimism burning in him, Gram packed up Margaret and a few friends, along with a healthy stash of liquor and weed, and headed out to the desert, reaching the Joshua Tree Inn before the sun had set on September 17, 1973.

By the next afternoon, the party was in full gear, with a friend heading back to LA to score more pot and a local connection arriving with a delivery of morphine. Gram took a dose, adding more opiates to a system that had already been pushed to the limit by a late lunch of Jack Daniels shots and the prescription medication he was taking for his seizures. By late afternoon, he was neck deep in an altogether pleasant stupor.

As evening arrived, an inky desert darkness began to settle in around the small hotel, blanketing the simple cement structure with foreboding calm, a yawning silence. But Gram didn't notice. He felt good, a liquid warmth inside him, the desert air soft on his skin. He strummed his guitar and watched Margaret swim in the pool, her body pale under blue water.

Finally, tired and content, Gram went to lie down, swaying a bit on the way, stumbling onto the bedspread of his favorite suite— room eight. He felt heavy, made of stone. Everything was slowly darkening around the edges, the ceiling giving way, floating upward. He heard Margaret calling him from some faraway place, but he was already dreaming, already gone.

He dreamt of Gretchen's white cheeks, the blue veins just under her skin, of Nancy's silken hair, of sweet Polly's big eyes watching him, her tiny hand in his. He dreamt of the arc of his mother's neck, his father's melancholy smile, dreamt of heat and swampland and music, of the light shooting diamonds off of Lake Eloise, the smell of sugar cookies and a girl's hair.

And then, something inside him went still, and he felt himself sinking, slowly, into cool dark water, felt himself let go. He dreamt on, of a golden thread breaking, of his soul floating up high, and finally, of silence, of sweet and welcome release.

Margaret Fisher Interview #2
Interview by Polly Parsons

Old friend and high-school sweetheart Margaret Fisher remembers meeting Gram again and discusses what happened in the last moments before his death.

Q: So how old were you when you met up with him again?

A: I was, well, he died two days before my twenty-fifth birthday.

Q: How long had it been since you'd seen him?

A: Since high school. Since the day he graduated.

Q: So he saw your picture and recognized you?

A: No, he didn't. He had no clue. He thought that was a pretty girl, that she looked a little familiar and he wanted to meet her. It was just a little bit too much coincidence to me. I was scared. I had had such a crush on him in high school. I was scared of meeting him. I thought, "I don't know what to say."

Q: He had a crush on you twice.

A: Well, he should have. I was perfect. But not as big as the crush I had on him. I mean, butter would not melt in my mouth. And I did see him before that, I saw him at Altamont because they were one of the opening acts for the Stones. But I'm probably the only person I know that had a terrible time at Altamont. I loathed it. It was cold, it was wet. The first fifty junkies that had gotten to the portable had shut themselves in there to shoot dope. I could not go to the bathroom, I was miserable. And my friends I was with kept saying, "Why don't you go up and talk to Gram Parsons?" and I just kept saying "Nope." I was still too shy.

Q: Do you mind telling me about what happened in Joshua Tree?

A: He called me when he finished *Grievous Angel* and said, "Come on down, we're gonna go out to Joshua Tree." And we'd already been out there once with Phil Kaufman. So I flew down and Phil couldn't go, which was a tragedy. I don't think anything would've happened if Phil could've gone. Phil Kaufman is a good man. Gram had moved from the Chateau Marmont to Philip's house. So I went down there. And Gram and I, and I think Michael Murphy and Dale, went out to Joshua Tree. And Gram was doing a lot of pills, but he really wasn't shooting dope. But some girl out there sold him some dope. And that was when he OD'd.

Q: You were the only one with him?

A: Well, Dale was there, but she had gone back to her room. And when I saw he was in trouble I went and got Dale and I said, "Look, I'm gonna go get some coffee." I brought him around once and got him on his feet.

Q: And he was just on pills and what?

A: He took a shot of morphine. Some girl had sold us some liquid morphine from Pendleton Marine Base. The thing I remember about it is the girl who delivered it had a two-year-old toddler running around. I'm thinking, "I cannot believe this. This is so trashy. How could she have her child watching people shoot up dope?" When I saw Gram was in trouble I put him in the shower and I brought him around. I put him to bed and I went out to get him some coffee. Now I was gone for about thirty minutes. I took his Jaguar, and when I got back he was really in trouble. I told Dale to call the ambulance. I was so appalled. I kept thinking nothing, nothing in my whole life is ever going to be this intense. And it was the worst thing that ever happened to me. Twenty-nine Palms hospital was about forty minutes away and there just wasn't anything they could do. And also, of course, I was stupid. I didn't realize how much trouble he was in. I had never seen anybody OD. I brought him around once and I thought it was going to be okay. Off and on I have blamed myself. Even realizing there wasn't anything you could do. You were a witness to it, and you felt bad. And then when they took him to the hospital I went back and cleaned up his room. I got rid of all the pills I found and all the morphine I found and everything I found. And I sat with him until the ambulance came. I think he was dead then. But I just sat by him.

Q: Do you remember watching the woman distribute the morphine and thinking that it was too much?

A: The first one I did some, too. Well, the thing was he wasn't a junkie. If he had been a junkie at that time, like everybody said, no, he wouldn't have OD'd. Junkies don't often OD. But he had been clean.

Q: He had been clean off that stuff for a while.

A: Right. And we both did one shot and then he wanted to do another one. And I said, "No, I don't think you better." But you know, trying to talk him out of doing something . . . and he did another one. As soon as he did the second shot I knew he was in trouble and she knew it, too, because that chick split, immediately. And I took him back to the room, put him in the shower and did the ice cubes. And he came around, then he went under again. What it was was he hadn't been doing junk, he'd had a lot to drink, he had some pills and it was a combination. But I didn't know. This was perhaps the fourth time I'd ever done morphine. I didn't have pills. I was just stupid. And it's something I've thought about my whole life. The thing was, I never could tell Gram Parsons not to do something anyway. He wouldn't have paid any attention to me, and he didn't that night. But he was nice to me. He was a nice boy. And I really, really loved him. I really did. I'm not sure it would've lasted. I'm pretty certain he would've pissed me off and I would have walked. I mean, I would like to tell you this was the love affair of the century and it would have lasted forever. But there was one thing about your dad, he never gave a woman a second chance. I have a half brother and sister who were raised by an alcoholic, and they don't give people much of a chance either. If you did something to make him think you weren't totally loyal, you really didn't get a second chance. In high school he saw me talking to another boy one day and didn't speak to me for six months. You just did not make mistakes with that boy. He had what we would call today "trust issues." I realized his mother was a very damaged person. And with his father dying and her remarrying, of course he couldn't trust women. Why should he? But other than that, he was a southern gentleman. He did not discuss past girl-friends. And you had better not bring up past boyfriends. I mean what we had was totally in the moment. We either talked about high school, or we talked about each other. He didn't talk about living with the Rolling Stones. It's a very southern thing. You don't run down your past women. But he did talk about you.

Q: He did talk about me?

A: Oh yes, he told me he had the prettiest little girl. And he did say he didn't see her enough. You were the only other woman he ever mentioned. As far as I knew he was a virgin. But he was nice like that, you could tell he had been raised by people with manners. And I think that was probably what women found so appealing about him. He was very, very nice to me. But when we were together, at the end, we mostly talked about high school and he mostly laughed about it.

Q: What do you think about what happened after he died?

A: I heard them make that promise. When Clarence White died we were out in Joshua Tree. When we came back we found out Clarence had died and we went to Clarence's funeral and it was after Phil and Gram got seriously drunk. At that time I didn't drink, I was like one of those people forced to bear witness wher-ever I went. That was when he and Gram decided, whoever died first, the other would take him out to Joshua Tree. So when Philip called me, after Gram died, and told me what he'd done, I wasn't even surprised. I knew Philip would do it. After Gram died, Phil came and sent me back to San Francisco. And I went and crawled into bed and had me a nice nervous breakdown. Didn't get out of bed for two weeks. But that Sunday I turned on the news and there's Walter Cronkite saying, "A curious thing

happened out in the California desert this weekend." And I listened to him tell the story and I thought, "Fucking Phil." Then
the phone rang and it was Philip. And he said, "I'm here. I'm
waiting for the FBI to come and get me." And I said, "You
didn't." And he said, "Of course I did."

Joshua Tree National Park.
PHOTO BY JEANEEN LUND.

Now I'm Leaving
— Epilogue —

I loved you every day and now I'm leaving
And I can see the sorrow in your eyes
I hope you know a lot more than you're believing
Just so the sun don't hurt you when you cry

So take me down to your dance floor
And I won't mind the people when they stare
Paint a different color on your front door

And tomorrow we will still be there
And tomorrow we will still be there

From "A Song for You"
Words and music by Gram Parsons

IN SOUTHERN CALIFORNIA, September is a month of
winds. A few weeks in and a shivering, electric breeze grabs hold
of the magic that lurks in the Mojave and drags it west, into the
Los Angeles flatlands, tearing through the city, pushing at palm
leaf and spreading mischief, a tugging, an anxious pull at the skin.

Phil Kaufman was in the Valley, sitting on the ragged, busted-
beam front porch of his home, drinking a warm beer, when Margaret
Fisher called him to tell him that Gram was dead. She had to say it

Joshua Tree National Park. PHOTO BY JEANEEN LUND.

twice, the connection was bad, a crackle of static pulling her words apart. "Gram is dead," like a mantra, the sentence thick in her mouth.

Phil sat with the phone heavy in his hand and said what he was supposed to say. "Sit tight. Don't talk to anyone. Get rid of the drugs, shut your mouth and wait for me." Within the hour he was closing in on Joshua Tree, the night moonless, too many thoughts jumbling around in his head. He rolled the windows down to keep awake, breathed in warm autumn, pulled at his beard and blinked back the heavy wave of fury and sorrow and regret that was building behind his eyes.

A few days later—back in the Valley, Margaret safe, Gram poked and prodded and packed up—and that wave in Phil's head had yet to hit shore. The coffin, waxed and polished and lined with silk, had been paid for by Gretchen's father and was waiting, with Gram inside, waiting in some drafty airport warehouse, waiting for Bob Parsons to arrive from New Orleans and claim the body of his stepson.

Meanwhile, Phil was soaking himself through with whiskey,

Phil Kaufman Interview #2
Interview by Jessica Hundley

Phil Kaufman remembers his infamous actions following Gram's death.

Q: Tell me what you remember about the day you took Gram's body out to Joshua Tree.

A: We were very drunk. When we got the body out of the airport, we hit the wall, hit a wall with the hearse. The wall of the hanger! I mean they park 747s in there. But that didn't deter us. We just kept plodding on until we got him out to the desert and had a few words with him and sent him off to Valhalla or Pittsburgh, or wherever the hell he ended up.

Q: What did you love most about Gram?

A: Gram wasn't always a nice person, but I liked him very much. He was quite frustrated about not having a large fan base. He was quite respected by his contemporaries, but he wasn't all that successful at that time, although I think he probably would have been. Gram's music touched people. It had that kind of special kind of cosmic cowboy thing. So many people were influenced by him and there is the mystique of his death and his funeral, if you will, which adds to that.

Q: Do you feel like his music still has influence today?

A: You know, I think it does. It's strange because we were very close, Gram and I. He lived with me at the time when he died. We had some great times together. I know we were together for a really special time in music history, but to us, it was just another day. We didn't realize that it was a special time. To us, it was just the way it was.

Joshua Tree Inn, and the
room where Gram died.
PHOTOS BY JEANEEN LUND

staring glazed-eyed into the sun and trying to find enough gumption to do what he had promised. He remembered Clarence
White's funeral, remembered the set in Gram's jaw when he'd told
Phil he didn't want to go out that way, that he'd want desert and
blue flame and night sky and not some hollow-hearted ceremony
with Bob Parsons and the Snivelys throwing daggers over his grave.

Phil, alive still, a survivor in the Valley, the sun high—Phil spat
in the dirt, took a few more sips from his bottle and went into
action. Almost as soon as he stood, his mind made up, almost
immediately everything began to move faster, a blur, the ease of
things to come a surprise even to Phil. There was the call to the
airport for information. Which airline? What time? Then there
was the friend with the hearse, a battered, rusted-out hulk of a
hearse, but a hearse nonetheless. Phil in the driver's seat without
knowing quite how he got there, heading toward LAX in his torn
denim and muttonchops to get Gram the hell out, to get Gram
where he needed to be.

The guy at the desk took in Phil's slur, the reek of Jack Daniels,
the cracked passenger window of the hearse and . . . shrugged. Phil
was babbling. He needed to take the body to another airport, a
smaller one, private plane, family's wishes . . . years of straight-
faced bullshitting, telling tall tales to travel agents and hotel clerks,
those years coming in handy, taking the waver from his voice.
When the clerk asked him to sign, Phil scrawled "Jeremy Nobody"
with a flourish, winked and was off, the hearse's tires squealing.

Joshua Tree Park was quiet on a weekday, hikers and campers
few and scattered and no one saw the hearse or the man in the
worn jean jacket dragging a coffin through the dust. When Phil
got close enough to Cap Rock he sat down and wiped away the
sweat and opened the coffin. Gram was there, waiting for Phil to
do what he'd said he'd do, to pour on the gas and light the flame
and say the right words, to say "goodbye" into blue desert dusk.

Phil blinked.

The sun was just setting, orange and huge. There was no sound,
just silence and somewhere below it, that low, distant hum, that

Polly Parsons in Gram's guitar case. COURTESY OF BEN FONG-TORRES.

Jonathan Richman Interview #2
Interview by Christian Bruno

Jonathan Richman remembers Gram's death and the funeral party at Phil Kaufman's.

Q: When he died, do you feel like you learned some sort of lesson? Did you feel like there was something you got out of the fact that someone so talented died so young?

A: No, no I already knew that lesson, which is there's no need to fuck things up. Nah, we were just sad. It would've been nicer if he'd been around. No lesson.

Q: Now there was the funeral party. . . .

A: It wasn't quite a funeral party. It was a benefit party to raise money for restitution for the coffin that Phil Kaufman stole. Phil Kaufman and a pal of his went out to the airport and dressed up as undertakers. Phil had his own hearse anyway. That was easy.

Q: He had his own hearse?

A: Yeah, they signed for the papers and took the body. There were a lot of things that the people at the airport didn't notice, like that the hearse was a 1953 Pontiac hot-rod hearse. There were probably a few other things out of order. But off they went to Cap Rock at Joshua Tree and burned the body which was sort of a deal that they had, that whoever died first that the other guy would burn his body.

Q: Did you know Phil was going out to do this or did you find this out after the fact?

A: Oh it had to be secret. He could've gotten in trouble. In fact he did, later. But the charges got reduced to restitution of the coffin.

Q: Just to pay for the coffin?

A: Yeah, if he didn't do that he was going to have to spend ninety days in jail. Which was no big deal to him, but we wanted to help him out. So he had another great party. Bobby "Boris" Pickett played "Monster Mash." That was great. That was a great band. Whole other bunch of people played and we volunteered to play, too. We played some songs. We missed him. It was a sad thing that he died. It affected all of us.

vibration that Gram had heard himself, that first day in Pear Blossom, the day of the Burritos photo shoot, the day he'd decided that there was something in the space and stretch of desert that felt like home.

Phil had a swig from the bottle. Another. Then he took a deep breath, poured a shot for Gram and toasted into the soft air, "To you, friend." Phil watched the sun sink, let out a whoop, flicked a lit match and then it was done—the lick of flame catching, bursting—good old Gram going out in just the same way he had lived, in high romantic style, with a bright yellow-gold burning. There was a flash of light and a cloud of dust, and then, nearly twenty-seven years after he'd first arrived, Gram Parsons was gone.

PHOTO BY ANDEE COHEN NATHANSON.

Thank-Yous

JESSICA GIVES A BIG THANKS TO—

Sweet Polly, for standing by my side, giving her encouragement, insight, and enthusiasm. Shirley Halperin, for her vast music knowledge and indispensable interview contributions. Mark Olsen and Christian Bruno for their interview expertise. Trent Buckroyd at *Flaunt* magazine for making me feel like a decent enough writer to wrestle with a subject such as Gram. Gandulf Henning for all his help and support, for his fine documentary *Fallen Angel*, and for his knowledge and love for Gram. Ben Fong-Torres for his graciousness and wise words. Lawrence Dunlop and Peggy Hanson for their kind help. Jack Snively and the Snively family for welcoming Polly and me to Winter Haven and for sharing their past with us so generously. Chad Brown for introducing me to Gram's music and for

PHOTO BY JEANEEN LUND.

inducting me into the fine art of Country Bachelor Living. Jack Guilderson for sitting next to me on my living room floor and saying, "Yes. Do it." Jeaneen Lund for her amazing photo skills and her utterly beautiful presence. Steve Salardino for his patience and support and for letting me use our kitchen as my office. Hillary Frileck for her photo research and her incredible friendship. Michelle Lanz and Emily Sunderland for working so hard and so well. Jofie Ferrari-Adler for his amazing editorial skills and much-appreciated enthusiasm. Alex Smithline for nurturing this project from inception and playing midwife; without you this book would not have existed. Thanks also to my amazing friends and family and to Sebastian, my own "old boy," who makes me stronger and wiser each and every day. And lastly, thank you to all the incredible photographers, writers, and musicians who were kind enough to take part in this book and share their thoughts and images. And thanks, of course, to Gram himself, my dear, sweet, Cosmic American cowboy. I blow you a kiss. . . .

POLLY THANKS—

I would like to thank God and my father, for seeing fit to love and guide me anyway. Congratulations on being a grandfather, dad. I love you.

And Jessica Hundley, for without her tenacity and love for the subject matter, this story never would have had a chance to be told.

PHOTO BY
JEANEEN LUND.

Photographers

ONE OF THE most seductive elements of Gram Parsons's persona was his utterly unique aesthetic, and we have the wonderful photographers who contributed to this book to thank for capturing his style and grace. All photos included in this book are available directly through the photographers. If you're looking for a print, track it down and say I sent you. . . .

—JESSICA

Andee Cohen Nathanson was Gram's dear friend and compatriot, fellow adventurer, and partner-in-mischief. Her photos of Gram reveal a playful sensitivity, an intimate side that few were able to truly capture. www.andeenathanson.com

Earl Crabb is a man of many talents—artist, photographer, actor, and adventurer. He appeared in Peter Fonda's 1973 film *Idaho Transfer*. His photos can be found at www.humbead.com.

Jeff Gold is a former record exec turned full-time audiophile and memorabilia collector. You can find his incredible array of music memories at www.recordmecca.com.

Kim Gottlieb-Walker graduated from UCLA in the late 1960s with a BA in Motion Picture Production. She shot stills for numerous magazines, including *Music World, Feature, Crawdaddy, Rolling Stone, Newsweek,* and *People,* and she has worked for over twenty-five years as a still photographer on motion pictures and in television. She is an elected representative for still photographers on the National Executive Board of the International Cinematographers Guild, IATSE Local 600. Her Web site is www.lenswoman.com.

Jeaneen Lund is one of the finest of a new crop of LA photographers. Her lens has captured celebrity, fashion, music, documentary film, and many beautiful places. You can find her at www.jeaneenlund.com.

Jim McCrary has been taking incredible photos for nearly half a century. In addition to his classic images of Gram and the Burritos, McCrary has also been responsible for some of the most unforgettable album covers of the past few decades, including several covers for the Carpenters, Carol King's *Tapestry*, and Keith Moon's *Two Sides of the Moon*. www.jimmccrary.com

Tom Wilkes is one of the finest of Gram's documentarians, his images capturing a colorful time with the intimacy and poignancy that came from Tom's long-standing friendship with his subject. Wilkes has just completed his own book, *Tommy Geeked a Chicken*, an outrageous autobiography that is illustrated with amazing classic graphics and photos. www.wilkesworks.com

Contributors

Christian Bruno is a San Franciscan man-about-town, a writer/director/cinematographer and documentarian. He is currently working on a documentary about movie theaters and urban decline, writing articles for various prestigious publications, and teaching filmmaking to eager students. He loves shooting 16mm film, and he feels grateful that there are people like Jonathan Richman in the world.

Shirley Halperin is a music fan first and a writer/editor to keep a roof over her head. Since 2002 she's been the music editor of *US Weekly* and a frequent contributor to *Rolling Stone*. She has also been published in *Blender*, the *Washington Post*, and *CosmoGIRL!* in addition to starting her own magazine, *Smug*. At the latter, Halperin covered bands on the fringe—Radiohead and Guided by Voices in the early years, Korn and Rage Against the Machine later on—for five years until she was forced to get a "real" job. Halperin was then tapped to relaunch the teen magazine *Bop*, one of her childhood favorites. A cowgirl at heart, Shirley (who was born in Israel and whose name means "sing to me" in Hebrew) has been singing the "Gospel of Gram" to anyone who will listen for years.

Mark Olsen was born in White Plains, New York, and raised in Overland Park, Kansas. In 1994, he graduated from the beautiful and historic University of Kansas. In 1996 he moved to New York City and eventually earned a master's degree at New York University. In 2001, he moved to Los Angeles. He is currently a contributing editor to *Film Comment*, as well as a frequent contributor to the *Los Angeles Times, Sight & Sound, L.A. Weekly, Interview*, and other publications.

W/THE SHILOS:

Gram Parsons: The Early Years, Volume I (1963–1965)
  Sierra
  February 1979
  Contains tracks recorded with the Shilos, one in '64, the others
  in early 1965.

W/THE INTERNATIONAL SUBMARINE BAND:

"The Russians Are Coming"/"Truck Driving Man"
  Ascot 2218
  1966

"Sum Up Broke"/"One Day Week"
  Columbia 4-43935
  1966

Safe at Home
  LHI-S-12001
  April 1968
  Rereleased as ***Gram Parsons***
  Shiloh RI 4088
  May 1979

W/THE BYRDS:

Sweetheart of the Rodeo
  Columbia CS-9670/CK-9670
  July 22, 1968

"I Am A Pilgrim"/"Pretty Boy Floyd"
  Columbia 44643
  September 2, 1968

W/THE FLYING BURRITO BROTHERS:

The Gilded Palace of Sin
  A&M SP 4175
  March 1969

"The Train Song"/"Hot Burrito #1"
  A&M 1067
  1969

Burrito Deluxe
A&M SP-4258
April 1970

Close Up the Honky Tonks
A&M SP-3631
July 1974
Contains songs from the first three Burritos albums, plus several
unreleased tracks.

Honky Tonk Heaven
Ariola 87-585 XDT (Dutch)
1974
Contains several previously unreleased tracks.

Sleepless Nights
A&M SP-4578
May 1976
Contains unreleased tracks from 1970 Burritos, with Gram Parsons.

Dim Lights, Thick Smoke
Edsel
March 1987
Contains some hard-to-find Burritos tracks, including "Bony
Maronie" and "The Train Song."

Farther Along
A&M CD 5216
1988
Contains best of Gram Parsons–era Burritos, with some previously unreleased tracks.

Out of the Blue (UK)
A&M 540408-22
April 1996
Contains songs from the first three Burritos albums, plus several
unreleased tracks.

GRAM PARSONS/Solo:
"She"/"That's All It Took" (US)
Reprise
January 1973

GP

Reprise MS 2123
March 1973
Rereleased on *GP/Grievous Angel*
Reprise 9 26108-2
February 1990

"The New Soft Shoe"/"She" (UK)
Reprise
March 1973

Cosmic American Music: The Rehearsal Tapes 1972

Magnum America
1995
Demos for *GP*

"Love Hurts"/"In My Hour of Darkness" (US)
Reprise
January 1974

GRAM PARSONS & THE FALLEN ANGELS:
Live 1973

Sierra GP 1973
February 1982

More Gram Parsons & the Fallen Angels Live 1973

Sierra GP/EP 104
September 1982

Live 1973

Sierra SXCD 6003
December 1994
Contains the entire unedited broadcast that made up the earlier
LP and EP.

GRAM PARSONS & EMMYLOU HARRIS/FALLEN ANGELS:
Grievous Angel

Reprise MS 2171
January 1974

Rereleased as double album *GP/Grievous Angel*
Reprise 9 26108-2
February 1990

GRAM PARSONS:
Warm Evenings, Pale Mornings 1963–1973
Raven
August 1992
Australian compilation that covers each phase of Parsons's career.

OTHERS:
Sony rereleased a deluxe version of the Byrds' *Sweetheart of the Rodeo* in January 2004.

There have been nearly twenty tribute albums dedicated to Parsons since his death in 1973. The most recent of these, *Return of the Grievous Angel*, was released in 2001 and featured tracks from Beck, Elvis Costello, Lucinda Williams, and Wilco.

In the summer of 2004, Polly Parsons produced two incredible tribute concerts for her father in southern California. Many of the interviews for this book were conducted backstage at these amazing shows. Keith Richards, Norah Jones, Steve Earle, Dwight Yoakum, Lucinda Williams, and many others came together for two nights to remember Gram's legacy and to sing his songs in their own unique way. A DVD release of these concerts, *Return to Sin City: A Tribute to Gram Parsons*, is available through Image Entertainment.

Index